Rebels

Rebels is an exciting and innovative new series looking at contemporary rebel groups and their place in global politics. Written by leading experts, and published in conjunction with the Department of Peace Studies at the University of Bradford, the books serve as definitive introductions to the individual organizations, whilst seeking to place them within a broader geographical and political framework. They examine the origins, ideology and future direction of each group, whilst posting such questions as 'When does a "rebel" political movement become a "terrorist" organization?' and 'What are the social-economic drivers behind political violence?' Provocative and original, the series is essential reading for anyone interested in how rebel groups operate today.

The Department of Peace Studies is a world-class centre which since 1973 has developed a unique interdisciplinary research culture. Its mission is to engage in empirical, theoretical and applied research in order to prevent and resolve conflicts and develop peaceful societies; and to provide an enabling environment for international research excellence involving diverse and critical approaches.

The editors of Rebels are Nana K. Poku and Anna Mdee.

ALREADY PUBLISHED

Alex Khasnabish, *Zapatistas: Rebellion from the Grassroots to the Global*

Garry Leech, *The FARC: The Longest Insurgency*

FORTHCOMING

Ram Manikkalingam, *Tamil Tigers: Dialogue, Terrorism and Nationalism*

About the Author

CHRISTINA HELLMICH is Lecturer in International Relations at the University of Reading, UK, and co-author of *Knowing Al-Qaeda: The Epistemology of Terrorism* (2011).

AL-QAEDA

From Global Network to Local Franchise

CHRISTINA HELLMICH

Fernwood Publishing
HALIFAX & WINNIPEG

Department of Peace Studies

Zed Books
LONDON & NEW YORK

Al-Qaeda: From Global Network to Local Franchise
was first published in 2011

Published in Canada by Fernwood Publishing Ltd,
32 Oceanvista Lane, Black Point, Nova Scotia BOJ 1BO
www.fernwoodpublishing.ca

Published in the rest of the world by Zed Books Ltd,
7 Cynthia Street, London N1 9JF, UK and
Room 400, 175 Fifth Avenue, New York, NY 10010, USA
www.zedbooks.co.uk

Copyright © Christina Hellmich 2011

The right of Christina Hellmich to be identified as the
author of this work has been asserted by her in accordance
with the Copyright, Designs and Patents Act, 1988

Designed and typeset in 11 on 14 Monotype Bulmer
by illuminati, Grosmont, www.illuminatibooks.co.uk
Index: Rohan Bolton, Rohan.Indexing@gmail.com
Cover designed by www.alice-marwick.co.uk
Printed and bound in Great Britain
by CPI Antony Rowe, Chippenham and Eastbourne

Distributed in the USA exclusively by Palgrave Macmillan, a division
of St Martin's Press, LLC, 175 Fifth Avenue, New York, NY 10010, USA

A catalogue record for this book is available from the British Library
Library of Congress Cataloging in Publication Data available

Library and Archives Canada Cataloguing in Publication
    Hellmich, Christina, 1978–
        Al-Qaeda : from global network to local
    franchise / Christina Hellmich.
    Includes bibliographical references.
    ISBN 978-1-55266-458-2
        1. Qaida (Organization). I. Title.
    HV6431.H45 2011   303.6′25   C2011-902742-9

ISBN 978 1 84813 909 1 hb   (Zed Books)
ISBN 978 1 84813 908 4 pb   (Zed Books)
ISBN 978 1 55266 458 2   (Fernwood Publishing)

Contents

Acknowledgements

This book is the result of countless conversations about al-Qaeda and the generous support of the Leverhulme Trust through the University of Reading's Liberal Way of War Programme. The former forced me to make sense of conflicting narratives; the latter enabled me to commit my thoughts to paper. It is due to Andreas Behnke that I ended the search for the 'truth' and began to appreciate the value of 'yet another story' – even the 'bad' ones. I am indebted to James Piscatori, Nelly Lahoud and Ali Parchami for our ongoing discussion of Muslim politics, their detailed comments on draft chapters (often at short notice) and for being living proof that metrics fall short of measuring 'impact' in a meaningful manner. My proofreader extraordinaire, Jeremy Legg, and my editor at Zed, Ken Barlow, went out of their way to keep me focused during the busiest times. My husband Andrew made sure I remain grounded in reality: 'Al-Qaeda, one might conclude, has much in common with cardiac tumours: the associated symptoms are undeniable proof of their existence, even if we cannot see them.'

ONE

9/11 and the
anxious search for answers

On 23 February 1998, Osama bin Ladin and his associates issued a religious ruling (*fatwa*) that called on every Muslim to kill Americans, both civilians and military personnel, in every country in which it was possible to do so, in order to liberate al-Aqsa Mosque and the Holy Mosque and to drive the US armies out of all the lands of Islam, to the point where they would be defeated and unable to threaten any Muslim. Three and a half years later, on the morning of 11 September 2001, al-Qaeda demonstrated the magnitude of its threat and the sophistication of its methods by organizing and perpetrating the world's greatest terrorist outrage: for the first time in history, transnational teams, united in their belief that they were defending Islam, hijacked four planes to use as flying suicide bombs. Two were directed into the iconic Twin Towers of the World Trade Center, New York, one into the Pentagon, and the fourth crashed outside Pittsburgh after its passengers attempted to regain control of the plane. What happened next is, as they say, history.

Al-Qaeda, the first global terrorist group of the twenty-first century, embodies the enigmatic new face of global terrorism.

Since perpetrating the most destructive act of terrorism to date on 11 September 2001, it has dominated discussion of national and international security in the media as well as in academic and policymaking circles. Who would do such a thing, and why? Ten years into the global war against terrorism, one would expect to find clear answers to these basic, though critically important, questions. Yet, despite the fact that few issues have generated more substantial debate than the task of explaining the rationale and appeal of spectacular mass murder in the name of Islam, speculation about the strength and extent of the group continues to run rife. Bewildering descriptions – eagerly seized upon and broadcast by the mass media – of a shadowy network and undercover terrorist cells, televised reports of new arrests of suspected terrorists and urgent warnings of imminent dangers continue to create alarm but bring little by way of clarity, whilst heightened security threat levels and hitherto unheard-of restrictions endured by the travelling public have become an accepted feature of life in the post-9/11 world.

That the threat of so-called 'Islamic' terrorism dominates the collective consciousness of the Western world is plain to see: a quick Internet search of the term 'al-Qaeda' on Google generates over 12 million links to articles, interviews, books and commentaries in a wide variety of languages. Yet a closer look at the extant literature on the subject generates more questions than answers. Is al-Qaeda a rigidly structured organization, a global network of semi-independent cells, a franchise, or simply an idea whose time has come? Was Osama bin Ladin an engineer, a business-school graduate, a playboy or a university dropout? What is meant by talk of the 'global Salafi jihad' that is confronting the West? On closer examination, 'facts' about the nature of the terrorist group which permanently branded its name into the Manhattan skyline begin to sink all too quickly in a proverbial sea of assertions and unsubstantiated truth claims.

Why is this so? How can a subject of such importance be so riven by uncertainties? A first attempt to explain the ambiguity surrounding the most notorious terrorist organization to date necessarily begins with a closer look at the state of the information that was available prior to September 11 and the rapid development of the literature that followed immediately thereafter. In the 1990s, only a handful of people were conducting research on what was to become one of the most widely discussed security issues in the years ahead. As surprising as it may seem with the benefit of hindsight, the spectacular destruction of the Twin Towers against a bright blue September sky took the Western world by surprise: terrorism experts, security specialists and academics alike had failed to predict an attack of such magnitude.[1] As Magnus Ranstorp aptly pointed out in his extensive review of the terrorism studies literature, 'there was extraordinarily limited research on al-Qaeda related topics before 11 September 2001.'[2]

Naturally, then, the events of September 11, at once the most spectacular case of propaganda ever carried out, instantly launched a rollercoaster of uncertainty, fear and speculation as the most obvious and pressing of questions begged to be answered: Who would do such a thing and why? Meaningful answers, however, were nowhere to be found. Indeed, a striking feature of the early days following the attacks was the circulation and recirculation of spectacular images of destruction that engrained the reality of what had literally come out of the blue into the consciousness of all those who could not escape the reach of the media. At the same time, little, if any, room was allocated to text – analysis and explanations of what had happened. Yet the prevalence of the sensational over the analytical was not an act of media propaganda or even, as some voices have claimed, the outworking of some sort of government conspiracy. Rather, the inescapable presence of those horrifying images in our newspapers and on our television screens was merely the visual evidence of a mounting confrontation of the bewildered Western world with questions to which there were no answers at that time. At risk of further sensationalizing the issue, September 11 could be said to be the opening of a blank page on which the biography of al-Qaeda had yet to be written.

That the circumstances in the aftermath of September 2001 were so bewildering and so urgent explains why there then came a rush to fill the vacuum left by Ground Zero with answers. What ensued was a widespread suspension of critical faculties as commentators rushed headlong to generate explanations. The corollary of this was that the most attention was paid to those who shouted loudest and appeared to provide the most satisfying, if not the most sophisticated, answers. Virtually overnight, journalists became the most influential commentators in the field, not because of the superior quality of their knowledge, but because their words and their analyses of the situation reached most people first. In turn, some analysts – especially those who were soon to be hailed as experts – were quoting 'facts' about al-Qaeda, the true nature of Islam and the meaning of jihad drawn from what they had picked up from CNN, the *New York Times* and Fox News. They began to talk of al-Qaeda's vision of a fantasy world, propounded by religious fanatics, hypocrites and madmen. Some argued that al-Qaeda was totally devoid of ideology, while others traced the origins of Osama bin Ladin's ideas to a variety of Islamic scholars such as Taqi ad-Din Ahmad Ibn Taymiyyah (d. 1328), Muhammad Ibn

Abd al-Wahhab (d. 1792) or Jamal al-Din al-Afghani (d. 1897), without having first engaged in any meaningful analysis of either the messages of bin Ladin or the writings of those who were supposed to have influenced him.[3] It mattered little that many of the popular stories about 'global jihadism' were told by individuals with little expertise in the subject area, who relied on questionable sources and abandoned established academic procedures of analysis and even critical thought. Indeed, with the launch of the all-out global war against terror, in which freedom and democracy confronted their worst enemy – and which demanded a clear, uncompromising alignment with 'us' or 'them'[4] – concerns about academic rigour and method, the 'but ifs...', 'not quites', and observations that 'we need to put matters into broader perspective', were largely sidelined and consequently failed to receive the attention they deserved. Marc Sageman makes an important point when he observes that most of the early efforts at explaining al-Qaeda amount to little more than 'arguments made for the sake of scoring political points and have no role in a scientific study'.[5] Fear and overreaction have historically not been the best foundation for rational consideration, reflection and debate, and September 11 and the uncritical kill-and-capture approach that underlay much of the strategy in the war against terror sit comfortably with a long line of historical precedents. In that sense, both the violent nature of the West's response and the reactionary climate that still prevails are unsurprising in the face of what was seen to be a new kind of 'terrorism', unprecedented in both the scale of the violence and destruction it seeks to inflict and the globality of its reach.

To explain fully the controversy surrounding al-Qaeda, it is useful to look beyond the immediate circumstances of 9/11 and to consider the state of terrorism studies and its concept of the issue it seeks to investigate: terrorism itself. During the thirty years before the 9/11 attacks, the field of terrorism studies occupied a somewhat marginal position within the social sciences, with only a limited number of researchers contributing assessments of a variety of terrorist incidents that occurred at different times and in different geographic and socio-cultural contexts. Indeed, most of the extant terrorism literature clusters around individual terrorist incidents and includes – perhaps unsurprisingly, in the light of post-9/11 experience – a large proportion written by individuals with little to no background or expertise in the subject area.[6] In numerical terms, of the 490 articles published in the two core terrorism journals *Studies in Conflict and Terrorism* and *Terrorism and Political Violence*, between 1990 and 1999, a total of 406 (83 per cent) were written by one-time authors.[7] This body of literature is bedevilled by a number of shortcomings: the analytical efforts of various individual authors lacked rigour and were devoid of adequate theory, short of accurate data and in want of appropriate investigative methods. Many of the articles attempted to identify the causes of terrorism and to chart the evolution and dynamics of different terrorist groups, but their authors were typically too preoccupied with recent events to be able to devote adequate analysis to the bigger picture. Assessments of future security risks failed to include a real understanding of the terrorists' rationale, whilst any counter-terrorism strategies that were formulated tended to be founded on an ad hoc approach rather than long-term planning. The consequence of this is what Martha Crenshaw described as the 'construction of general categories of terrorist actors that lump together dissimilar motivations, organizations, resources and contexts'.[8] The now infamous connection of al-Qaeda – as proclaimed by the US government – with Hamas, the Shia schools of Qom, the hard-line Islamic traditionalist Deobandi seminaries of northern Pakistan, and secular Arab nationalist Ba'ath Party regimes is but a contemporary example of a long-standing problem in the field.[9] As lamented by Ted Gurr in 1988, 'most of the [terrorism] literature consists of naïve description, speculative commentary, and prescriptions for dealing with terrorism which could not meet minimum research standards in the more established branches of conflict and policy analysis.'[10]

The same methodological shortcomings continued to be reflected in the literature that was published after 9/11. Although a record number of books related to terrorism were published within a year of the event, there is little reason to believe that the overall pattern has substantially changed. Again, Magnus Ranstorp's analysis of the state of terrorism studies post-9/11 points out the development of a worrying trend that not only further undermines the esteem in which the field is held, but also – more importantly in the light of the subject under investigation in this book – has not only obscured but also at times literally *created* what we know about al-Qaeda. In the absence of the kind of quality control to which academic literature is normally subject, the quest for answers has provided a fertile breeding ground for pseudo-academics and at times outright fraudsters claiming to be experts. Many claim privileged access to information, often from sources which are at first presented as 'secret', but which investigation has revealed to be unverifiable, unreliable or even non-existent.

One of the most egregious examples is the case of Alexis Debat, a former journalist who managed to rise to the prestigious positions of director of the Terrorism and National Security Program at the Nixon Center in Washington DC and editor of *The National Interest* on the basis of a faked Ph.D. from the

Sorbonne, Paris and fraudulent claims regarding his professional background, experience and expertise.[11] His case, unfortunately, is no exception. Indeed, many so-called 'experts' who in reality have little if any in-depth knowledge of al-Qaeda happen to be the very same people whose opinions on the organization have been most widely relied upon and quoted in public debate, and whose contributions in the field form a significant proportion of our 'intelligence' about the organization. A case in point is that of Evan Kohlmann, author of *Al-Qaeda's Jihad in Europe: The Afghan–Bosnian Network*, who, without any obvious expertise beyond a first degree in law and an internship, rose to the rank of a leading expert on Islamist terrorism in both media and government circles. Boasting 'factual expertise' seemingly gleaned from little more than Internet resources, he became a consultant to the US Department of Defense, the Department of Justice, the FBI, the Crown Prosecution Service and Scotland Yard's SO-15 Counter Terrorism Command.[12] The true extent of his 'expertise' was revealed during a trial (*United States* v. *Haref and Hossein*), in which he served as an expert witness on the Bangladeshi Islamist party Jamaat-e-Islami, the oldest religious party in Pakistan:

> Under cross examination it transpired that [Kohlmann] had never written any papers on the party, nor been interviewed about the group. He had never been to Bangladesh, could not name the country's Prime Minister nor the name of the leader of *Jamaat-e-Islami*.[13]

In 2008, Kohlmann testified before the first Guantánamo military commission in the case of bin Ladin's chauffeur that the Office of Military Commission had asked him to produce a 90-minute video about the evolution of al-Qaeda. Having received $45,000 in compensation for the film and the testimony, Kohlmann confessed at the OMC that he had changed his proposed name of the film from the 'Rise of al-Qaeda' to 'The al-Qaeda Plan' in order to draw closer comparison to 'The Nazi Plan', a famous documentary movie produced during the Nuremberg trials.[14]

The reliance on such questionable expertise undermines the credibility of the proceedings. Yet, despite this record, Kohlmann's assertions continue to influence the debate on al-Qaeda in terrorism studies and security circles alike: his most recent contribution on 'Al-Qa'ida's Yemeni Expatriate Faction in Pakistan', seemingly based on information taken from dubious Internet sources, featured prominently in the January 2011 edition of the *CTC Sentinel*, the journal of 'The Combating Terrorism Center' based at the United States Military Academy, West Point.[15]

Delving further into the academic field, one of the early and best-known al-Qaeda experts is Rohan Gunaratna, author of *Inside Al Qaeda*, one of the first and, as the following chapters will show, most widely read and cited books dedicated to exposing the origins, nature and inner workings of the group. It is unfortunate that many of the factual statements made in the book rely on classified sources that cannot be verified or substantiated, as well as interviews with terrorists the author claimed to have conducted in Yemen, Lebanon, Egypt and Saudi Arabia – places he later confessed never to have visited and whose languages he does not speak.[16] Pressed by defence lawyers as to the nature of the sources used in the book, during the trial *United States* v. *Hassoun Jayyousi and Jose Padilla* in 2007, in which he served as the main prosecution witness, Gunaratna explicitly agreed when it was put to him that 'a huge number of sources in your book cannot be checked by other authorities unless they have inside information from you.'[17] The implications for Gunaratna's testimony in al-Qaeda-related trials are well worth bearing in mind even today. That he should have been relied upon to so great an extent is surprising, to say the least, given that as early as 2003 his expertise had been called into question, with the British *Observer* describing Gunaratna as 'probably the least reliable expert on al-Qaeda'.[18]

Overall, these individuals are but a few examples of the many commentators whose expertise on the subject is now known to be questionable, but whose statements have nonetheless been taken at face value and have shaped our understanding – or lack thereof – of al-Qaeda. In the big picture they constitute but a fraction of the most infamous assertions and unsubstantiated truth claims. Yet the very same statements have subsequently been cited, and indeed are often relied upon as a key source of evidence, in publications on al-Qaeda such as the *The 9/11 Commission Report: The Final Report of the National Commission on Terrorist Attacks upon the United States*[19] and Marc Sageman's *Understanding Terror Networks*.[20] By virtue of repetition, many of those claims that were of questionable value from the very beginning have entrenched themselves as facts. There exists a major methodological problem in terrorism studies literature, which Edna Reid described in 1997 as 'circular research systems'.[21] These are created in the form of a 'feedback loop', which continually reinforces itself as authors uncritically rely on and cite each other's work, and this is a pattern which has clearly continued into the post-9/11 era. This in turn highlights the fundamental problem in any discussion about al-Qaeda: how to distinguish facts from fiction. Does a statement become truth because we have heard it so many times?

Although it is clear that the study of terrorism in general, and much of the extant literature on al-Qaeda in particular, suffer from a number of problems regarding the generation of reliable information, the issue is complicated further by difficulties that arise with formulating a clear concept of the very subject under investigation: terrorism itself. The assumption in the mainstream (or what Miller and Mills refer to as 'orthodox')[22] terrorism studies literature is that terrorism is 'extra-normal', and doomed to eventual defeat, an assumption which has been obscured by the literature's focus on issues that appear to be more pressing, such as the need to explain particular violent incidents, their causes, and strategies for predicting and responding to future threats. Indeed, the question of how terrorism can be brought to an end has been, and continues to be, a key question that has generated as much debate as state funding of terrorism. The objection might be raised that significant efforts have been made, albeit unsuccessfully, to find an acceptable definition of terrorism, and that in the face of continued disagreement we must put up with a certain level of ambiguity. Ultimately, as a seemingly widely accepted but nonetheless problematic view has it, we will know terrorism when we see it: it is the deliberate use, or threat of use, of violence against civilians in the pursuit of political goals by non-state actors, which in the modern world frequently involves the use of bombs and other weapons in targeting public places, aeroplanes or other forms of transportation. This definition, which is not exhaustive and is open to expansion, illustrates the extent to which the commonly held view of terrorism is shaped by the latest experiences and placed outside the historical continuum.[23] It is a working definition, flawed and by no means universally accepted, but a definition that nonetheless goes some way towards providing a framework within which the phenomenon can be discussed.

In more theoretical terms, the very preoccupation with finding a definition, even just a working definition, in the first place is itself an expression of an inherently liberal view of political order and state sovereignty, particularly the view of the state as the legitimate arbiter that mediates between the competing interests of its individual residents.[24] Within this scheme, where the balance of power and the use of violence are subject to particular rules, an act of unsanctioned violence by a non-state actor to contest the legitimacy of the existing order is not acceptable. The legitimacy of the liberal state cannot be questioned because it is already premissed upon a consensual social contract. As such, both terrorists and terrorism operate outside the established rules of engagement, and, if the global war against terror is an indicator of the full extent to which the liberal state holds terrorism to be unacceptable, stand to be defeated at all costs. Put differently, most of the work in mainstream terrorism studies is both ideologically committed to and practically engaged in supporting the authority of the Western state. As Miller and Mills have carefully demonstrated, 'The ideas prominent in orthodox terrorism studies, and often the theorists themselves, have strong roots in counterinsurgency doctrine and practice.'[25] The result is, in the words of James Der Derian, that in order 'to gain official entry into the terrorist debate one must check critical weapons at the door, and join the chorus of condemnation.'[26] However, the perception of terrorism as extra-normal that is inherent to the liberal-state viewpoint, and the simultaneous condemnation of terrorism that necessarily results from this perception, prevent what might be a simpler, and arguably more meaningful, observation, namely that terrorism – and counter-terrorism for that matter, whereby the terrorist is the illegal combatant and the counter-terrorist the legal warrior – is at its very core a violent struggle for and over political legitimacy. In other words, the nub of the matter is this: who has the right to use violence in the international system?

Moving on to the case of al-Qaeda, the immediate condemnation of the terrorists and their actions – however understandable this reaction might have been in the tragic shadow of the Twin Towers massacre – meant the absence of any meaningful engagement with the wider message of Osama bin Ladin. Until the publication of his central public speeches, letters and interviews in 2005, only fragments of his statements were available in English translation.[27] Similar to the way that former First Lady Laura Bush urged parents to shield their children from the horrific images of 9/11,[28] the adult Western audience has largely been shielded from the voice of bin Ladin, almost as if hearing him unedited posed a threat to the national well-being. The selected parts of his statements that have been reproduced in the Western media tended to highlight his controversial proclamations that call for the use of violence against Western targets and hence provided only a partial glimpse of his agenda rather than accurately representing it in its entirety. As a result, bin Ladin was easily and all too quickly written off as an evil lunatic spouting ideas that were too radical to be taken seriously. Indeed, a commonly held view was that al-Qaeda's goals are so unrealistic that they do not warrant closer attention. Regardless of content or context, however, what was broadcast of bin Ladin's public statements instantly triggered fear and unease. In broad terms, bin Ladin's vision was a militant Islamist group seeking to eradicate Western influences and restore the glory of the *umma* (the community of all Muslims) through the re-creation of the caliphate – the pan-Islamic state, combining political and religious authority in a single ruler (caliph) – across the whole of the Muslim world, ultimately reaching across Europe and all of the Western world, including the USA. It is an agenda that has become closely associated with a complete rejection of Western values and the Western way of life, employing forced conversions and violent Islamization and calling for an end to freedom and democracy. As Audrey Cronin, author of *How Terrorism Ends*, makes abundantly clear: 'You cannot negotiate with a terrorist group who seeks nothing less than the complete destruction of everything we are.'[29] Her argument is compelling. Al-Qaeda is not the IRA and Osama bin Ladin was not Gerry Adams. It would be a stretch of the imagination of even the most idealistic diplomat to envision something remotely close to the Good Friday agreement being negotiated in Tora Bora or the mountains of Pakistan. But this is only part of the story.

A simple point easily overlooked is that the pan-Islamist ambition pursued by bin Ladin is never cast in specific terms, – that is, how or by whom the *umma* is to be governed – and thereby firmly remains in the realm of the ideal rather than presenting a well-defined plan or agenda. Moreover, neither the nature of the perceived threat, pan-Islamist ambitions in various forms, nor Western overreactions to the idea and its various manifestations are new or unique to the appearance of al-Qaeda. Yet little effort has thus far been made to place the goals and ideals of bin Ladin in the larger context of the history of pan-Islam in order to gain a more nuanced perspective on the issues at stake. Instead, much of the analytical efforts in terrorism studies have been directed at tracing the origins of al-Qaeda to a variety of radical Islamist thinkers of the distant past. Although one might question the analytical value of looking for the ideological roots of a highly contemporary phenomenon in the early thirteenth, eighteenth or nineteenth centuries, not to mention that such a practice lacks the basic requirements of sound historical enquiry, the conceptualization of the 'Salafi jihad' and 'Salafi jihadis' as distinct categories by which to clearly identify bin Ladin and his followers filled a void in the terrorism studies discourse. Comforting though it may be, however, to have created a label and arguably a definition for one's enemy, the use of the description 'Salafi' is expedient only inasmuch as it is convenient. What it means to be a 'Salafi jihadi', alias 'al-Qaeda member or affiliate', ultimately remains in the eye of the beholder and does not provide a reliable profile by which to identify and monitor potential terrorists.

A further unforeseen consequence of attributing not only bin Ladin's actions but also his ideas to the fringes of Islam and the darkness beyond is that this has prevented any meaningful engagement with the question of why ordinary Muslims would relate to his broader messages. In the context of a political climate that demanded clear allegiance – 'either you are with us or you are with the terrorists' – it has not been possible to separate actions from ideas. Although there is a widely shared agreement among Muslim legal scholars that, for example, suicide bombings, the indiscriminate killing of women and children, or the designation of fellow Muslims as 'unbelievers' (the practice of *takfir*) are not acceptable under sharia law and have had devastating consequences for groups embracing these practices in the past,[30] the rationale that has motivated such actions has a broader appeal. In defence of the violence committed in the name of the global jihad, bin Ladin points out the suffering of Muslims from Iraq and Palestine to Kashmir and Bosnia as a direct consequence of aggressive US/Western policies. While it is clear that he exaggerates the numbers of the actual casualties, and that the causalities are not as clear-cut as he presents them, his narrative is not entirely without merit. A prominent, frequently mentioned example is the well-documented death of 500,000 children as a consequence of economic sanctions imposed on Iraq in the aftermath of the second Gulf War in 1991.[31] Former US Secretary of State

Madeleine Albright's calm assertion that US policy objectives were worth the sacrifice of half a million Iraqi children has not only been oft repeated in the Arabic press.[32] It also features prominently in Osama bin Ladin's statements, while al-Qaeda recruitment videos show pictures of Iraqi babies wasting away from malnutrition and lack of medicine.[33]

Of course, an obvious and immediate objection to bin Ladin's presentation of these events would emphasize the difference between collateral damage arising from a 'legal' action such as war or economic sanctions and the intentional targeting of civilians. The former is viewed as 'regrettable', the latter as an unacceptable 'atrocity' in the civilized world. To be clear, the intention here is not to condone 'terrorism' or the use of violence to settle otherwise legitimate grievances. Rather, the objective is to illustrate the different picture that emerges when one looks beyond instinctive condemnation of acts of terror, condemnation born of the assumption that state-sanctioned violence is legitimate while that which challenges or operates independently of the existing state structure is not. The inference that can be drawn here is that states and terrorists share a common rationale – the belief that the deaths of thousands of innocents are a price worth paying to achieve one's political ends. Meaningful engagement with the ideas of Osama bin Ladin that underlie al-Qaeda's global jihad – a critical analysis of causes and consequences – requires suspension, at least temporarily, of judgement regarding the legitimacy of one kind of violence over the other. In other words, for analysis of the terrorist's rationale to be effective, it has to be dispassionate, impartial: it requires that one set aside one's justified sense of outrage at 9/11 and other atrocities and consider the other side's point of view. Only then is it possible to evaluate the role of the historical sense of the suffering and victimhood of the *umma* that is central to the rationale of the global jihad, and from that starting point to begin to explore al-Qaeda's justification for its actions. In practical terms, one is then at liberty to contemplate, without fear of political incorrectness, not the question of *whether* the death of 500,000 Arab children justifies the killing of 3,000 Americans, but the fact that, for one side at least, it *has* justified it.

This book investigates the nature and appeal of al-Qaeda in the light of these methodological and conceptual observations. However, rather than simply offering yet another view from yet another angle, particular attention is paid both to the discrepancies between the most common explanations and to the limits of what can realistically be known. In addition to the source criticism mentioned above, this also includes a critical take on the material that is published by or in the name of al-Qaeda. As a group that is engaged in an inherently asymmetric confrontation with the USA and the West, the strength of al-Qaeda is not based on physical might in the traditional sense that can readily be measured, quantified and countered. Rather, it lies in its ability to manipulate the audience, to instil fear and to provoke a response. This means that public statements advocating the global jihad, from videos to online journals, cannot be taken at face value and have to be seen, first and foremost, as an attempt to establish a certain status quo among a wider audience. What can be said with certainty is that the jihadis will attempt to appear as unified, competent and powerful as possible. The extent to which this amounts to wishful thinking and mere pretence is another question entirely.

It is clear that these dynamics pose a particular problem to the task of identifying who and what al-Qaeda really is. Is it an organization, a global network, a dispersed and amorphous foe, a random bunch of men? Does it consist of cells, operatives, members and a leadership? Is it more (or, some would say, less) than an organization – an ideology and a process? Chapter 2 begins with an overview of the main discourses regarding the origins and manifestations of al-Qaeda, and traces the development of what allegedly began as a regional struggle against the Soviets in Afghanistan to the declaration of the global jihad and the attacks of 11 September.

From questions about the 'who?' and the 'what?', the subsequent chapters turn to a detailed examination of the 'why?' What is the rationale for the global jihad? How can we explain violent, indiscriminate attacks against civilian targets in the name of Islam? Chapter 3 offers a critical assessment of various attempts to explain al-Qaeda's *raison d'être*. Whilst commentators have variously attempted to portray al-Qaeda adherents as madmen, religious hypocrites, Wahhabis of the twenty-first century or Salafi jihadists, what these approaches have in common is what might be described as an 'outside in' perspective that assumes a concept of the underlying logic of al-Qaeda without sufficient reference to the primary sources of evidence and at the exclusion of alternative approaches that would have offered a different reality. The chapter argues that particularly those explanations that seem to have become the official wisdom regarding the ideology of al-Qaeda, Wahhabism and the notion of the Salafi jihadist are distinguished schools of thought only within the realm of terrorism studies, and are in fact subject to much controversy in the broader fields of Middle East and Islamic studies. In the anxious quest to explain al-Qaeda, the terrorism studies community deviated from the guidelines of academic conduct and instead contented itself with recycling old oversimplifications of the complexity of Islamic thought and positing new ones, thereby granting those oversimplifications a lease of life they do not deserve. But while the 'Salafi-jihadi' label continues to stick, it offers no explanation of the lingering appeal of bin Ladin's messages among a wide sector of the Islamic faithful or of the fact that many ordinary Muslims across the world have declared him a Muslim hero.

Explaining the appeal of the broader ideas associated with al-Qaeda and the global jihad is the objective of Chapter 4. By means of reference to primary sources relating to the ideology at the core of al-Qaeda's global jihad, this chapter investigates in depth Osama bin Ladin's writings and public statements issued between 1994 and 2009, and sets them in relation to the development of Islamic thought and changing socio-political realities in the late nineteenth and twentieth centuries. In contrast to current notions of the 'Salafi jihad', it reveals an idealistic, pan-Islamic sentiment at the core of his messages that is not based on the main schools of Islamic theology, but is rather the result of the intellectual crisis of modern Islam. The historical perspective demonstrates that bin Ladin's rationale is probably best understood as a contemporary expression of pan-Islamism, an ideology that first emerged in the late nineteeth century, and that Western overreactions to its perceived threat have existed for a similar length of time.

Taking up the more concrete question of the nature and threat of al-Qaeda, Chapter 5 investigates the state of the organization in the post-9/11 world, discussing the spate of terrorist incidents that have occurred since September 2001, and examining the arguments for and against the notions that al-Qaeda exists as a structured organization and is a considerable global security threat. Has it, as some commentators have claimed, been reduced to a 'leaderless jihad' carried out on an ad hoc basis by radicalized individuals, or is al-Qaeda 'on the march', with its leadership regrouping in the remote areas of Pakistan and Afghanistan and returning to the international scene through local franchises in the Maghreb, Iraq and, most recently, the Republic of Yemen? The case of Yemen will be examined in greater detail, providing valuable insights into the current state of the jihadist movement in a region which is rapidly becoming a focus of international attention due to its increasing political instability, evident at the time of this volume going to press.

Chapter 6 looks to the future of the global jihad – one that is characterized by individualist attacks inspired by the jihadist ideology, yet unrelated to a grand organization, and provides a critical assessment of the way al-Qaeda has been and continues to be conceptualized and responded to by the international community. Has al-Qaeda's call to violent defence of the community of believers been overshadowed by more peaceful – or, at least, more democratic – actions in North Africa and the Middle East? The death of bin Ladin has been seen by some as the end of an era. Will al-Qaeda soon find itself more marginalized and isolated from the Islamic political mainstream than ever before?

TWO

What is al-Qaeda?
From Afghanistan to 9/11

Al-Qaeda was formed in 1988 by veterans of the anti-Soviet civil war in Afghanistan, with the purpose of exporting the victory Islam had won over the communists to other theatres of conflict around the world. At the head of the new movement were Abdullah Azzam and his deputy, Osama bin Ladin, who may have differed as to how their objectives were to be achieved. When Azzam was killed in 1989, bin Ladin assumed full control of the organization. Between 1991 and 1996, al-Qaeda was headquartered in Sudan, where it enjoyed friendly relations with the governing National Islamic Front. International pressure forced bin Ladin to relocate back to Afghanistan in 1996, where al-Qaeda allied itself with the then-nascent Taliban. In late 2001, most of al-Qaeda's training camps were destroyed, and the group became somewhat diffuse, with much of its leadership relocating either to Iran, the mountainous region along the Afghanistan–Pakistan border, or to Pakistan's cities. Many of those who were in Pakistan's cities were caught. The status of the leadership in Iran remains unclear. Al-Qaeda's purpose is to spread jihad worldwide through a number of means, including funding and training Islamic and ethnic guerilla movements, issuing propaganda aimed at inspiring freelance jihadists to commit acts of terrorism, and organizing and conducting complex attacks on countries it sees opposing it.

Homeland Security, 2010[1]

So goes the story of the origins and nature of al-Qaeda. Or, to be more precise, so goes one version of events. The questions surrounding the origins and development of al-Qaeda, coupled with a growing concern that its true identity should be clearly established, have resulted in a number of different theories being formulated. Indeed, the variety of different descriptions and explanations that surfaced as early as 2003 led Xavier Raufer to exclaim: 'al-Qaeda is floating between contradictory descriptions, comparisons and metaphors.'[2] Far from being resolved, the controversy has only intensified over the years, and has led to the creation of different schools of thought regarding both the make-up of al-Qaeda and, consequently, the nature of the threat it poses. A closer analysis of the leading discourses reveals a variety of discrepancies, unsubstantiated assertions and truth claims that often appear plausible at first sight, but that prove upon further examination to be incoherent or to lack a strong basis in fact. The story of one of the most significant challenges to international security in the twenty-first century is also one of the most distorted and ambiguous.

1986–91: the 'birth' of al-Qaeda

Most accounts of the origins of al-Qaeda begin with the legacy of the Soviet invasion of Afghanistan in late 1979 in support of the communist Afghan government. Opposition to the communists led to creation of the well-documented Afghan National Resistance movement that would ultimately defeat the Soviet forces. The call to arms was answered not only by native Afghans. The conflict soon attracted young Muslims from around the world, particularly from the Middle East, who volunteered to join what was seen as a holy war, or *jihad*: a righteous war of defence against the godless invader. Among these volunteers, also referred to as *mujahideen* (those engaged in jihad, sometimes referred to as 'holy warriors') or 'Afghan Arabs' (the name given to mujahideen from the Arab World), was Osama bin Ladin, son of a wealthy Saudi businessman, who would become the emir (leader) of al-Qaeda. Also among them were the Egyptian Dr Ayman al-Zawahiri, a surgeon, leader of the Egyptian Islamic Jihad and al-Qaeda's number two, considered by some to have been the real leader and mastermind of the group, and the Jordanian-Palestinian Dr Abdullah Azzam, a disciple of Egyptian author and Islamist Sayyid Qutb and a leading Islamist of his generation, who formulated much of the doctrine of the jihad against the Soviets and also served as mentor to bin Ladin. The three men who would unite in the fight against the Soviets each came to the task with different motivations and long-term goals, and each contributed distinctive skills.

Abdullah Azzam, who distinguished himself early on by urging the Afghan resistance leaders and opposition groups to unite against their common enemy, was one of the first Arabs to join the jihad. His main contribution to its success, however, was his worldwide promotion of the jihad, both through his ideological communications and later, jointly with bin Ladin, through the establishment of an infrastructure for the recruitment of volunteers. Azzam communicated a simple message. To him, coming to the defence of a Muslim country against invasion by non-Muslim forces was a clear case of personal obligation (*fard 'ayn*): it was every Muslim's duty to join the jihad. Indeed, it has sometimes been argued that he saw Afghanistan as the first step in a worldwide jihad to recapture Muslim lands lost to infidels, especially his native Palestine.

> This duty shall not lapse with victory in Afghanistan, and the jihad will remain an individual obligation until all other lands which were formerly Muslim come back to us and Islam reigns within them once again. Before us lie Palestine, Bukhara, Lebanon, Chad,

Eritrea, Somalia, the Philippines, Burma, South Yemen, Tashkent, Andalusia... Our presence in Afghanistan today, which is the accomplishment of the imperative of jihad and our devotion to the struggle, does not mean that we have forgotten Palestine. Palestine is our beating heart.[3]

Although Azzam was an aggressive advocate of jihad, demanding the return of formerly Muslim lands, it is important to note that he refrained from demanding the overthrow of secular Muslim governments on the grounds of apostasy and strongly rejected internecine Muslim conflict. His views would later clash with the ambitions of Ayman al-Zawahiri and other members of the Egyptian Islamic Jihad, who aimed to overthrow the Egyptian government and in whose minds condemnation of the apostasy of secular Muslim states was inseparable from true Islamic faith.[4] Indeed, Azzam's comparatively moderate viewpoint may have led to his untimely death in the second of two bomb attacks carried out against him in 1989. Initially, however, it was Azzam who exercised a strong ideological influence on the much younger Osama bin Ladin, with whom he would coordinate the task of international recruitment. To that end, bin Ladin was an outstanding addition: although he would eventually become highly respected and lionized in tales of his bravery, his unique contribution to the jihad in its early days was his commitment to global recruitment and his provision of financial assistance out of his inherited family fortune.[5] The *9/11 Commission Report* emphasizes the role of bin Ladin, claiming that he 'understood better than most of the volunteers the extent to which the continuation and eventual success of the jihad in Afghanistan depended on an increasingly complex, almost worldwide organization'.[6]

General agreement exists that it was during this period that the idea of al-Qaeda began to take shape, although opinions differ as to exactly when, how and by whom al-Qaeda was founded. Initially, however, both Osama bin Ladin and Abdullah Azzam became actively involved in the task of recruiting volunteers for the ongoing struggle for Afghanistan. Jointly they set up Maktab al-Khidamat – the 'Afghan Service Bureau', also known as the Bureau of Services, or MAK – which channelled international recruits and funding into the conflict in Afghanistan.[7] Gunaratna provides specific details about the MAK's role and the extent of its reach:

> As an organization staffed and managed by the *mujahidin*, it played a decisive role in the anti-Soviet resistance. In addition to recruiting, indoctrinating and training *tens of thousands* of Arab and Muslim youths from countries ranging from the US to the Philippines, MAK disbursed $200 million of Middle Eastern and Western, mainly American and British, aid destined for the Afghan *jihad*. Osama also channelled substantial resources of his own to the cause, a gesture that resonated with his fighters, raising his credibility and allowing him to raise even more funds and recruit even more volunteers.[8]

What Gunaratna does not provide, however, is references to support these claims. By contrast, journalist Lawrence Wright, drawing on an extensive number of personal interviews, offers an overall more modest description, although he too fails to provide any details of his sources:

> [They] set up what they called the Services Bureau (Makhtab al Khadamat) in a house bin Ladin was renting in the University Town section of Peshawar. Bin Ladin provided twenty-five thousand dollars a month to keep the office running. The house also served as a hostel for Arab mujahideen and the headquarters of Azzam's magazine and book publishing efforts. The service Bureau was essentially a repository for the money that the two men were sweeping in through their fundraising efforts.[9]

By contrast, the *9/11 Commission Report* is somewhat vague in its assessment of the extent of the MAK, noting in fairly general terms that 'mosques, schools, and boarding houses served as recruiting stations in many parts of the world, including the United States'[10] – creating the impression of an extensive, but overall rather informal operation. The *Report* gives a similar impression of loose affiliation with regard to the financing of the operation, with references made to a financial support network consisting of financiers in Saudi Arabia and the Gulf, with monies flowing through charities and nongovernmental organizations. Its vagueness regarding the make-up of the MAK notwithstanding, the *Commission Report* is quite specific in refuting the popular allegation that it was US money that effectively fostered al-Qaeda. Despite the billions of dollars secretly supplied by the USA in support of rebel groups fighting the Soviet occupation, 'Bin Ladin and his comrades had their own sources of support and received little or no assistance from the United States.'[11]

Whatever the full extent of the MAK, it is widely considered to be the forerunner of al-Qaeda. In the words of Alexander and Swetnam, '*Al-Qaida* emerged from the *mekhtab al khidemat* (MAK), the Afghan Mujahideen "services office", around 1989.'[12] Indeed, once victory had been achieved by the Afghan jihad and Soviet forces were beginning their withdrawal from the country, its leaders were beginning to contemplate what to do next. Allegedly, 'Bin Ladin and Azzam agreed that the organization successfully created for Afghanistan should not be allowed to dissolve. They established what they called a base or foundation (al-Qaeda) as a potential *general headquarters* for future jihad.'[13] Sageman, who offers no details as to the extent of the MAK, advances the same rationale but fundamentally differs in his view of what was created. To him, 'the consensus among the hardcore leaders of the mujahedin was to establish a base (al-qaeda), or *a social movement*[14] – rather than a general headquarters – to carry out a worldwide jihad.

Although a variety of different interpretations have since evolved regarding the particulars of the group, a number of US legal and government documents are specific about the fact that the 'birth' of al-Qaeda took place in 1989. Clear and reliable as the date of al-Qaeda's foundation is, a detailed history of its formation is more difficult to come by. For example, in the indictment of bin Ladin and various cohorts such as Ayman al-Zawahiri, the US District Court of New York notes, 'From in or about 1989 until the present, the group called itself "al-Qaeda" ("the Base"). From 1989 until in or about 1991, the group ... was headquartered in Afghanistan and Peshawar, Pakistan.'[15] Similarly, a congressional report published in 2005 maintains that 'al-Qaeda was founded by Osama bin Ladin in Afghanistan in 1988.'[16] In the light of these assertions, Raufer makes an important point when he concludes that,

> surprisingly, and even if al-Qaeda constitutes the most serious imme-
> diate threat to the security of the United States and has committed
> the worst terrorist attack ever, no one in the United States seems to
> be really sure of what al-Qaeda is. Even worse, the question 'What
> is al-Qaeda?' seems futile, even meaningless to an American admin-
> istration persuaded it knows what al-Qaeda really is: a well-known
> entity, clearly defined and devoid of mystery.[17]

In other words, the US government's working definition of al-Qaeda was – and continues to be – that it is a dangerous terrorist organization founded and run by Osama bin Ladin.

Contradicting this commonly held and, as noted above, formally documented view of Osama bin Ladin as the 'founder' of al-Qaeda, there seems to be a general agreement in the extant literature that al-Qaeda was in fact conceived by Azzam. As noted by Gunaratna, 'al-Qaeda was conceptualised by Azzam, not Osama, and hence the former's imprint is firmly embedded in the psyche of its leadership.'[18] Migaux expands upon this, explaining that it was 'Abdullah Azzam who named the organization ... he decided he would not disband the army of Arab volunteers he had created for years but would undertake a much wider, vaster mission – the re-conquest of the Muslim world... He coined the term *al-qaeda al-sulbah* (the solid base) for this.'[19] Almost all of these claims refer to an article that Azzam wrote for a magazine aimed at the mujahideen, *al Jihad*, in which he stated 'It is *al-qaeda al-sulbah* that constitutes this vanguard for the hoped-for society.'[20] Moreover, bin Ladin himself is on record as saying that 'the name "al-Qaeda" was established a long time ago by mere chance. The late Abu Ubaida Al Bashiri established training camps for our Mujahideen against Russia's terrorism. We used to call the training camp "al-Qaeda" ["The Base"], and the name stayed.'[21]

The controversy surrounding its genesis notwithstanding, the image that emerges at this stage is that rather than actually being 'created', in the sense of being planned with the specific goal of creating an entity to fight the USA and the West, al-Qaeda evolved from the structures that were originally put into place to recruit volunteers for the fighting in Afghanistan. Much debate and disagreement continue to surround the details of both the original structure and the entity it later became. Broadly speaking, there are two schools of thought. One of these holds that al-Qaeda was planned from its inception to be a tightly knit organization, with distinct divisions of labour assigned to different branches and with recognized forms of entry such as the by now infamous oath of allegiance to bin Ladin, the existence of which continues to be disputed. The contrasting theory holds that the essence of al-Qaeda was some-thing much more vague: a network of individuals affiliated to different Islamist groups that could well have aspired to become highly organized and boast a strong chain of command, but that in fact consisted of much looser associations. Thus, while it may lack a coherent structure in reality, the group benefits from pretending or appearing to be more organized and structured than it really is, essentially creating a propaganda image which strikes fear into national governments and the general public, but is disproportionate to the group's true size and effectiveness.

The *9/11 Commission Report*, reflecting if not representing the formal US perspective, offers the clearest picture of the structure of al-Qaeda:

> [Al-Qaeda's] structure includes as its operating arms an intelligence component, a military committee, a financial committee, a political committee, and a committee in charge of media affairs and propaganda. It also had an Advisory Council (*Shura*) made up of Bin Ladin's inner circle.[22]

Other commentators, however, depict al-Qaeda in much less concrete and structured terms. According to Gunaratna,

> Al-Qaeda's global network, as we know it today, was created while it was based in Khartoum, from December 1991 till May 1996. To co-ordinate its overt and covert operations as al-Qaeda's ambitions and resources increased, it developed a decentralised, regional structure. Although its *modus operandi* is cellular, familial relationships play a key role.[23]

For Sageman, as has been noted above, al-Qaeda was from the beginning conceptualized as a base or social movement sup-porting the global jihad, although he has since distanced himself from his original position, acknowledging the existence and continued importance of the central organization of al-Qaeda.

For Raufer, and indeed a number of other analysts, the make-up of al-Qaeda is something more amorphous.

> Since the beginning, Al-Qaeda is nothing more than a nebula, a protoplasm with not one mold, no unique way to organize, but rather each group (i.e. the Egyptians or Pakistanis) creating its own cells within the nebula, out of its own jihadi culture, its own local habits.[24]

Or, in the words of criminologist R.T Naylor,

> In reality, al-Qaeda seems less an organization than a loose association of independent, cell-like entities that change form and personnel ad hoc in response to threat and opportunities. Al-Qaeda seems less an entity than a shared state of mind, less a political organization than a cult of personality.[25]

But what is the rationale for these conflicting perceptions? And is it possible to establish which scenario is true? A closer look at the sources that underlie these different assertions offers insights that are both interesting and unsatisfying in equal measure. Arguably the most convincing case is made by Burke, who maintains that 'To see [al-Qaeda] as a coherent and tight-knit organization, with "tentacles everywhere", with a defined ideology and personnel, *that has emerged as early as the late 1980s,* is to misunderstand not only its true nature but the nature of Islamic radicalism then and now.'[26] He makes a strong case for his assessment, which is based on a critical view of the sources of evidence and their selective utilization by the US Federal Bureau of Investigation all too eager to present a clear case for al-Qaeda being a structured organization. The weight of Burke's argument further rests on the observation that the term 'al-Qaeda' was not used by either bin Ladin or his associates to refer to an organization at the time. Indeed, as late as 1998, following the double bombings of American embassies in the East African cities of Dar es Salaam, Tanzania, and Nairobi, Kenya, then US president Clinton still talked of the 'bin Laden network', not of 'al-Qaeda' the organization.[27] It was only during the FBI-led investigation into the bombings that the term was used to describe a traditionally structured terrorist organization. For Burke, the reasons behind this development are obvious:

> The culture of the FBI is focused on achieving convictions, and the teams working on the prosecution of those responsible for the east African embassy bombings of August 1998 had to work within the extant laws, particularly those of conspiracy. Such laws were designed to deal with coherent and structured criminal enterprises, not with amorphous and dispersed politico-religious movements where responsibility for any one single act is difficult to pin down. ... Unfortunately, in the case of 'al-Qaeda', it completely misrepresents the nature of the entity under investigation.[28]

Furthermore, most of the accounts that portray al-Qaeda as a tightly structured entity formed in 1989 are based on the testimony of a single individual, Dr Jamal al-Fadl, a Sudanese militant who is believed to have been recruited to the Afghan mujahideen through the Farouq Mosque in Brooklyn, New York, in the early 1980s and who subsequently became a senior member of al-Qaeda. Al-Fadl defected from bin Ladin's inner circle after being caught siphoning off large amounts of al-Qaeda's money for personal use, and subsequently switched sides to become the principal informant for the US intelligence services. As Burke explains,

> He ... hawked himself around a series of Middle Eastern security agencies before being picked up by the Americans in 1996. As such, he is not a particularly reliable source, and it is clear that, as a prosecution witness in *USA* v. *Usama bin Laden*, he had a strong interest in exaggerating the role of the main defendant.[29]

Reliable or not, al-Fadl served as a key prosecution witness in the January 2001 trial (*United States* v. *Usama bin Laden*) that led to the conviction of four men involved in the 1998 US embassy bombings in East Africa. The attacks, which have been linked to members of the Egyptian Islamic Jihad, brought Osama bin Ladin and Ayman al-Zawahiri to the centre of attention of the US government for the first time and led the FBI to place bin Ladin on its 'Ten Most Wanted' list. At the time of the trial, the intention was to prosecute bin Ladin in his absence under the Racketeer Influenced and Corrupt Organizations Act (RICO), which legally required that the prosecutors provide evidence of the existence of a 'criminal' organization, which would allow for the prosecution of its leader, even if he or she could not be linked directly to the 'crime'.

It would indeed appear convenient that al-Fadl delivered the evidence required of him when he testified that Osama bin Ladin was the leader of a large international terrorist organization known as 'al-Qaeda'. It mattered little that his claim was challenged at a later stage of the trial by the testimony of Khalfan Khamis Muhamed, one of the bombers. Muhamed is on record as explaining that he had not taken a *bayat* (oath) to join a group called al-Qaeda. Indeed he claimed not to have heard of any such organization and merely commented that 'al-Qaeda was a formula system they used to carry out the bombing.'[30] In the light of these contradictory accounts, Burke deems the narrative of the tightly structured make-up to be closer to wishful thinking than reality, coming to the conclusion that al-Qaeda at that time is best understood as a tactic and that Azzam primarily saw it as a 'mode of activism and not an organization'.[31]

A similar criticism of the notion of al-Qaeda as a tightly structured organization is made by Adam Curtis in a four-hour BBC documentary, *The Power of Nightmares*. Like Burke, Curtis contends that Osama bin Ladin and Ayman al-Zawahiri were 'on the fringes of the Islamist movement', and that their role has been exaggerated to suit the purposes of the FBI, who were looking to prosecute bin Ladin *in absentia*.[32] Here again, al-Fadl's testimony is seen as both central and convenient to this objective as he paints a picture of a formidable terrorist structure with bin Ladin at its head. Sam Schmidt, attorney for one of the defendants on trial in *United States* v. *Usama bin Ladin*, states: 'There were selective portions of al-Fadl's testimony that were false ... [which] made [al-Qaeda] identifiable as a group and therefore [made it] easier to prosecute a person associated with al-Qaeda for any acts or statements made by bin Ladin, who talked a lot.'[33]

Whether or not Burke and Curtis are ultimately correct in their assessments, they do well to emphasize that the evidence describing al-Qaeda as an organization is drawn from a limited number of questionable sources. In addition to al-Fadl and Muhamed, evidence was also heard from L'Houssaine Kherchtou, who pleaded guilty to conspiracy to murder in the embassy bombings, but was granted immunity from prosecution and entered into a witness protection programme in exchange for testifying against his former colleagues. Like al-Fadl, he thus had a considerable incentive to play into the hands of the prosecution. Together, their testimonies form the bulk of the information known about the early years of al-Qaeda. Although their respective testimonies offered conflicting images of the structural make-up of al-Qaeda, the description of a structured terrorist organization has been accepted as accurate. There was, however, no hard evidence to justify this acceptance; the statements of al-Fadl and Kherchtou were simply taken at face value at trial and accepted as truth from then on. It therefore

seems legitimate to conclude that by early 2001 the truth about
the nature of al-Qaeda had become a hostage to the determination of the United States authorities to build a prosecution
case against bin Ladin at all costs, and that al-Qaeda became
known as a complex terrorist organization because it suited the
purposes of the United States to portray it as such.

Of particular interest with regard to the reliability of sources
is the case of Enaam Arnaout (*United States* v. *Enaam Arnaout*),
a Syrian American and former director of the charity Bene-
volence International Foundation (BIF) in Sarajevo, who was
arrested on charges of terrorism based on the allegation that he
had worked for bin Ladin and made use of donations received
by BIF to fund the jihad in Bosnia.[34] Much attention was given
at the trial to a file labelled 'Tareekh Osama' – a collection of
memos, letters and notes recovered from Arnaout's office at
the BIF, which allegedly contained detailed information as to
when al-Qaeda was established, what its structure was and
who the key members were. In the court proceedings, the file
is specifically referred to as evidence for al-Qaeda being an
organization. It is interesting to observe, however, that despite
the insistence that an organizational structure existed, the
evidence itself points to something that was more diffuse:

> As remarkable materials archived by BIF prove, Bin Laden formed
> *al Qaeda* in 1988 with others, including Salim (Abu Hajer) and
> Bayazid (Abu Rida). *Al Qaeda* maintained personnel files and mem-
> bers pledged a *bayat* (oath of allegiance) and signed a contract....
> Defendant Arnaout himself is not known to have made *bayat*, though
> evidence demonstrates he was very important to the *al Qaeda* net-
> work. Many key members of the *al Qaeda* network, including Abu
> Hajer, may not have become formal members.[35]

The proceedings specifically record in a footnote:

Members did not always know who else signed a contract or swore a *bayat*. Moreover, many key members of the *al Qaeda* network … may not have become formal members of the group by making *bayat* even though they played a controlling role in the work of *al Qaeda*.[34]

Indeed, upon closer analysis of the evidence given in the *Arnaout* case, which, as the following extract illustrates, is far from clear, at times poorly presented and difficult to read, the data found in the Tareekh Osama file appears to be more reflective of an ongoing attempt at the creation of an organization rather than depicting a well-structured organization already in existence.

In addition to discussing fund-raising, the list contains numerous entries calling for the establishment of a leadership council and determining the best places to work. *Id.* It calls for:
A printed declaration which will explain the following:
a. The East's and West's agreement to prevent the establishment of an Islamic nation and thorn.
b. The only solution is the continuation of the armed Jihad.
c. Taking interest in the training and seizing the opportunity.
d. Supporting the Mujahideen believers and… [illegible].
e. Specifying the locations where we want the brethren to be. Will be signed by Yunis Khallis, Ansar Al -Jihad ['supporter of *jihad'*]
f. Urging the brethren to be patient, pious, obedient, and to practice abstinence (Abu Hajir). *Id.* [parentheses in original]. Near the end of the list the following entry appears ominously: 'Keeping alive the Jihadist spirit among Muslims in general, and the Arabs in particular, by opening bases for their Jihad along with maintaining contact lines with them. The Sudan is recommended.'[37]

Although it is difficult to judge the content of the Tareekh Osama file solely on the basis of the translations and summaries provided in the court case, even this second-hand view does not fit neatly with the notion of al-Qaeda the organization. Furthermore, it is by no means clear that those commentators who subsequently refer to the file as evidence have actually seen the original data or in fact draw their conclusions on the basis of what the file allegedly contains. For example, the *9/11 Commission Report* relies to a great extent upon the content of the Tareekh Osama file in its characterization of al-Qaeda as a coherent organization, and effectively treats the court proceedings as a reliable source.[38] To support these claims, in the 'Notes to Chapters' the report states:

> A wealth of information on al-Qaeda's evolution and history has been obtained from material seized in recent years, including files labelled 'Tareekh Usama' (Usama's history) and 'Tareekh al Musadat' (History of the Services Bureau). For descriptions of and substantial excerpts from these files, see ... *United States* v. *Arnaout*.[39]

Another outspoken supporter of the notion of 'al-Qaeda, the organization', journalist Peter Bergen, rejects the claims of Burke and Curtis as 'nonsense'.[40] In his opinion, there is overwhelming evidence to support the assertions that al-Qaeda was established in the late 1980s, and that it had a clear chain of command with bin Ladin at the very top.[41] He goes on to quote the Tareekh Osama file as evidence to substantiate his claim. Bergen, who gives no indication as to whether he had ever seen the original file, maintains that

> BIF had in its Sarajevo office a computer file labelled 'Tareekh Osama' or 'Osama's History.' The file contains scanned images of documents which chronicle Usama bin Ladin's activities in Afghanistan which led to the formation of al-Qaeda and even includes later reports of the threat bin Ladin poses to the US.[42]

Bergen also adds that 'Some of the letters bear bin Ladin's signature at the bottom of the originals',[43] whereas the court case indicates that letters attributed to bin Ladin were in effect written by an alias.

Thus, to the puzzlement of the attentive observer, the official debate as to the true identity of al-Qaeda continues to go round in circles. In the end, there remain two differing interpretations of the nature of al-Qaeda in late 1989. Should it be regarded as a fully fledged terrorist organization with cells all over the world, or is it instead something more amorphous which gained some kind of coherence during the years preceding the September 11 attacks? To a great extent, the truth remains obscured by conflicting interpretations and fabrications that have grown up in the absence of sufficient reliable evidence.

Whether or the not the end of the Soviet–Afghan war saw the establishment of al-Qaeda qua organization, it certainly witnessed the growing ideological divide between bin Ladin and his mentor, Abdullah Azzam. This was due to the growing influence of the Egyptians, especially Ayman al-Zawahiri, who advanced new ideas and agendas for the jihad. Gunaratna expands on this point:

> Although Osama and Azzam agreed on the principal issues of supporting Muslims who were persecuted ... they disagreed on tactics. The tension between the two came to a head over a proposal by MAK's Egyptian fighters to train the Mujahideen in terrorist techniques. The Egyptians were keen to build a force to mount a campaign back home... Having lived in Egypt, [Azzam] knew the futility, danger and limits of launching a terrorist campaign there and hence issued a *fatwa* stating that using jihadi funds to train in terrorist tactics would violate Islamic law.[44]

Indeed Azzam has categorically rejected any move that would spread discord, or *fitna*, among Muslims. According to Bergen, Egyptian militants wanted 'the violent overthrow of governments across the Islamic world they deemed "apostate", a concept of Jihad that Azzam and many of his followers rejected, as they wanted no part in conflicts against Muslims.'[45] Wright agrees, expressing in unambiguous terms that 'Azzam fiercely opposed a war of Muslim against Muslim.'[46] Abdullah Anas, a mujahideen commander and confidant of Azzam, claims that Zawahiri was keen to recruit bin Ladin because of the money he brought with him.[47] Subsequently Anas also accuses Zawahiri of running a smear campaign against Azzam to remove him and undermine his authority. Azzam was assassinated in November 1989; his killers have never been identified. Gunaratna claims that bin Ladin was involved in the plot against Azzam: 'The Egyptians had won over Osama to their cause before assassinating Azzam, on the condition that he backed the strategic shift towards terrorism, a move he wholeheartedly endorsed.'[48] Others disagree with this assessment, including Abdel Bari Atwan, who recognizes the breach between the two men but dismisses the idea that bin Ladin had a hand in Azzam's death.[49] As with so much of the history of al-Qaeda, the controversy regarding the circumstances surrounding the death of Azzam remains unresolved.

With Azzam dead and the war over, Osama bin Ladin allegedly went back to Saudi Arabia as something of a hero. 'The young idealist returned to the Kingdom with a sense of divine mission... He had gone an acolyte of an iconic Muslim warrior, and he had returned as the undisputed leader of the Arab Afghans.'[50] With his new status, bin Ladin's aims became ever more elevated. To illustrate this point, Wright accuses bin Ladin of financing guerrilla war in the newly unified Yemen in a bid to rid the Arabian Peninsula of 'foreign elements'.[51] At the same time, bin Ladin also became ever more vocal about America and its corrupting role in the Islamic world. Atwan asserts that bin Ladin was placed under house arrest because of a growing concern about his activities.

The Saudi government had security concerns about him even at this early stage. His very outspoken public speeches had been recorded on cassette tapes and widely distributed; in them he warned the Saudi people about the threat posed by Iraqi Ba'athist regime, which he believed had plans to invade the whole Gulf region.[52]

Gilles Kepel supports this idea when he states that bin Ladin was so concerned about the Ba'athist threat that he offered King Fahd the use of his jihadi forces.[53] Indeed, the invasion of Kuwait by Iraq in 1990 marks something of a turning point for bin Ladin and al-Qaeda. First, bin Ladin was vindicated over his concerns about Saddam Hussein's expansionist aims – an observation that seems ironic in the light of post-9/11 allegations by the United States of cooperation between Saddam and Osama. More significant by far was the Saudi Arabian rejection of bin Ladin's offer of jihadi troops to protect the kingdom against Saddam's expansionism in favour of American financial and military help. This caused an irreconcilable rift between bin Ladin and the kingdom, as Atwan articulates:

> Bin Ladin told me that the Saudi government's decision to invite US troops to defend the Kingdom and liberate Kuwait was the biggest shock of his entire life. He could not believe that the House of Al Saud could welcome the deployment of 'infidel' forces on Arabian Peninsula soil, within the proximity of the Holy Places, for the first time since the inception of Islam.[54]

Indeed, this event appeared to mark the beginning of an antagonistic and confrontational relationship between bin Ladin and Saudi Arabia and the beginning of a new chapter in the contested history of al-Qaeda.

1992–96: al-Qaeda in Sudan and Afghanistan

In the aftermath of the Gulf War, Osama bin Ladin decamped to Sudan after a brief sojourn in Pakistan. There appears to be a consensus in the literature which asserts that bin Ladin and

Zawahiri had been invited to Sudan at the behest of Hassan al-Turabi, a Sudanese Islamist and prominent figure in the Council for National Salvation, headed by President Omar al-Bashir. The new Islamic regime had swept to power in a coup in 1989 and Turabi was a hugely influential figure, although he was later to be arrested and imprisoned a number of times for alleged conspiracies against the Bashir regime. Bergen quotes Jamal Ismail of *al Jihad* magazine: 'The Sudan government extended an invitation for [bin Ladin]. They opened the borders for Arabs and Muslims to invest and to visit Sudan... Dr al Turabi, played a very, very important role in convincing Omar Bashir to bring Osama.'[55] Apparently it was hoped that bin Ladin would bring a lot of money and thus investment to the impoverished country. Indeed, Burke notes that 'Most of bin Ladin's time in Sudan appears to have been devoted to setting up and running a sprawling and less than successful business empire.'[56]

Initial agreement aside, this period has raised plenty of speculation as to how much money bin Ladin had, what amounts he invested in Sudan, and whether his ventures were profitable or in fact a significant waste of money. Opinions differ widely as to the total amount of capital involved. Gunaratna, relying on unnamed sources of intelligence, claims that bin Ladin inherited only $25–$30 million.[57] At the other end of the spectrum, Atwan argues that bin Ladin spent $300 million[58] of his own money in Sudan, of which $200 million was devoted to 'large-scale construction projects such as the Port Sudan airport and the 400-km "Defiance Highway" between Port Sudan and Khartoum'.[59] Taking a more cautious stance, Wright observes: 'Exaggerated claims about his [bin Ladin's] wealth were circulating; people said that he was investing $350 million – or more – in the country, which would certainly be its salvation.'[60] Thus there is a great deal of confusion as to how much money bin Ladin actually had invested, although there is agreement that he spent a great deal of money in Sudan during this time. Gunaratna describes him as 'prudent'[61] whereas Burke[62] and Wright[63] paint a less flattering picture. In fact, Wright goes so far as to argue that bin Ladin was 'broke' due to the chronic mismanagement of his Sudanese businesses and the discontinuation of the stipend he received from his family in Saudi Arabia. This was evidenced by the aforementioned L'Houssaine Kherchtou, who needed money to pay for his wife's Caesarean section but was told there was none.[64] Furthermore, according to Wright, the actions of al-Fadl, who siphoned off money from al-Qaeda operations, were motivated by a lack of parity between what Egyptian and Sudanese operatives were paid.[65] There simply was not enough money.

Osama Bin Ladin was not only investing in Sudanese infrastructure, but in the process was also helping to fund a wider group of Islamic fighters. Richard Clarke, author of *Against All Enemies*, describes him as a 'philanthropist of terror',[66] and Burke claims that al-Qaeda acted like a 'venture capitalist firm' in bankrolling prospective terrorists in ideologically similar causes.[67] Gunaratna paints a picture of an ever growing and strengthening organization, claiming that al-Qaeda had 1,000–1,500 fighters who were able to train by means of an extensive infrastructure in Pakistan and Afghanistan and then went on to fight in places such as Bosnia.[68] Richard Clarke also comments on the emergence of al-Qaeda-trained fighters in Bosnia, albeit with a minor caveat: 'We didn't know they were al-Qaeda, but we knew they were international terrorists.'[69] Gunaratna adds that al-Qaeda fighters were trained in making explosives on an al-Qaeda-owned farm, and that the Sudanese gave them land to set up training camps.[70] In summary: 'From Sudan, Al-Qaeda began to spread its network worldwide, developing [an] unprecedented communications network linking its regional offices in London, New York, Turkey and other centres.'[71] Wright, however, assesses the activities of the period very differently, claiming that during this time 'al-Qaeda had come to nothing' and had 'no leadership and no clear direction'.[72]

These conflicting accounts of al-Qaeda's origins and growth form the background to the Western world's understanding of both al-Qaeda's ideological development and its involvement in acts of terrorism that followed. On one hand, the *9/11 Commission Report* claims that by 1992 al-Qaeda's mission had turned global, referring to a fatwa issued by the al-Qaeda leadership, calling for jihad against western forces' 'occupation' of Islamic lands.[73] On the other hand, Sageman maintains that during this period, the strategy of al-Qaeda was to target the 'near enemy': secular Arab regimes and Western targets in Islamic countries.[74] Hence the fatwa can be seen within a context of defensive jihad. Sageman further remarks that 'The skirmishes against the US were still a minor aspect of the jihad during the Sudanese exile.'[75] The *9/11 Commission Report*, however, insisting on the growing threat of al-Qaeda, claims that bin Ladin was already preoccupied with the 'head of the snake' – the United States – and that this was evidenced by the fatwa and subsequent terrorist acts. In fact, one of the first al-Qaeda-attributed terrorist incidents was the bombing of a hotel in Aden, Yemen, in 1992. The outbreak of a humanitarian disaster in Somalia led the Americans to deploy a small-scale humanitarian mission ('Operation: Restore Hope', begun December 1992) to facilitate the delivery of aid. Bin Ladin took this as a sign that the USA was looking to move into the region and expand its operations and perhaps target Sudan. The bombing of the hotel was aimed at American troops en route to Somalia, but in fact they were not there to be bombed, having left two days prior to the explosions. The *9/11 Commission Report* states: 'The perpetrators are reported to have belonged to a group from southern Yemen headed by a Yemeni member of Bin Ladin's Islamic Army Shura; some in the group had trained in an al-Qaeda run camp in Sudan.'[76] Atwan also claims that 'Bin Ladin also told me that his Afghan Arabs had been involved in the 1993 ambush on American troops in Mogadishu, Somalia' and that he was disappointed when the Americans withdrew following the 'Black Hawk Down' incident.[77] Burke contradicts this view as 'almost certainly untrue'.[78] He goes on to say that 'journalists who worked in Somalia at the time found little evidence of any "al-Qaeda" involvement in the "Black Hawk Down" episode.'[79]

Arguably the most significant event related to al-Qaeda in this period was the 1993 bombing of the World Trade Center by a man called Ramzi Yousef, although there is a dispute in the relevant literature as to the extent to which this event can be attributed to al-Qaeda. The *9/11 Commission Report* states that although bin Ladin had links to Yousef and the so-called 'Blind Sheikh' (Omar Abdel-Rahman, alleged leader of militant Egyptian Islamic group Al-Gama'a al-Islamiyya, later convicted of 'seditious conspiracy' in relation to the 1993 World Trade Center bombing), al-Qaeda's 'involvement is at best cloudy'.[80] Wright does not directly link bin Ladin to the bombing but does state that Yousef had been trained in al-Qaeda camps.[81] For Gunaratna, however, bin Ladin's involvement is more explicit:

Although the US at the time was unaware that the British-educated bomber Ramzi Ahmed Yousef was financed by Osama, they knew of the threat posed to it by the Pakistan- and Afghanistan-based Mujahideen. As Osama concealed his hand in most operations, including the 1993 bombing, the multinational nature of his organization had escaped the attention of the CIA.[82]

Bergen strongly contradicts this claim. He is categorical in his dismissal of the notion that bin Ladin was involved with the World Trade Center bombing, despite being initially convinced that a greater hand was behind the attacks. He asserts: 'bin Ladin had nothing to do with that attack.'[83]

One terrorist incident more or less unanimously attributed to al-Qaeda is the bombing of the Khobar Towers in Saudi Arabia in 1996. Yet before this attack could be carried out, bin Ladin faced new pressures from his hosts, the Sudanese, to leave the country. In 1995, an assassination attempt on the Egyptian president, Hosni Mubarak, in Ethiopia led to renewed pressure on the Sudanese to expel bin Ladin. It was suspected that Egyptian Islamic Jihad fighters stationed in Sudan were responsible for the failed attempt on Mubarak's life. There also appeared to be continued tensions between bin Ladin and the Saudi authorities, who sent envoys to Sudan to entreat the emir to return home. None of these attempts was crowned with success, and in 1994 the Saudi authorities revoked bin Ladin's citizenship and he was publicly disowned by his family. Bergen cites the comments of Prince Turki al-Faisal, head of Saudi intelligence:

[We monitored bin Ladin] recruiting persons from different parts of the Islamic world... It was an unacceptable activity. So remarks were made and the [Sudanese] authorities were informed and we were given assurances that Osama would not be allowed to harm Saudi interests.[84]

Consequently it would appear that the pressure placed on the Sudanese compelled them to persuade bin Ladin to leave the country.

Osama bin Ladin left Sudan and returned to Afghanistan in 1996. During this time the Taliban, led by Mullah Omar, had control over large parts of the country. Migaux sets out how bin Ladin exploited the situation, including the weaknesses of the Taliban, to create a symbiotic relationship:

> A delicate network of alliances, based on honorary positions, marriage ties, administrative functions, financial support, and involvement in trafficking, was gradually being woven between the Taliban and bin Ladin's movement. Bin Ladin was a member of the Taliban council of elders, and Mullah Omar was accorded an honorary position in al-Qaeda's Majlis al-Shura.[85]

Bergen reinforces this view by citing the comments of Vahid Mojdeh, who had previously worked under Abdullah Azzam for the MAK:

> Osama and his loyalists were of course well aware of how to influence the Taliban, relying on their previous experience with the Mujahideen leaders.... Financial support in the war against the Taliban's opposition, in particular buying off opposing commanders, proved to be an effective strategy. Osama thus established himself far above the mere guest. Osama bin Ladin successfully positioned himself among the Taliban.

Gunaratna is more specific:

> Osama was quick to consolidate his links with the Taliban leadership, and by financing and materially assisting the regime he soon had widespread influence over it. After a while, Al Qaeda developed a guerrilla unit especially to assist the Taliban in the fight against the Northern Alliance. Known as the 055 brigade, Al Qaeda's guerrilla component of 1,500–2,000 Arabs was integrated into the Taliban fighting forces.... The regime reciprocated Osama's assistance by giving him and Al Qaeda sanctuary, and by providing weapons, equipment and training facilities. Furthermore, Al Qaeda was permitted to use Afghanistan's national aircraft to transport members,

recruits and supplies from overseas. As such, their relationship was reciprocal.[86]

It is, however, difficult to understand fully how bin Ladin was able to become an influential figure on such a grand scale in Afghanistan by means of his wealth when, if Burke and Wright are correct, he was effectively broke after his Sudanese foray. Indeed, Burke gives a very different account of the situation in Afghanistan. He asserts that there was already an array of Islamist groups based in the country and that, as a consequence, training camps had already been established.[87] More specifically,

> Bin Ladin arrived back in Afghanistan with an ideology but no way of prosecuting it.... But though bin Laden lacked manpower and security, there were several groups in Afghanistan which did not.[88]

1996-2001: 'gaining strength'

Notwithstanding the debate about the internal coherence of al-Qaeda and the questionable extent of its involvement in the acts of terrorism with which it is credited, the 'organization' is perceived to have gained strength during the five years preceding the events of 9/11. Even Burke concedes that 'The nearest thing to al-Qaeda, as popularly understood, existed for a short period between 1996 and 2001.'[89] Nonetheless, the extent to which it ever resembled a tightly knit organization remains unclear. What is clear is that the period preceding the attacks of 9/11 witnessed an increasing level of 'al-Qaeda propaganda': interviews with Western-based journalists, fatwas, open letters and public statements aired via Al Jazeera, by which bin Ladin was attempting to establish a public image. Peter Bergen's account of his first encounter with the 'financier of Islamic extremism' depicts a man who knew how to use the media to his advantage and to leave a lasting impression:

I met with Osama bin Laden in 1997. ... At the time bin Laden was regarded only as a financier of Islamic extremism. ... I had always believed that the first World Trade Center attack in 1993 ... might have some larger organization behind it, perhaps led by someone like bin Laden. That hunch would turn out to be wrong. Bin Laden had nothing to do with the attack, *but the Saudi exile did lead a global terrorist organization, as we would find out when we met with him in Afghanistan.*[90]

... Osama bin Laden arrived out of the darkness ... he wasn't the fire-breathing terrorist, he comported himself like a cleric. ... Bin Laden was not going to answer questions about his family, his money or his personal story; he just wanted to get his political message out.

In the light of the relatively limited attention that the CNN report received at the time, the goal of 'getting the political message out' may have been only partially successful. Bin Ladin had not yet reached the level of international notoriety that would follow in the years ahead. It is a sad irony that it was through acts of violence that his message would eventually reach a wider audience. His second attempt to establish his media presence, the 90-minute interview with Al Jazeera that was aired in December of 1998 in the aftermath of the East African US embassy bombings, was clearly more successful to that end.[91] In more analytical terms, whilst it remains questionable whether bin Ladin was truly the leader of a global terrorist network at this point, it is clear that this was precisely the image he wanted to communicate to both the journalists and the wider audience.

The period before 9/11 is also significant in that it witnessed al-Qaeda's ideological transition from a more regional focus towards a more global dimension. It is particularly notable, however, for its widening of the range of legitimate targets. In August 1996, bin Ladin issued a fatwa entitled 'Declaration

of Jihad against Americans Occupying the Land of the Two
Holy Mosques', which authorized defensive war (jihad) against
the American government and specifically the US military for
their continued presence or 'occupation' of Saudi Arabia. Bin
Ladin expressed this clearly in the aforementioned interview
with CNN:

> We have focused our declaration on striking at the [US] soldiers in
> Saudi Arabia. ... Even though American civilians are not targeted in
> our plan, they must leave. We do not guarantee their safety.[92]

The fatwa also broadens the framework of bin Ladin's
appeals, addressed now to Muslims across the world rather
than limited to those in the Arabian peninsula, and invok-
ing their sufferings at the hands of the Americans from the
Balkans to Southeast Asia. At this juncture, bin Ladin continues to focus on Saudi Arabia, the occupation of which he
describes as 'the greatest disaster to befall Muslims since the
death of the Prophet'.[93] So bad is the situation in the kingdom
that it has begun to 'resemble a huge volcano that is about to
explode and destroy unbelief and corruption'.[94] To illustrate
the rising resistance, he specifically refers to the two bomb
attacks which took place in Riyadh in November 1995. The
first of these was a car bombing which killed five Americans.
The second, much larger, explosion occurred at the Khobar
Towers in June 1996, where a massive 1,500 kg (3,000 lb) of
dynamite exploded in a military complex housing American
Forces, killing nineteen soldiers and injuring some 500 people
of many nationalities. In the fatwa, bin Ladin describes these
two bombings as mere 'warning signs'. Implying that al-Qaeda
was in some way responsible for the two attacks would appear
to have been a canny piece of propaganda on the part of bin
Ladin, and indeed al-Qaeda's attempts to project itself as an

organization on the rise seem to have benefited from the fact that the attacks were frequently attributed to al-Qaeda. Atwan, for example, interprets the statement as a confession, stating that 'Bin Ladin confirmed that al-Qa'ida was behind the June 1996 bombing of the American base at Khobar Towers in Dharan, Saudi Arabia.'[95] Yet five years after the attack, thirteen members of Saudi Arabia's Hezbollah were indicted in the USA for the bombing. In the words of Burke, Osama bin Ladin was 'wrongly blamed': 'Though suspicion had initially focused on Afghan veterans ... investigation swiftly showed that an Iranian-backed Shia group within Saudi Arabia was responsible.'[96] In a similar way, bin Ladin later denied direct responsibility for the Riyadh attacks, attributing them instead to his role as an inciter to jihad. Whether or not al-Qaeda was directly responsible, the idea of al-Qaeda as a dangerous organization was gaining strength. Indeed, al-Qaeda's ability either to claim acts of terrorism as its handiwork, or at least to *appear* to be the culprit, continues to be an effective way for the organization – in so far as al-Qaeda can be described as such – to advertise itself, both to its supporters and to the world at large.

By almost all accounts, 1998 witnessed significant progress in al-Qaeda's attempts to establish itself as a global player. On 23 February, the newly formed World Islamic Front announced a 'Jihad against the Jews and the Crusaders', which has become particularly well known and is generally referred to as 'the 1998 fatwa'. Unlike previous fatwas, it bore four co-signatories in addition to bin Ladin: Ayman al-Zawahiri, leader of Egyptian Islamic Jihad (EIJ); Abu-Yasir Rif'ai Ahmad Taha, a representative of al-Gamaa al-Islamiyya (another Egyptian Islamist movement); Mir Hamzah, secretary general of Jamiat Ulema-e-Pakistan (a political party in Pakistan, part of the

Islamic Muttahida Majlis-e-Amal, which won the legislative elections of 20 October 2002); and Falzur Rahman, leader of the Jihad Movement in Bangladesh.[97] According to a number of sources, Jihad against the Jews and the Crusaders was the result of the merger of bin Ladin's al-Qaeda and Ayman al-Zawahiri's EIJ. Richard Clarke, then counterterrorism adviser to Bill Clinton, remarks,

> As 1998 dawned, al-Qaeda grew stronger, thanks to a merger with Egyptian Islamic Jihad... In February 1998, EIJ and al-Qaeda were among several groups that jointly issued a declaration of war against Egypt, the United States and other governments.[98]

Clarke argues that this was a result of the crackdown on EIJ and affiliated jihadis after they had perpetrated atrocities such as the 1997 Luxor bombing,[99] which had a devastating effect on the Egyptian tourism industry.[100] Although Zawahiri is often credited as the mastermind of this operation, Bergen argues that in fact this merger saw the influence of bin Ladin extend over his Egyptian colleague. Indeed, Zawahiri had to overcome internal group resistance to joining al-Qaeda from his EIJ members.[101]

Often Zawahiri is seen as the real brains of al-Qaeda, who provided bin Ladin with the political/theological arguments underlying the organization's attacks, and, while there is certainly some element of truth to this, it was bin Ladin who focused Zawahiri's attention away from his Egyptian 'near enemy' to attacking the 'far enemy', the United States.[102]

Wright further supports this view and claims that the infighting between the Egyptian factions and their ineffectual operations in their homeland, in bin Ladin's mind, had to cease.[103] According to an assistant of Zawahiri, 'I myself heard bin Ladin say that our main objective is now limited to one state only, the United States, and involves waging guerrilla war against U.S. interests, not only in the Arab region but throughout the world.'[104] Contradicting this rationale, Atwan asserts that it was Zawahiri who was behind the targeting of Americans and is reported to have said, 'Let the Americans become your personal media agents – they've got the biggest PR machine in the whole world.'[107] Indeed, Atwan goes so far as to argue that bin Ladin was opposed to the indiscriminate targeting of American and Jewish interests and needed some persuading.[106]

Despite these differences of opinion regarding the internal dynamics, general agreement exists as to the change in direction the newly aligned al-Qaeda was beginning to take. The fatwa of 1996 was still primarily concerned with the illegitimate occupation of Saudi Arabia, exemplified by the unlawful presence of American troops and the deterioration of moral standards of socio-political affairs within the kingdom. The 1998 fatwa, however, moves on from there to focus on the sins of the United States, condemning its policies in the Middle East as acts of war against God, his messenger and the community of the believers. It is particularly strong in its insistence that religious Islamic scholars throughout history have agreed that jihad becomes the duty of each believer when an enemy attacks Muslim countries, highlighting Iraq as a target of intensifying aggression. It specifically warns of the United States' determination to destroy Iraq and to weaken all the other countries within the region:

> For seven years America has occupied the holiest parts of the Islamic lands ... turning its bases there into a spearhead with which to fight the neighbouring Muslims peoples. There is no clearer proof than America's excessive aggression against the people of Iraq. ... Despite the terrible number of Iraqi deaths – over one million – ... they are not satisfied with the long period of sanctions.... There is no better

proof than their eagerness to destroy Iraq ... and their efforts to fragment all the states in the region ... into paper mini-states whose weakness and disunity will guarantee Israel's survival.

All these crimes and sins committed by the Americans are a clear declaration of war on God, his messenger, and Muslims. And *ulema* have throughout Islamic history unanimously agreed that jihad is an individual duty if the enemy destroys Muslim countries. ... We must agree collectively on how best to settle the issue.[107]

The ruling[108] that followed states that it is the individual obligation of every believer to wage jihad against Americans – notably *both* military and civilian – until the land of the *umma* is liberated:

The ruling to kill the Americans and their allies – civilians and military – is an individual duty of every Muslim who can do it in any country in which it is possible to do it. ... We call on everyone who believes in God and wants reward to comply with His will to kill the Americans and seize their money wherever and whenever they find them.[109]

The content of the 1998 fatwa represents a significant ideological and theological leap from Osama bin Ladin's previous edicts. The scale of the strategic shift, from targeting the US government and its armed forces based in Saudi Arabia towards the use of violence against all US citizens, military and non-combatants alike – cast as an individual religious obligation – cannot be overstated. Sageman views the fatwa as the consolidation of the 'global Salafi jihad' and the completion of the transition to targeting the 'far' enemy as opposed to the 'near' enemy.[110] Thus what began, in the terms of the 1996 fatwa, as a fight against the American military presence in Saudi Arabia, targeting only the 'occupation forces', now became a global struggle to be taken up by all Muslims against all Americans, everywhere. Under the 1998 fatwa, American civilians in all countries, not just those that were theatres of

US military activity, were added to the American armed forces in being identified as a legitimate enemy, and the entire world became the battlefield upon which the righteous war to liberate the *umma* might be waged. The *9/11 Commission Report* further describes this development in terms of the structure and organization of al-Qaeda:

> The February 1998 fatwa thus seems to have been a kind of public launch of a renewed and stronger al-Qaeda, after a year and a half of work. Having rebuilt his fund-raising network, Bin Ladin had again become the rich man of the jihad movement. He had maintained or restored links with terrorists elsewhere in the world. And he had strengthened the internal ties in his own organization.[111]

The report then goes on to assert that bin Ladin had around him an inner core of loyal supporters who had sworn the *bayat* to him, but that he was also supported by a fluctuating outer circle. The inner core is described as consisting of a 'hierarchical top-down group with well-defined positions, tasks, and salaries.'[112] Migaux states that during this time, al-Qaeda's structure was modified to facilitate attacks against the USA.[113] Gunaratna also expands on this point:

> To further advance the Islamist project, in 1998 Al-Qaeda was reorganized into four distinct but interlinked entities. The first was a pyramidal structure to facilitate strategic and tactical direction; the second was a global terrorist network; the third was a base force for guerrilla warfare inside Afghanistan; and the fourth was a loose coalition of transnational terrorists and guerrilla groups.[114]

Although these claims appear in both Migaux's and Gunaratna's work, both fail to provide references or other insights into the sources on which the allegations are based, and there is no mention of this restructuring elsewhere. Nonetheless, the *9/11 Commission Report* cites the 1998 US embassy bombings in Nairobi and Dar es

Salaam as evidence of the changing strategy and role of al-Qaeda,
as they were conducted by the group and its key members.[115]
Sageman appears to agree with the *9/11 Commission Report*, in
so far as the embassy bombings were the prelude to a worldwide
campaign against the United States. He comments: 'The East
Africa operations, which inaugurated a worldwide wave of bombings and plots against Western targets, involved a great deal of
centralised planning by full time al-Qaeda staff.'[116] For Wright,
although the operation 'bore the hallmarks of [al-Qaeda's] future
actions', it also 'betrayed al-Qaeda's inexperience': he claims that
the attack had been marred by problems, including the capture
of its bombers.[117]

For Burke, however, this is a fundamental misreading of
the situation, and he cites Bill Clinton to emphasize that these
attacks were financed by 'the bin Ladin network' and not 'al-
Qaeda.'[118] Richard Clarke, on the other hand, illustrates that
the search for and attempted prosecution of al-Qaeda preceded
the 1998 embassy bombings. He quotes the head of the CIA,
who is reported to have said in no uncertain terms, 'This one
is a slam dunk, Mr. President. There is no doubt that this was
an al-Qaeda operation. Both we and the Bureau have plenty of
evidence.'[119] In the bigger picture, it would appear that much
of the controversy over attributing certain acts of terrorism
to al-Qaeda stems from the fact that no clear consensus has
been reached as to what al-Qaeda actually is in the first place.
What Burke refers to as the 'bin Ladin network' is 'al-Qaeda'
in Clarke's account. On the whole, the East Africa embassy
bombings, more than any previous attack, have been clearly
attributed to 'al-Qaeda' – in spite of the fact that al-Qaeda's
precise identity had not been clearly determined.

The embassy bombings were followed by a series of terrorist incidents that have been linked to al-Qaeda. But, as

Sageman points out, 'Over the next two years, operations were more decentralized, and planned with a great deal of local autonomy. Instead of direct participation, al-Qaeda's involvement consisted of training potential terrorists...'[120] Sageman uses the 1999 attack on the USS *The Sullivans* and the attack on the USS *Cole* in Aden in October 2000, the Christmas Eve 2000 bombing of churches in Indonesia and the Rizal Day bombings, which targeted five locations in Manila on 30 December 2000, as examples of this strategy in action.[121] Abu Jandal, bin Ladin's bodyguard, is quoted by Bergen as saying that 'al-Qaeda pursues a method or principle that calls for the 'centralization of decision and the decentralization of execution. The decision was made centrally, but the method of attack and execution was the duty of the field commander.'[122] His statement reinforces Sageman's conclusions regarding the modus operandi of al-Qaeda at this time. As such, it would seem that the period between 1998 and 2001 saw al-Qaeda at its most organized and potent. It appeared to be well financed and to have spread its reach into a number of states. Osama bin Ladin's authority over the global jihad seemed unimpeachable: 'The attack on the USS *Cole* confirmed bin Ladin's position at the helm of the global Islamist jihad... Indeed, something of a bin Ladin cult was taking shape.'[123]

This would all bode well for al-Qaeda's most audacious and deadly assault on the United States to date, when, on 11 September 2001, four aircraft belonging to United States airlines were hijacked, of which two were deliberately flown into the Twin Towers of the World Trade Center in New York, one was flown into the Pentagon, and the final aeroplane crashed in a field near Shanksville, Pennsylvania, as passengers attempted to overcome the terrorists. The *9/11 Commission Report* detailed the incidents and how the operation was orchestrated by al-

Qaeda and Osama bin Ladin.[124] According to Bergen, 'The 9/11 plot amply demonstrates the central importance that bin Ladin plays in al-Qaeda. While bin Ladin did not involve himself in the details of the 9/11 operation he was [its] ultimate commander.'[125] Whilst Burke stresses the extraordinary nature of bin Ladin and the al-Qaeda outfit, for him the event was somewhat more expected. 'In terms of their ambition, the complexity of their execution and their spectacular nature, the 11 September attacks were not so much a radical break with previous developments but a summation of them.'[126] Richard Clarke, after years of watching the progression of al-Qaeda, warned the incoming Bush administration of the dangers of al-Qaeda but claims that these admonitions were not taken seriously enough at the time.[127] Whether the attacks of 9/11 were entirely unexpected or simply the culmination of previous activities, the scale of the operation and the destruction and bloodshed that resulted entrenched the reality of al-Qaeda – in all its different, putative forms and shapes – in the minds of spectators around the world. To some, it was the deed of a well-structured global terrorist organization determined to defeat the USA and its allies, to others the spectacular and arguably somewhat unlikely success of a more amorphous alliance of like-minded individuals linked by a common cause.

Rethinking the analysis of al-Qaeda's structure

Although the attacks of 9/11 have often been linked to the notion of al-Qaeda as a tightly structured terrorist organization, it is an idea that does not stand up to rigorous examination. From al-Qaeda's early beginnings in Afghanistan in the 1980s to the spectacular attacks in 2001, the precise make-up of the group that is believed to pose one of the greatest security threats to the

Western world remains unclear. Whilst the analysts were driven by differing concerns and agendas – from the need to establish the existence of a clearly defined organization in order to meet US legal requirements for bin Ladin to be tried *in absentia* to the simple belief, suspicion or indeed fear that something bigger was out there somewhere that needed to be exposed – each of them faced the difficult task of explaining the phenomenon by means of finding sources of evidence such as witnesses, manuals, letters and so forth that would provide conclusive proof not only of the existence of al-Qaeda, but also of its identity and nature. This, however, turned out to be an undertaking resembling that of grabbing the proverbial piece of soap in the bathtub: al-Qaeda continually slipped away from any attempt at clear and unambiguous classification. This is not to say that the individual discourses are not logically congruent and convincing in their own right, although the evidence on which these discourses relied has, at times, been thin to the point of being unconvincing. Rather, the problem lies in their incompatibility, compounded further by the ultimate impossibility of establishing beyond doubt the validity of any particular one. Given the very nature of the entity at stake, none of this should really come as a surprise: al-Qaeda does not have to prove its existence. Bin Ladin and his allies merely need to hint at the extent of their organization to have their audience on the run, desperately seeking to defeat what might not exist in the first place. This places a double burden on the analysts: sources indicating the existence of a structured organization might well be found, giving those convinced of the threat something tangible to hold on to in support of their claim. Absences, however, are impossible to prove in such a manner: those unconvinced of the theory of the grand organization are left with the task of questioning the reliability of the evidence put forward by the 'organization' theorists. As Andreas Behnke aptly pointed out, 'The spectre-like nature of al-Qaeda that has produced so many fruitless discussions about its precise constitution (an organization, a franchise, a network, an ideology...) refuses and eludes any kind of fixation.'[128] Put simply, al-Qaeda is an epistemological challenge – a problem of knowledge – which, in point of fact, may never be solved.[129]

Yet while theorists might generally be content with discussing the ontology of al-Qaeda and have no difficulty accepting that the real truth about its nature might never be known, such critical analyses, relevant as they may be, are destined to be confined to the ivory towers of academia by the authorities of the policymaking world. They cannot provide the straightforward answers – depictions of the 'enemy' in this case – that are necessary to rationalize the conduct of a global war. Is there room for compromise – a careful, critical assessment of the make-up of al-Qaeda that acknowledges the theoretical conditions but nonetheless provides a working concept by which to comprehend the phenomenon; a middle ground between an organization and a random set of actors inspired by shared ideological goals but acting entirely under their own authority? Burke offers a useful starting point for such an approach, advancing the argument that al-Qaeda consisted of three distinct elements: first, a 'hard core' which consisted of bin Ladin and 'a dozen or so associates who had stayed with him since the late 1980s'; second, a 'network of co-opted groups' around the world that were somehow linked to the members of the hard core; and third, an ideology, the idea of the global jihad that effectively links disparate and otherwise unconnected adherents and that would become most important in the post-9/11 era.[130] This integrated view of the make-up of al-Qaeda offers a degree of fluidity that satisfies the demand for precision while leaving room for speculation and uncertainty. For example, analysis of the make-up and indeed changing membership, reach and dynamics of the core or the central leadership might never be entirely accurate. In fact, regardless of the nature of the core, which is widely regarded as having suffered a serious blow as a consequence of the war against terrorism, even its total defeat would not mean the end of 'al-Qaeda'. Its ideology – the idea that something has gone wrong with the state of the *umma* and that it needs to be reclaimed at all costs, even by violent means – remains intact and continues to inspire individual Muslims to answer the call to jihad. Indeed, the consensus is unanimous that the post-9/11 world is a more radicalized place now than it was before – ironically, one might add, as a direct consequence of the ongoing war on terror. The wars in Afghanistan and Iraq, the abuse of prisoners at Abu Ghraib and the orange suits of Guantánamo are but the most easily recalled examples of incidents and behaviours that have added fuel to the flames of Islamic hostility to the West, playing into the hands of terrorist recruiters by aggrieving young Muslims. In spite of – even because of – the harsh measures put in place to prevent Islamist terrorism, the rationale that inspires it has become more compelling than ever before. As Burke puts it, 'Bin Laden's messages make sense to millions.'[131] Burke predicts that it will be individuals from among those millions who will carry out attacks in the name of Islam in the future. And although they are 'freelance operators' who have no obvious connection to any central group in the traditional sense, they are likely to see themselves as part of a bigger scheme or movement that is reclaiming the *umma* from oppression and restoring the true Islam. Viewed in this manner, al-Qaeda exists in the likelihood – or, more accurately, the fear of such potentiality – that something is out there that will strike again. It is the notion of an organization of sorts, a network of like-minded individuals, that fosters the global jihad movement through the formulation of ideas and propaganda as well as physical support wherever possible. It is through individual acts, attempted attacks or even simply the threat of such attacks and their subsequent consequences in the form of increased security measures and a permanent climate of fear of terrorism that al-Qaeda finds its physical manifestation – one that has become a daily reality for hundreds of millions of people over the last decade.

Before taking a closer look at the state of al-Qaeda in the post-9/11 world, however, a natural next step is to look more closely at the idea itself. What are the ideological underpinnings of the global jihad that has inspired the most destructive acts of terrorism ever committed? What is the rationale that explains such indiscriminate violence in the name of Allah and in defence of Islam itself? What are its origins, and on what does it found its authority?

THREE

Hypocrites, Wahhabis and Salafi jihadis: post-9/11 explanations of al-Qaeda's ideology

Al Qaeda not driven by ideology.

> Finding of a Pentagon intelligence team,
> *Washington Times*, 5 June 2003

Al-Qaeda corrupts, misrepresents and misinterprets the Koranic text.

> Rohan Gunaratna, *Inside Al Qaeda*

Ideology of Al-Qaeda to be traced back to the origins of Wahhabism.

> Stephen Schwartz, *The Two Faces of Islam*

The Global Salafi jihad is a worldwide religious revivalist movement with the goal of re-establishing past Muslim glory in a great Islamist state stretching from Morocco to the Philippines, eliminating present national boundaries. Al Qaeda is the vanguard of this movement. Salafi ideology determines its mission, sets its goals, and guides its tactics.

> Marc Sageman, *Understanding Terror Networks*

'Who would do such a thing – and *why*?' '*Why* do they hate the United States and the Western way of life so much?' '*Why* were they prepared to commit suicide in pursuit of their goals?' Since the attacks of September 11, few issues have been more urgently and widely debated than the need to explain the acts of violence and bloodshed on a grand scale that have taken place in the name of Islam in recent years – and numerous interpretations have surfaced. These include suggestions that the terrorists' actions are irrational, potentially resulting from a variety of mental disorders; that the religious rhetoric is merely a veil for political ambition; or that the explanation lies in different theories of Islamic extremism. 'Al-Qaeda not driven by ideology' is the conclusion reached by a Pentagon intelligence team,[1] while according to Stephen Schwartz, 'Osama bin Ladin and his followers belong to a puritanical variant of Islam known as Wahhabism, an extreme and intolerant Islamo-Fascist sect that became the official cult of Saudi Arabia.'[2] Still others prefer to present al-Qaeda as a group of hypocrites or even fascists – embodiments of 'pure evil'. As Rohan Gunaratna puts it, 'aiming to galvanize the spirit of its supporters, al-Qaeda corrupts, misrepresents or misinterprets the Koranic text.'[3] More recently, there appears to be some consensus that al-Qaeda is the vanguard of 'the global Salafi jihad, a worldwide religious revivalist movement with the goal of re-establishing past Muslim glory in a great Islamist state.'[4] In fact, the notion of the Salafi jihad appears to have entered the mainstream vocabulary to the extent that it now features regularly in newspaper articles, government reports and television talk shows discussing the ideological underpinnings of al-Qaeda. The term conveys the impression that considerable efforts have been made to analyse and understand the religious, philosophical and historical influences that are at the core of al-Qaeda's rationale. Without doubt, the ease with which al-Qaeda can be described in this manner lends the label a certain amount of popular appeal: both the media and political authorities are able to benefit from its expediency, and ultimately the general public are comforted thereby. Nevertheless, the fact that there appears to be a definition for the ideology of al-Qaeda, whilst the nature of the organization itself continues to evade certain classification, raises concern. Is it possible that, much like 'al-Qaeda', the 'Salafi jihad' is but a name or a label that either lacks substance or bears little relation to reality? Do any of the attempts that have been made to define al-Qaeda's ideology offer a comprehensive and trustworthy explanation of the logic and appeal of the global jihad advocated by Osama bin Ladin?

Explaining the ideology of al-Qaeda in the shadow of the 'war on terror'

To obtain meaningful answers to these questions it is useful to recall the state of information regarding al-Qaeda prior to September 11 and the rapid generation of information that followed. In addition to the overall lack of information regarding the rationale of the attackers, it was the nature of the political context that fundamentally shaped the explanations and strategies that would ensue. The horrors inflicted upon New York and Washington had scarcely unfolded before the United States quickly moved to declare an open-ended 'war against terrorism'.[5] It was arguably an uncalculated, instinctive response that would become nothing less than a global military, political, legal and ideological campaign against individuals and organizations designated as 'terrorists', as well as regimes that were accused of supporting them or otherwise appeared to pose a threat to the USA and its allies. In the context of this broad definition of the enemy, then US president George W. Bush soon began to talk of 'a terrorist underworld', including groups like Hamas, Hezbollah, Islamic Jihad, Jaish-i-Mohammed, that 'operates in remote jungles and deserts, and hides in the centers of large cities' and is aided by regimes, including North Korea and Iraq,

that seek to export terrorism and threaten America.[6] 'States like
these, and their terrorist allies, constitute an axis of evil, arming
to threaten the peace of the world.'[7] Potential targets of the 'War
on Terror' would soon include a wide range of Islamist groups
and actors, as well as regimes that differ remarkably in their
ideological constructs and political objectives, all united by the
fact that they could reasonably or conveniently be accused of
having links with al-Qaeda. Although it may, at first glance, seem
quite astonishing that the United States government, with all of
its intelligence resources, should lump al-Qaeda together with a
range of disparate groupings such as Hamas, the 'disputatious
schoolmen of Qom', the Deobandi seminaries of northern Pakistan
that trained the Taliban, and then, elsewhere, relate them all to
secular Arab nationalist Ba'ath Party regimes, with the benefit
of hindsight it is not so surprising. Against the backdrop of an
overall political climate that divided the world into 'good' and
'evil', the US government assumed the existence of an underlying
Islamist terrorist agenda and focused on superficial similari-
ties such as suicide attacks and aeroplane hijackings that were
somehow related to the Middle East and Islam. It was, in a sense,
nothing short of the creation of new Orientalist stereotypes,
this time seeing the Middle East and Islam represented not by
harems and veils, but by bearded suicide bombers born and raised
in a geographic cradle of anti-Americanism. This new form of
Orientalism has been strongly criticized by scholars, who refer
to it as the 'neo-Orientalist terrorism discourse', taking as their
reference the late Edward Said, in whose work the West's view
of the Eastern world and thought is censured for being based
on preconceptions and a limited understanding of Eastern and
Islamic culture.[8] Thus neo-Orientalism is deeply rooted in clas-
sical Orientalist ideas such as 'the Arab mind' and 'the nature
of Islam', enabling the construction of an 'Arab-Islamic terrorist

other', which – in keeping with Huntington's theory of the clash of civilizations – seeks to negate Western culture and values.[9] Dag Tuastad has identified the neo-Orientalist narrative as an instrument of 'symbolic power' that sustains neo-colonial interests through 'presentations of political violence that omit political and economic interests and contexts ... and present the violence as resulting from traits embedded in local cultures.'[10] In this Manichean model, al-Qaeda is essentially not very different from Hamas, Hezbollah, Islamic Jihad or the Moro Islamic Liberation Front (MILF): they are, first and foremost, enemies of the USA and the civilized Western world.

Particularly telling illustrations of this outlook – many of them not so much enlightening as demeaning, both to their subjects and to those involved in producing them – can be found in psychological profiling efforts that fuel the image of Islamic terrorists as 'crazy madmen' acting under the influence of mental disorders and deprived of any rational logic related to social, political or religious conditions. At first sight, the attribution of terrorism to some underlying mental pathology might appear to provide an immediate, scientific and acceptable explanation at a time when straightforward answers are in great demand. The logic is simple: normal, healthy people do not have an urge to kill vast numbers of other people.[11] Those afflicted with some kind of severe mental illness occasionally do. On the other hand, 'crazy' people usually make poor leaders of complex technical operations and even worse communicators – genuine severe mental illness would in all likelihood deprive individuals of the very capacities they would need in order to become successful terrorists.[12] However, the concept of 'crazy terrorists' has been found not just to provide easy answers by describing the behaviour of selected individuals, but also to posit a diagnosis by which to discriminate against an entire society, bringing to mind the image of 'native culture as patient in need of Western medicine'.[13] A notable proponent of this theory is Joan Lachkar, who concluded that suicide bombers suffer from borderline personality disorders brought on by 'Islamic child-rearing practices'.[14] Terrorism at the hands of Islamists is thereby transformed into the terminal stage of a general Muslim malady – with al-Qaeda a particularly malignant development of the condition.

It is obvious to the critical observer, however, that the stereotyping and oversimplification inherent in this perception of extreme or pathological behaviour somehow being related to the nature of Arab-Islamic culture, while complementing the notion of fundamentally incompatible, geographically bound ideals, effectively obscure the socio-political and religious diversity that must necessarily be taken into account in any cross-cultural analysis. For as long as the dust was still settling at Ground Zero, the failure of the international community to grasp fully the complexities of the situation was forgivable. As Bernhard Lewis elegantly explains, intercivilizational contacts have often been difficult.[15] Yet to continue to view the intricate dynamics, problems and prospects of an entire region within the general framework of a clash between Islam and the West is to become preoccupied with a balance sheet that tells, at best, only part of the story. The neo-Orientalist narrative can only be sustained for as long as it is removed from the local and specific. Its perception of a homogenous Islamist terrorist enemy falls apart when the nature and objectives of al-Qaeda are compared, however briefly, to those of other fundamentalist groups.[16] In contrast to the territorial struggle against a specific enemy that underlies, for example, the reality of Palestinian rejectionist movements, al-Qaeda's mission is first and foremost transnational, neither limited to any specific nation-state context nor driven by the needs and aspirations of specific peoples. As Olivier Roy puts it, the adherents of al-Qaeda 'are indifferent to their own nationalities. Some have several … they all define themselves as Muslim internationalists and link their militancy to no particular national cause.'[17] In other words, they are committed to all Muslim causes, and aim for nothing less than the end of all Muslim suffering at the hands of the ultimate enemy of Islam: the USA and its allies, also referred to as the Crusader–Zionist alliance. Thus both sides can in a sense be said to be engaged in the same process of stereotyping.

Further explanations of al-Qaeda's ideology can be found in frequently encountered notions characterising its members variously as criminals, religious hypocrites or political players who calculatingly make use of religion to manipulate the sensibilities of others in order to achieve political, rather than religious, goals.[18] Rohan Gunaratna, who argues that bin Ladin intentionally invokes Islamic symbolism and rhetoric to create an image of religious authority, arrives at the conclusion that in 'aiming to galvanise the spirit of its supporters, al-Qaeda corrupts, misrepresents or misinterprets the Koranic text'.[19] The publication of Gunaratna's *Inside Al Qaeda* as one of the first extensive works on al-Qaeda post-9/11 resulted in wide acceptance of this view of bin Ladin and his followers as political actors whose apparent commitment to Islam is in fact a clever propaganda tool to rally popular support and legitimize terrorism in the pursuit of purely political ends. One might note, however, that appealing to religious sensibilities is by no means unique to the case of Osama bin Ladin, but rather a common feature of Muslim politics in the ongoing contest over religious and political legitimacy.[20] An important point that is easily overlooked – and that will be addressed in greater detail in the following chapter – is that both bin Ladin and his followers perceive themselves to be true believers and see no contradiction between their religious views and political actions.

Other analysts choose to paint Islamic terrorists as religious hypocrites who speak the language of Islam with conviction, yet still resort to making their point with the bomb, whilst some commentators deny the absence of any kind of underlying ideology altogether. In 2003, a Pentagon intelligence concluded that al-Qaeda was not bound to a particular view and would cooperate 'across ideological, philosophical lines'.[21] Such a logic is in many ways as apparently convenient and as actually deceptive as the 'crazy madmen' hypothesis, for both imply the same solution: capture or destroy the misguided few and the problem goes away. Yet the lack of final success in the war against terrorism might be an indication that this explanatory model is not entirely accurate. It seems more likely that the perpetrators of September 11 who so willingly went to their own deaths had grander motives for doing so than are generally available to rational, political actors. Indeed, even a glance at anthropological research quickly reveals that religious fundamentalists throughout the world, including the followers of al-Qaeda, consider themselves to belong to a strictly defined community of true believers, guided by the will of God and eligible for divine rewards for their obedience.[22]

Towards an 'Islamic' explanation of al-Qaeda: the Wahhabi debate

Acknowledging the existence of a greater source of meaning than 'this-worldly incentives' to explain the ideology of al-Qaeda, researchers like Stephen Schwartz argue that Osama bin Ladin and his followers belong to a puritanical variant of Islam known as Wahhabism, an extreme and intolerant Islamo-Fascist sect which, allegedly, is also the official cult of the Saudi state.[23] This view typifies Wahhabism as an extremist and latently dangerous, monolithic school of thought. Such an assumption is readily supported by an initial online search of the term 'Wahhabism', which generates thousands of links – mainly to anti-Wahhabism sites. However, the *Encyclopedia of Islam* – a far more authoritative source on this matter – indicates that the term 'Wahhabism' is in fact an outsider's designation for a religious movement within Islam, founded by the eighteenth-century scholar Muhammad Ibn Abd al-Wahhab. Its followers, according to the *Encyclopedia*, regard themselves as Sunnis, follow the school of Ibn Taymiyya and advocate a strict literalism in which the Qur'an is the primary source of legitimacy. The Wahhabi manifesto is simple: ridding Islam of all innovations (*bida'*) later than the third century of Islam. It also confirms that Wahhabis went on uncompromising campaigns against Sufis and Shiites, labelling those who held differing views heretics and apostates and effectively legitimizing the use of violence against them.[24]

This sanctioned use of violence against other Muslims tends to be the focus of those who link Wahhabism to al-Qaeda, but this appears somewhat short-sighted, as it ignores fundamental differences between the two ideologies as well as the complex development of Wahhabism during the centuries following its genesis. At the most basic level, one can but wonder to what extent Abd al-Wahhab, whose strong beliefs about *tawhid* led him to assert that 'the overwhelming majority of Muslims ... had fallen into a state of religious ignorance no better than that of the *djahiliyya*',[25] would have embraced the comparatively tolerant rhetoric of pan-Islam proclaimed by Osama bin Ladin, who seeks to reclaim the whole of the *umma* from foreign oppression, regardless of religious differences that are bound to exist.[26] Furthermore, despite its legacy of violent campaigns

against all those who did not share its views, Wahhabism has
evolved from its traditional, fundamentalist beginnings, and
its standards have moderated to a certain degree over the past
century. While Osama bin Ladin and other Islamic fundamentalists may be inspired by the violent tradition and spirit
espoused by Muhammad Ibn Abd al-Wahhab, it is equally
true that Wahhabi sheikhs in Saudi Arabia have unequivocally
stated that suicide bombings are un-Islamic.[27] These observations, brief as they may be, give rise to an important question:
how much is really known about the origins and subsequent
development of Wahhabi thought by those who claim that it is
essential to al-Qaeda's vision?[28] How accurate, as a matter of
fact, is our reading of Islamic history?

To illustrate this point, it is helpful to return to the debate
around the influence of Ibn Taymiyya, whose supposedly radical
interpretations of Islam inspired not only 'Abd al-Wahhab but
also the modern Islamic fundamentalists, including Osama bin
Ladin. The arguments are readily available: Delong-Bas admon-
ishes Ibn Taymiyya for 'his espousal of the division of the world
into two absolute and mutually exclusive spheres – the land
of Islam (*dar al Islam)* and the land of unbelief *(dar al-kufr)*,
which for him described both a status (Muslim or unbeliever)
and a necessarily hostile relationship between the two.'[29] According to Bernhard Haykel, 'Ibn Taymiyya's importance lies
in that he was willing to hereticise fellow Muslims who did not
share his views, and, more important, he declared permissible
war against Muslim rulers who did not apply the Shari'ah.'[30]
Taking this argument one step further, Milson argues that
'according to Ibn Taymiyya, a Muslim ruler who commits
grave sins or applies alien laws is no better than an apostate
(*murtadd*) and should be put to death. Hence waging *jihad*
against such rulers is a religious duty.'[31] Following the same

logic, Guy Sorman concludes that Ibn Taymiyya 'inaugurated a theological and political revolution: there is no fundamentalist Islamic movement that does not refer back to it.'[32]

In contrast to what seems to have become popular knowledge about the origins of Wahhabism, Yahya Michot presents a much more balanced perspective in his careful and unemotional reading of Ibn Taymiyya's fatwa of Mardin, from which this debate originates, and his subsequent comparison of the ways in which it was interpreted by, among others, Muhammad Abd al-Salam Faraj and Shaykh Abd Allah Yusuf 'Azzam.[33] Indeed, Michot's analysis serves as an important reminder that a present-day reading of Ibn Taymiyya needs to be disciplined by the historical context in which he operated. In doing just that, Michot brings to life a scholar who was far from the arch-radical that many analysts and commentators would like him to have been. Moreover, it also becomes clear that the modern authors, whose interpretations of Ibn Taymiyya's fatwa of Mardin Michot proceeds to examine, 'commit the sin of (at least) anachronism in giving modern connotations to the words of Ibn Taymiyya or, more precisely, in tying their version of Ibn Taymiyya to modern circumstances'.[34]

If one considers the possibility that Ibn Taymyya was not the origin of radical Islamic thought, then the question that immediately follows is this: when, and with whom, did it begin?[35] The most obvious suspect is of course Muhammad 'Abd al-Wahhab.[36] Once again, however, on closer examination, it appears that, notwithstanding the works of Henri Laoust, Thomas Michel and Bashier N. Nafi, a systematic historical inquiry into the development of Islamic thought during the centuries prior to the emergence of 'Abd al-Wahhab, and its progress thereafter, remains a task yet to be accomplished.[37] With all of this said, the answer to whether the ideology of al-Qaeda originates from 'a puritanical variant of Islam known as Wahhabism' can be little more than a definite 'maybe'. In the development of the debate surrounding the ideology of al-Qaeda, however, the Wahhabi theory was soon to become part of a theory that achieved much wider recognition.

Al-Qaeda: 'The vanguard of the global Salafi jihad'

Against this background, some consensus eventually emerged within the field of terrorism studies that al-Qaeda is the vanguard of 'the global Salafi jihad'.[38] It is a term that is widely used to depict the ideology of al-Qaeda, giving the impression of representing an unambiguous school of thought within the Islamic tradition. While the term is frequently used to refer to the nature of al-Qaeda's ideology, it is not clear what it really means other than the vague notion that the ideology is of a particularly radical kind, and hence the label is something of a gloss over concepts that have not been adequately explored, rather than a distinctive appellation for a phenomenon which has been clearly and reliably identified. Although it is difficult to locate the first usage of the term, Marc Sageman's book *Understanding Terror Networks* is a particularly frequently cited source that allegedly offers insights into the Salafi jihad. Sageman views al-Qaeda as

> a worldwide religious revivalist movement with the goal of reestablishing past Muslim glory in a great Islamist state stretching from Morocco to the Philippines, eliminating present national boundaries. It preaches *salafiyyah* (from *salaf,* Arabic for 'ancient one', referring to the companions of the Prophet Muhammad), the restoration of authentic Islam, and advocates a strategy of violent jihad, resulting in an explosion of terror to wipe out what it regards as local heresy. The global version of this movement advocates the defeat of the Western powers that prevent the establishment of a true Islamist state.[39]

To further emphasise the threat, Sageman goes on to state that the West is confronted with a large movement 'which includes many other terrorist groups that collaborate in their operations and share a large support base'.[40] Sageman does not, however, proceed to name these other terrorist organizations; nor does he give any details of the sources from which he has obtained his information. The remainder of his examination of the 'origins of the jihad' provides no further insights of any value; nor does it include a working definition of the 'Salafi phenomenon'. Sageman maintains that Mohammad ibn Abd' al-Wahhab, who 'based many of his Qur'anic interpretations on the fatwas of Ibn Taymiyya', had a critical influence on the development of radical Islamist thought that underlies the ideology of al-Qaeda.[41] Unfortunately, there is no reference to particular fatwas that might illustrate this. However, the subsequent description of the circumstances that surrounded the incident, namely during 'one of the most disruptive periods of Muslim history – the conquest of Muslim lands by the Mongols ... when the question was put to Ibn Taymiyya whether it was legitimate for Muslims to declare a jihad against other Muslims', gives reason to think that Sageman is referring to the fatwa of Mardin discussed in the previous section. His conclusion that 'the Mongols were not real Muslims ... but apostates who should be punished with death according to the Sharia' and that 'it was the right, indeed the duty, of Muslims to wage jihad against them' is much in line with the views of other contemporary scholars previously mentioned.[42] Yet the uncomfortable question remains: does a statement become truth because it has been said so many times? More important, however, is the conclusion one comes to even after a thorough reading of Sageman's first chapter: that the idea of the 'global Salafi jihad' – which for many seems to have become the new truth about the ideology of al-Qaeda – remains vague at best.

A look at Wiktorowicz's 'Anatomy of the Salafi Movement' promises some clarification of this issue. Wiktorowicz states that 'the Salafi movement (often referred to as the Wahhabis) represents a diverse community' that 'includes such diverse figures as Osama bin Laden and the Mufti of Saudi Arabia and reflects a broad array of positions regarding issues related to politics and violence'.[43] In spite of numerous differences, however, 'Salafis are united by a common religious creed', which revolves around strict adherence to the concept of *tawhid* (the oneness of God) and ardent rejection of a role for human reason, logic, and desire.[44] More specifically, 'Salafis believe that by strictly following the rules and guidance in the Qur'an and Sunna (path or example of the Prophet Muhammad) they eliminate the biases of human subjectivity and self-interest, thereby allowing them to identify the singular truth of God's commands.'[45] From this perspective, there is only one legitimate religious interpretation, in which there is no place for Islamic pluralism. In his subsequent discussion, Wiktorowicz divides the diversity of thought within the Salafi movement into three main categories: the purists, the politicos and the jihadists. At first sight, this categorization seems to offer a means by which to conceptualize the diversity within a movement that has evolved greatly since its inception. However, Wiktorowicz is not alone in his quest to define the Salafi movement. Elsewhere, we read about 'neo-traditional Salafis', 'conservative reformists' and 'radical secularists', to name but a few.[46] While a thorough comparison of these different approaches is beyond the scope of this book, this observation raises two interesting questions. First, to what extent is there any kind of consensus on the Salafi-discourse? And, second, therefore what exactly is meant by the terms 'Salafi' and 'Salafism'?

Again the *Encyclopedia of Islam* describes a very complex, often contradictory, process of development of Salafi thought. If nothing else, 'the issue of who is considered a member of the *salaf* is a controversial one'.[47] In literary terms, the word *salafiyah* is derived from the Arabic root *salaf,* which means 'to proceed'. While the Qur'an uses *salaf* to refer to the past, according to Arabic lexicons, the *salaf* are the virtuous forefathers (*al-salaf al-salih*), where the *salafi* is the one who draws on the Qur'an and the Sunna as the only sources for religious rulings. Although most Muslim scholars agree that the *salaf* comprise the first three generations of Muslims, which span three centuries and include the companions of the Prophet, their followers, *al-Tabi'in*, and the followers of their followers, *Tabi' al-Tabi'i*, neither the literal nor the chronological definition is sufficient to explain the term fully. The *Encyclopedia* specifically states that the '*salaf* are not confined to a specific group nor to a certain era'.[48] Rather, prominent scholars and independent figures of later times are considered members of the *salaf,* including Ahmad ibn Hanbal, Abu Hamid al-Ghazali, Ibn Taymiyyah, Ibn Qayyim al-Jawziyah, Muhammad Ibn Abd al-Wahhab, Jamal al-Din al-Afghani, Muhammad 'Abduh and others. Here it deserves to be mentioned that the views of even the earliest generations of Muslims were far from homogeneous, and that the ideological components of the Salafiyah further changed over time and in response to the myriad challenges the Muslim community faced as its dedication to reform and revival persisted.[49] Thus the widespread assumption that the Salafi-jihadist discourse is a well-defined, monolithic school of thought is very much open to debate, as is the fashion in which Salafism is portrayed, in the literature on terrorism in general, and with regard to the ideology of al-Qaeda in particular.[50]

To emphasize this point, it is useful to investigate the frequently encountered argument that Salafis shun human reasoning and desire just a little bit more – whilst keeping in mind that interpretation is necessarily part of all *tafsir* (exegesis of the Qur'an). At first sight, the *Encyclopedia of Islam* confirms that Ahmad Ibn Hanbal, for example, advocated the primacy of the revealed text over reason, although he saw no contradiction between reason and scripture.[51] It is further confirmed that the modern Salafiyah, as established by Jamal al-Din al-Afghani and Muhammad 'Abduh, share the belief that the Qur'an is the uncreated word of God – that is, that it is divinely inspired, as opposed to simply being written by men – and rejected the interpretation of its verses. They equally considered revelation and reason to be in full consonance, but whenever there seemed to be a contradiction between the two, they employed reasoning to interpret the text.[52] Does that mean that human reason is permissible under certain circumstances? If so, what are these circumstances? Is the kind of subjectivity that inevitably accompanies human contemplations of divine concepts admissible? And, finally, if only the divine can truly speak for the divine, who has the right to speak for the 'true Islam'?

At this point it is interesting to return once more to Sageman's argument, which, among others, notes that '[Egyptian author and Islamist] Sayyid Qutb's influence on the Salafi jihad was crucial.'[53] Before developing this thought any further, one must first establish by what definition Qutb might be said to be a Salafi. The first link of the aforementioned Internet search reveals that 'most Salafis reject what they call Qutbism as a deviation from true Salafism.'[54] The article, however, does not state who these 'Salafis' are, nor where they express such opinions; nor indeed does it provide a greater sense of objectivity by defining the 'true Salafism' of Qutb's critics. Wiktorowicz's argument that Salafis reject any role for human reason and interpretation leaves Sageman's attempt to connect Qutb and al-Qaeda with Salafism looking even weaker: simultaneous – and supposedly mutually exclusive – denial of reason and demonstration of cognitive adaptation of the Qur'anic text to reality are evident, for example, in Sayyid Qutb's well-known political interpretation of the Qur'an, *Fi Zilal al-Qur'an* (In the Shade of the Qur'an). While a certain level of interpretation, as mentioned before, is common to all *tafsir*, in reading Qutb's commentary one is continually struck by the interplay between his own ideas and the Qur'anic text, showing that he did not find the truth in the script itself but rather in what he believed to be its meaning.[55]

The same process is evinced when bin Ladin calls upon fellow Muslims to wage jihad against the enemies of Islam and envisions the creation of something that resembles the modern idea of an Islamic state: he has transferred the words of the holy text into the current political situation and interpreted their meaning within this novel context. Bin Ladin constructs his idea of Islam along the lines of an alternative interpretation which overcomes the ideological rifts within Islam and places the supposed community of faith (*umma*) well above individual states and governments and outside the influence of all that is un-Islamic. What he lacks in terms of coherent planning as to how this community of faith is to be organized in practice, he makes up for in fervour, the logic of which can be summarized as follows: first, we need to overcome the enemies of Islam, namely the Zionist–Crusader invasion, and then everything else will naturally, or maybe by divine intervention, fall into place. With this rationale, bin Ladin falls short of other pan-Islamists who have expressed their visions of Islam in significantly more concrete terms as to how the community of the believers is to be structured and governed.[56] As has become clear, however, in the previous discussion of al-Qaeda's existence as an organization, it is in its ideology that its real strength lies. In motivating individuals to pursue the physical struggle rather than engaging in nation-building, a focus on ideas is of particular importance. Beyond its relative simplicity, bin Ladin's vision is, above all else, idealistic, and it is arguable that this kind of idealism goes to the very heart of the issue of Muslim solidarity, and hence is hugely appealing to those who sympathize with bin Ladin and al-Qaeda. As such, a meaningful way to evaluate the ideological origins and broader appeal of al-Qaeda would be to place it in the larger context of the emergence of pan-Islam, a topic which will be explored in greater detail in the next chapter.

The validity of this alternative approach is further supported when the label 'Salafi' is applied to bin Ladin. By what definition does bin Ladin become a Salafi? Is it because of his denial of the validity of human reasoning in interpreting Islamic scripture, if that is a legitimate criterion, even though he effectively flies in the face of this prohibition by applying his own interpretation to the scriptures when advancing his argument? Is it because of his proclaimed effort and intention to return to the fundamental principles (*ususl*) of Islam? Or, rather, does this categorization result from the fact that he, much like other Islamic fundamentalists, perceives of himself as a true believer – or Salafi – strictly following the divine guidance of the Prophet and retrieving Islam's fundamental basics, whilst seemingly unaware of the ongoing process of his own interpretation? If for any or all of these reasons bin Ladin and his supporters are classified as Salafi jihadists, then maybe the more appropriate question to ask is, 'who is not a "modern" Salafi?'

Although it is beyond the scope of this chapter either to explore the diversity of the Salafi movement or to track the development of Wahhabism in full, it is worth noting that it is not rewarding to throw out the concept of Islamic fragmentation with the Orientalist bathwater. The perception that the Salafi discourse is a homogenous unit is challenged by the existence of a variety of strands of thought and differing interpretations, especially at a time of ongoing fragmentation of religious authority 'whereby the meaning of scripture no longer needs to be interpreted by a religious establishment but, rather, lies in the eyes of the beholder'.[57] The observation underlying this argument is that the Muslim world has not been isolated from either the processes of modernization or the advent of mass education, which, among other factors, have both influenced and permitted the development of new political societies, inequalities, identities and opportunities. While many Muslims would vehemently insist that the long-standing development of Islamic jurisprudence and Qur'anic exegesis provides definitive guidance to the believer, 'this tradition now confronts the proliferation of modern-educated individuals, who have direct access to the basic religious texts and question why they should automatically defer to the religious class.'[58] As a result of this ongoing development, it has become increasingly difficult to say what is Islamic and what is not. And it is both this shifting of goalposts and the ease with which individuals can presume to invoke and defend Muslim tradition that have allowed individuals such as Osama bin Ladin to claim to speak on behalf of Islam. But does this, in turn, mean that every Muslim who strives on behalf of the actual meaning of Islam can be said to be a Salafi?[59] Hassan al-Turabi, the Sorbonne-educated leader of the Muslim Brothers in Sudan, who exclaimed that 'because all knowledge is divine and religious, a chemist, an economist or a jurist are all 'ulama', would claim that this is so. In the words of James Piscatori, 'ideas concerning issues

from popular participation to social justice are far from stag-
nant, and Qur'anic meanings are nothing if not ambiguous.'[60]
In other words, the 'Salafi-jihadist' discourse that seems to have
become the underlying ideology of al-Qaeda lacks a definitional
basis and remains vague at best. Although one might regard
it as a convenient label for radical Islamists in the broadest of
terms, such a designation poses the problem of generalization
and the lumping together of a variety of movements with different geo-specific goals and agendas by focusing exclusively
on the violent means through which these different ends are
to be achieved. As such, it does not seem to be particularly
rewarding to use this term as a means to explaining the logic
that underlies al-Qaeda's global jihad.

Towards the ideology at the centre of al-Qaeda

As has already been seen, existing inquiries into the ideology of
al-Qaeda apparently originated from a state of crisis and were
carried out in a research climate gripped by urgency in the face
of sudden turmoil on the security and political scene. Whether
characterizing al-Qaeda's adherents as madmen, hypocrites,
religious fanatics, Wahhabis of the twenty-first century or Salafi
jihadists, what these different contributions have in common is
what one might call an 'outside-in' approach to analysis, which
concentrates on al-Qaeda's outward appearance and makes use
of existing paradigms to attempt to explain the phenomena under
investigation. By virtue of their focus on the use of violence,
terrorism analysts have turned to explanatory models such as
Wahhabism or the Salafi-jihadist discourse, which, as the previous discussion has shown, are concepts that are in themselves
nothing if not complex and subject to much controversy – and
which are by no means the straightforward, monolithic schools

of thought some would like them to be – in order to explain the rationale of al-Qaeda. Thus it would appear that much of the analysis has deviated from the established procedures of inquiry and created rather thin and shallow labels that give the illusion of answers but ultimately offer very little in terms of coherent meaning. Proceeding in such a manner risks not only misreading the rich history and development of Islamic thought, but also – more importantly – misinterpreting the very issue under investigation. While the Salafi-jihadi label might adequately capture the violent means that are pursued, it offers no insight into the rationale, the goals and justification, as well as the wider appeal, of al-Qaeda's global jihad.

A more pertinent line of inquiry into the mechanisms underlying al-Qaeda's politics of violence would be to focus specifically on questions that address the complex interplay of religion and politics in the Islamic tradition. More specifically, where does bin Ladin's global jihad fit within the modern political landscape of Islam? What is the connection between religious and political parameters blurred by the rhetoric of bin Ladin? How have these parameters been disrupted or affected by global socio-political changes? Consideration of these questions will shed a new light on both the rationale and the wider appeal of bin Ladin's global jihad and the threat that it poses to international stability.

FOUR

Reclaiming the *umma*:
the ideology of al-Qaeda in the context
of the pan-Islamic tradition

The people of Islam have been afflicted with oppression, hostility and injustice by the Judeo-Christian alliance and its supporters. This shows our enemies' belief that Muslims' blood is the cheapest and that their property and wealth is merely loot. Your blood has been spilt in Palestine and Iraq, and the horrific image of the massacre in Qana in Lebanon are [*sic*] still fresh in people's minds. The massacres that have taken place in Tajikistan, Burma, Kashmir, Assam, the Philippines, Fatani, Ogaden, Somalia, Eritrea, Chechnya, and Bosnia-Herzegovina send shivers down our spines and stir up our passions. All this has happened before the eyes and ears of the world, but the blatant imperial arrogance of America, under the cover of the immoral United Nations, has prevented the dispossessed from arming themselves. ...

We work to do away with the injustice that has befallen our umma at the hands of the Judeo crusader alliance.

Osama bin Ladin, Declaration of Jihad, 23 August 1996[1]

In contrast to popular perceptions of al-Qaeda as a group of radical Islamists on the fringes, if not outside the fold of Islam altogether, much of bin Ladin's rationale, albeit not necessarily the violent means, has broader appeal and resonates widely with Muslims around the world. The Pew Global Attitudes survey, released in July 2005, revealed that a surprising number of Muslims had confidence in bin Ladin's conduct in world affairs, regardless of the overall decline in support for the use of suicide bombing and other forms of terrorism and growing concern over the consequences of the war against terror.[2] While in Morocco and Indonesia public support for bin Ladin ranked at 26 per cent and 37 per cent respectively, marking an overall decline in support since 2003, this trend is not reflected in other countries. In Pakistan, for example, a narrow majority of 51 per cent placed some measure of confidence in bin Laden, a moderate increase from 45 per cent in 2003. In Jordan, support for the al-Qaeda leader rose in the same period from 55 per cent to 60 per cent, including 25 per cent who said they had a lot of confidence in him.[3] Notably, the sixteen nations covered in the survey did not include Iraq or Saudi Arabia, where support for bin Ladin was expected to be even greater than in other countries in the region. A subsequent report, published in 2007, revealed – or, some might say, confirmed – the existence of a deep and increasing resentment of the United States throughout the Muslim world. For example, only 21 per cent of Egyptians declared themselves to have a favourable view of the USA; in Pakistan the figure was 15 per cent; and in Turkey it was as low as 9 per cent.[4] The overwhelming sentiment in Muslim countries is one of little or no confidence in the way America handles world affairs. The conclusion that the public image of the United States is heavily tarnished is not limited to the Pew Global Attitudes Report but represents a recurring theme in other surveys of similar nature. For example, a Zogby International poll of six Arab countries in 2004 found that only 12 per cent had a favourable view of the USA, and a rather substantial 65 per cent rejected the suggestion that democracy is a genuine US objective in the Middle East.[5] The objection, however, is not to democracy and liberal values as such – a Gallup poll of ten Muslim-majority countries found overwhelming support for Western standards of freedom and democracy.[6] Instead, one of the key complaints is about US double standards in foreign affairs – an issue that is central to bin Ladin's critique of US foreign policy. This view holds that while America's international campaigns may be conducted in the name of freedom and democracy, they have very different consequences for those at the receiving end. If anything, the US administration under President Barack Obama has only led to a temporary improvement in America's opinion poll ratings: approval of US leadership in late 2010 was seen to be at a similar or lower level than in 2008 in several Middle Eastern and North African countries, erasing gains seen after the transition from the Bush administration to the Obama administration.[7]

Given this climate of antipathy towards the USA, it is hardly surprising that support for al-Qaeda has been growing. Not only did bin Ladin's messages make sense to a significant number of Muslims around the world, but, as has already been alluded to in references to anthropological research in previous chapters, the particular qualities of religious fundamentalists hold them up as examples for others to follow, namely that they consider themselves to be 'the' true believers and demonstrate their commitment to their faith not just by their piety, but by their actions.[8] In a world in which much of Islam finds itself, or perceives itself to be, under siege, both from foreign powers and from the insistent pervasion of secular values, groups and individuals who make a stand on religious principle and so boldly defend the faith against its foes become sources of great inspiration to those who are weary of the constant encroachment they are witnessing. Thus have al-Qaeda and bin Ladin won popular support for being the ones to stand up to America's Goliath. As Scheuer put it, 'bin Laden is seen by millions of his co-religionists ... as an Islamic hero.'[9] How did this come about?

Listening to Osama bin Ladin

A meaningful inquiry into both the ideological basis for and the appeal of al-Qaeda's global jihad begins with a careful examination of the rationale presented by Osama bin Ladin himself. As the discussion of the origins of al-Qaeda in the first chapter has indicated, Osama bin Ladin was vying for attention – publicly voicing his opinions and explaining his intentions before putting them into practice – from the early 1990s, albeit with limited success. His early interviews with the Western media received little attention, and he was not then taken seriously. As Bergen noted in response to the 1997 interview with CNN:

> [Bin Ladin] said, 'I predict a black day for America; a day after which American will never be the same and the States will not be united,' and he pretty much laid out that this would be a sustained battle.
>
> And at that point he went into one of the answers that we ended up playing a lot, which is he had this message for America – and the one that always struck me because it sounded hyperbolic at the time: 'I am declaring war on the United States. I'm going to attack your country.' And I thought, 'Yeah, you and what army?' If you took those words and played them on September 12 2001, as opposed to say September 9 2001, it went from sounding quite hyperbolic to – he was telling us all along.[10]

If bin Ladin's voice remained largely unheard before 9 September 2001, the attacks that took place that day came as the ultimate proof that actions speak louder than words. It was only through the attacks that bin Ladin eventually succeeded in his quest for public recognition[11] – although it was arguably not the kind of recognition he might have hoped for, namely an engagement with his political messages. While images of the fall of the Twin Towers instantly went around the world to become the ultimate symbol of freedom under attack, in the years that followed only fragments of bin Ladin's messages reached a wider Western audience. As has been mentioned before, the selected parts of his statements that were broadcast in the Western media in the aftermath of 9/11 tended to highlight his controversial proclamations calling for the use of violence against US/Western targets and hence provided only a partial insight into his agenda. Indeed, it was not until 2005 that a collection of bin Ladin's most important statements made between 1994 and 2004 finally became available in English translation.[12] However, the extent to which the long-awaited publication enabled a critical and unbiased engagement with the rationale of al-Qaeda's global jihad remains questionable. The arrest and subsequent detention of a Master's degree student researching terrorist tactics and a staff member of Nottingham University for downloading an al-Qaeda training manual that was deemed 'unfit' to be the subject of research raise a legitimate concern over the extent to which there is freedom to engage with the ideas of al-Qaeda.[13] It mattered little that the manual in question (*Al Qaeda Training Manual*, with the author listed as 'Al Qaeda') is also available from the Internet bookseller Amazon.com for US$14.95.[14] It is thus hardly surprising that the popular image of bin Ladin is one of a radical Islamist, the personification of evil and the representation of a 'group' or 'organization' ferociously hating the West for its liberal ways and determined to bring back the golden age of Islam at any cost. But if al-Qaeda is not the tightly knit organization it is believed to be, and if its main existence, strength and potential ultimately lie in the power of the idea – its ability to inspire, radicalize and motivate violence – then critical engagement with its messages is not only desirable but a basic necessity.

At present, as the bulk of his messages have been more readily available to an Arabic-speaking audience, it seems appropriate to speak of the existence of (at least) two bin Ladins: the evil enemy of freedom and democracy on the one hand, and the pious Muslim defending the faith on the other.[15] Yet a closer reading of bin Ladin's messages soon reveals – contrary to the popular image – that his war is less a response to what the West *is* (i.e. freedom and democracy, in itself a summary of 'the West' whose accuracy is questionable at best), and more about what it *does*. In a statement issued in 2003 he made explicitly clear that

> The White House misrepresents the truth, … claiming that we despise their way of life – although the truth that the Pharaoh of the age is hiding is that we strike them because of their injustice towards us in the Islamic world, especially in Palestine and in Iraq, and their occupation of Saudi Arabia.[16]

Indeed, as early as 1997 in the aforementioned interview with CNN, bin Ladin explained in no unclear terms to a Western audience that he had declared war against the United States because of the nature and the consequences of American foreign policy. Although at the time bin Ladin's particular concern was the presence of US military forces in Saudi Arabia, other reasons for his hostility included the sanctions in place against Iraq and US support for Israel – actions that all contribute to the suffering of Muslims in a variety of locations. According to bin Ladin, the USA maintains double standards by sowing terror in pursuit of its own interests and then calling those who resist 'terrorists'.

> We declared jihad against the U.S. government because the US government is unjust, criminal and tyrannical. It has committed acts that are extremely unjust, hideous and criminal whether directly or through its support of the Israeli occupation of the Land of the Prophet's Night Journey[17] (Palestine). And we believe that the US is

> directly responsible for those who were killed in Palestine, Lebanon and Iraq. The mention of the US reminds us before everything else of those innocent children who were dismembered, their heads and arms cut off in recent explosions. ... This US government abandoned even humanitarian feelings by these hideous crimes. It transgressed all bounds and behaved in a way not witnessed before by any power or imperialist power in the world. They should have been sensitive to the fact that the qibla[18] (Saudi Arabia) of the Muslims raises the emotion of the entire Muslim world. Due to its subordination to the Jews, the arrogance and haughtiness of the US regime has reached such an extent that they occupied the qibla of the Muslims (Arabia) who are more than a billion in the world today.[19]

Although bin Ladin's reasoning evolved over time to take account of socio-political changes and developments, he was consistent about why he was attacking the United States. The central theme invoked by Osama bin Ladin throughout his statements – from open letters and video messages to interviews and training manuals issued from the late 1980s to the present day – is the suffering and humiliation of the *umma*, the global community of all Muslims, at the hands of the unbelievers, namely the USA and its allies. At the core of his messages is a pan-Islamic world-view, according to which God's favoured community is facing an existential threat from the modern arch-enemies of Islam: the United States and Israel, also referred to as the Zionist–Crusader alliance. The primary means of communicating this message is the cataloguing of Muslim anguish by reference to symbolic situations such as in Palestine, Iraq, Chechnya, Kashmir and, above all, Saudi Arabia, where American military forces occupied and controlled the holy places of Islam. Thus the ultimate reason for the miserable and indeed intolerable state of the *umma*, evinced in both the physical suffering of Muslims and the widespread decline of Islamic standards and modes of conduct within the community, is found in the dual reality of US military occupation and cultural domination. In the words of bin Ladin:

> The Arabian Peninsula has never – since God made it flat, created its desert, and encircled it with seas – been stormed by any forces like the crusader armies spreading in it like locusts. For over seven years the United States has been occupying the lands of Islam, the holiest of places, the Arabian Peninsula, plundering its riches, dictating to its rulers, humiliating its people, terrorizing its neighbors....
>
> The world is on fire. Endless suffering, increasing corruption, horrendous abuse. Just look at Iraq. Look at Palestine. Look at Kashmir. Atrocities are committed against our brothers and sisters. Yet they are part of our community, and they deserve our sympathy and our support.[20]

The only way to defend the *umma* against this perceived aggression is through military (or, more precisely, paramilitary) confrontation with America, which bin Ladin presents in highly emotive terms as the rightful jihad of the present time against the principal enemy of God's favoured community, and by extension Islam itself. The ultimate goal of this jihad is to reclaim the *umma* from the United States' painful hold. The by now infamous fatwa of 1998 made unambiguously clear as to how this goal was to be achieved:

> To kill the Americans and their allies – civilian and military – is an individual duty incumbent upon every Muslim in all countries, in order to liberate al-Aqsa mosque and the Holy Mosque from their grip, so that their armies leave all the territory of Islam, defeated, broken and unable to threaten any Muslim.[21]

Explaining the appeal of bin Ladin

In many ways it is understandable that commentators and analysts should have focused on the violence displayed in both bin Ladin's rhetoric and the prosecution of his jihad, especially when even a glance at the history of Islam reveals many radical groups that separated from the established schools of thought and became famous for their use of violence against those who did not agree with their beliefs and practices. However, the same groups failed to survive for long due to their inability to attract and retain adequate support.[22] In contrast to such factions, whose manifestos were either so radical or so exclusive that they naturally alienated the vast majority of those they claimed to represent, bin Ladin advanced an ideology which achieved something that the campaigns of previous radical groupings did not: it struck a chord in the hearts of ordinary Muslim citizens. The appeal of bin Ladin's message lies not in the fact that it is radical, but that it is persuasive, because he speaks to something that is already present in the hearts of his listeners. Furthermore, rather than perceiving bin Ladin as too extreme to be taken seriously or too radical to be worth following, many Muslims around the world conceive of him as a sincere believer. In the words of a young Pakistani interviewed on Al Jazeera, 'Bin Ladin is not a terrorist. That is American rhetoric. He is a good Muslim fighting for Islam. I named my son Osama – I want him to become a believer just like him.' Does that mean that millions of ordinary Muslims condone the use of violence against civilians as the righteous jihad of our age, or is there something else to bin Ladin's message that would explain its broad appeal?

In his statements, bin Ladin stands by the acts of violence that have been carried out in the name of the global jihad and clearly intends to continue this fight in the future. Yet he is at pains to point out that his is a reactive kind of violence – an act of retaliation against what he perceives as the much greater form of aggression exercised by the West against the Muslim world over a far longer period of time. As he continually makes clear, the West stands out for having killed much larger numbers of Muslim civilians and inflicted more suffering upon the Muslim world than any other power. With the force of history on his side, it is difficult to deny, in principle, the legitimacy of his argument when bin Ladin recounts the impact of colonialism, from the first French invasion of Egypt to the artificial creation of state boundaries that redrew the map of the Middle East, and decries the betrayal of the Arabs, the West's unconditional support for Israel and American control of the entire region. Ever alert to the principle of reciprocity, bin Ladin dwells insistently on the enormity of Muslim suffering at the hands of the foreign invaders: the liberal use of poison gas by Churchill in the 1920s; the bloody crushing of the Palestinian uprisings from the 1930s to the present; the deaths through malnutrition and disease of Iraqi children in the 1990s; the growing number of civilian casualties in Afghanistan and Iraq and the latest atrocities committed in Gaza are but excerpts from the plethora of examples presented.[23] In the words of bin Ladin:

> Your (Muslim) blood has been spilt in Palestine and Iraq, and the horrific images of the massacre in Qana in Lebanon are still fresh in people's minds. The massacres that have taken place in Tajikistan, Burma, Kashmir, Assam, the Philippines, Fatani, Oaden, Somalia, Eritrea, Chechnya and Bosnia-Herzegovina send shivers down our spine and stir up our passions. All this has happened before the eyes and ears of the world.[24]

In their totality, the many examples illustrating the unjust suffering of the *umma*, coupled with the ultimate goal of reclaiming the same from the unholy oppressor and curing Islam of its stagnation, amount to the core tenets of bin Ladin's rationale. Bin Ladin's statements tap into a growing sense of Muslim solidarity that has become a prominent feature of the modern, globalized world.[25] Indeed, what set bin Ladin apart was his idealism, along with a truly transnational approach not bound to any particular nationalist project but uniting the entire spectrum of Muslim grievances as a single cause. And although not even the most legitimate grievances are capable of justifying bin Ladin's intentional killing of civilians – if anything, the brutality of his conduct served only to undermine the morality of his call – it is the universality of his appeal to Muslims' sense of injustice, as well as the indifference of the West to the atrocities it has committed, that helps explain why he continues to be so admired by ordinary Muslims, however much they may oppose the murder of innocents. He effectively utilized a growing sense of Muslim solidarity as a launching pad for violent action. In the words of Cairo-based journalist Yosri Fouda, 'there are very few people in the Middle East who do not to relate to his message.'[26]

The question which naturally follows is whether support for bin Ladin has been based purely on agreement with his political rationale. In other words, does his former position as the most radical anti-imperialist of the twenty-first century explain his appeal? Clearly, this view is not without merit. According to sociologist Michael Mann, 'despite the religious rhetoric and bloody means, bin Ladin is a rational man. There is a simple reason why he attacked the US: American imperialism. As long as America seeks to control the Middle East, he and people like him will be its enemy.'[27] Indeed, in an interview with the American network ABC bin Ladin effectively engages with the idea of terrorism in a distinctly secular manner:

> Terrorism can be commendable and it can be reprehensible. Terrifying an innocent person and terrorizing him is objectionable and unjust, also unjustly terrorizing people is not right. Whereas, terrorizing oppressors and criminals and thieves and robbers is necessary for the safety of people and for the protection of their property. There is no doubt in this. Every state and every civilization and culture has to resort to terrorism under certain circumstances for

the purpose of abolishing tyranny and corruption. Every country in the world has its own security system and its own security forces, its own police and its own army. They are all designed to terrorize whoever even contemplates to attack that country or its citizens. The terrorism we practice is of the commendable kind for it is directed at the tyrants and the aggressors and the enemies of Allah, the tyrants, the traitors who commit acts of treason against their own countries and their own faith and their own prophet and their own nation. Terrorizing those and punishing them are necessary measures to straighten things and to make them right.[28]

Here bin Ladin calls into question the meaning of 'terrorism' in the broader context of the question of who has the right to use violence in the international system, an argument that is likely to appeal to many in its own right. To see bin Ladin's cause as a matter of political philosophy, however, separated from religious concerns, is to see only one side of the story. An approach to bin Ladin's messages that focuses exclusively on the political leaves no room for the inherently religious dimension of his mission. Since this approach is implicitly founded upon the secular logic of the separation of state and religion, the application of this logic must lead to the conclusion that because the messages' reasoning is first and foremost political, it cannot be truly religious. What this position fails to acknowledge, however, is the intricate relationship between religion and politics in the history of Islam, as well as the related and ongoing, if not intensifying, controversy surrounding questions of the interpretation of Islamic scripture and the fragmentation of religious authority.

The separation of 'religion' and 'politics' and the ideal of Muslim unity

Most discussions of this issue – and this holds for both Western and, to a significant extent, Muslim scholarship – assume that

Islam makes no distinction between the religious and the political realms. The simple view is that all aspects of the lives of Muslims should be conducted according to the will of Allah, and thus there is no sense of matters of state lying without the purview of religion. Indeed, this widely held view of the inseparability of religious and political spheres finds support in over forty references in the Qur'an and in the Sunna of the Prophet, at once a spiritual leader and the head of a political community.[29] Closer examination quickly shows that this is an idealized version of Islam, denoting what should be rather than providing an accurate description of what it is or indeed ever was. In practice, as several authors have illustrated, the two spheres became separated soon after the death of the Prophet, although this observation could be qualified by adding that a degree of co-dependence continued to exist. The union of politics and religion only existed during the lifetime of the Prophet while he was able to provide direct guidance for the conduct of daily life on the basis of divine religious guidance to the ever-growing number of believers. With his death, the community of Muslims descended into a crisis of both political and religious leadership, and the complete union of religious and political spheres would never again exist in such a fashion, even if in retrospect certain periods in the history of Islam are considered to be closer to the ideal than others.

Notwithstanding the historically complex relationship of the two spheres, the fundamental principle that all Muslims should live by the will of Allah and that, by way of necessity, the *umma* should be governed by Islamic principles as prescribed by the Qur'an and the Sunna of the Prophet has always been seen as both legitimate and important. Thus the ideal stipulates that there is no contradiction between religion and politics, despite the fact that this has never fully been a practical reality. In fact, the Muslim world has not been insulated from global socio-political trends and has therefore moved further away from the ideal of Islamic unity and become more and more fragmented over time. In the face of this trend towards increasing secularism and division, the goal of contemporary Islamists is the fulfilment of what is perceived to be the most authentic and desirable state of existence: a return to the golden age of Islam, expressed in political terms as the re-creation of the caliphate, in which there will be the least possible divergence between the two spheres. Although it is not the intention of this book to assess the personal objectives of bin Ladin, in order to appreciate both the rationale and the appeal of his message it is crucial to acknowledge that he advanced a concept of Islam that not only sees no contradiction between religious belief and political action, but actually views political action as a necessary outworking of belief.

While it may be easy to concede that bin Ladin himself saw his mission as first and foremost Islamic (as has already been noted, religious fundamentalists of any faith regard themselves as the true believers),[30] the question as to why others should regard it in the same way remains more problematic. By curtailing any meaningful discussion from the outset, the post-9/11 political climate that divided the world into the forces of good and evil – 'If you are not with us, you are with them!' – has allowed for only one legitimate answer to the question of whether bin Ladin represents Islam: a definite 'no'. Yet, again, reality does not fit this starkly defined dichotomy. In fact, the only definite statement one can make about the term 'Islam' is that it is imprecise and means different things to different people. While Muslims agree to the profession 'There is no God but God and Muhammad is His Prophet' as an article of faith that is incapable of sustaining differing interpretations, the meaning of many, if not all, other principles and ideas, and whether they are unquestionable and immutable, is a different matter altogether. The obvious, and indeed frequently encountered, response would be to 'look at the Qur'an', but, like all fundamental documents, the meaning of the message lies in the eye of the beholder. And whilst scriptural interpretation is problematic in all religions, it is especially difficult in the case of Islam.[31]

The first observation to be made in this regard is that the Qur'an itself (despite the fact that generations of Muslim jurists have argued that no further legislation is possible in the face of the definitive guidance the Qur'an provides) encourages some degree of questioning by planting doubts as to the immutability of the revelation. It specifically states that certain verses are obscure and that only God knows what they really mean.[32] Moreover, the idea of the immutability of the revelation is challenged when it confirms that the message could change with divine whim: 'If We willed, We could take away that which we have revealed to you',[33] – and the challenge becomes even more apparent when it is considered that there were, in fact, systematic revisions to the Qur'an, as shown in verses 2:106, 13:37, 16:101 and 22:52. Furthermore, there is near-universal agreement among Muslims that, in interpreting the Qur'an, custom based on the example of the Prophet (Sunna) both clarifies and supplements it. However, the very pragmatism that defines the Sunna means that justifications of widely varying and even mutually exclusive positions occur in practice. Although this variability and inconsistency have attracted criticism,[34] the great majority of Muslims accept the authority of the Sunna as a whole and see nothing wrong with the Prophet having changed his positions and principles with the circumstances. Such precedents support the general idea in Islamic jurisprudence that whatever is *daruri* (necessary) and *maslaha* (in the public interest) can be deemed to be Islamic. At risk of oversimplification, the question of whether something is 'Islamic' may be said to depend on whether it is in the interest of the *umma*, and it is thus clear that this in turn may become subject to the interests and prejudices of the individual or group in charge of making political decisions.

Notwithstanding the flexibility that is reflected in the practice of the Prophet and the interpretation of the Qur'an, the question remains as to how and by whom the issue of what is 'necessary and in the public interest' is to be decided. Indeed, the problem of who decides is further complicated by the fact that 'although the individual's membership in the community of believers is emphasised, the sense of a definite spiritual authority over him is missing'.[35] Islamic legal scholarship builds on this idea with the concept of *ibaha*, whereby the individual's freedom of action outside the area of specific divine commands is acknowledged. Therefore, as long as the individual believes that there is only one God and that Muhammad is His Prophet and follows explicit scriptural injunctions, that individual ultimately becomes the arbiter of his own faith. Although the *'ulama* (Islamic legal scholars) may be prepared to exercise their independent judgement (*ijtihad*) to determine what the Word means – all the time following the same principle of there being no intermediaries between God and man – no ecclesiastical authority exists to settle disputes between them.

It is thus hardly surprising that the quest for the true way of Islam, from the appropriate conduct of daily life to the establishment of formal modes of governance for the growing number of believers, was a task that led to controversy and turmoil after the death of the Prophet. Islamic history testifies to the many differences that have gone unresolved: not only has there been the division between Sunni and Shi'i *'ulama*,

but there have been several divisions within each group, with
Sunnis dividing into four major legal schools – Hanafis, Malikis,
Shafi's and Hanbalis – and the Shi'a into Imamis, Isma'ilis,
Zaydis and their offshoots. The controversy over who speaks
authoritatively for Islam, far from ever being resolved, only
intensified with the processes of modernization and the advent
of mass education. Of the many implications of these global
trends, from the development of modern political societies to
the creation of new identities, opportunities and inequalities,
two interrelated issues are of particular importance for the
assessment of bin Ladin's rationale. One is the continuing and
increasing fragmentation of religious authority. With authoritative sources once confined to the educated few now readily
available to the literate masses, the meaning of sacred scripture
no longer needs to be interpreted by the *'ulama* but is now
there for interpretation by each individual.[36] Again, as Hassan
al-Turabi, leader of the Muslim Brothers in Sudan explained,
'because all knowledge is divine and religious, a chemist, and
engineer, an economist or a jurist are all 'ulama'.[37] These new
'ulama make up for what they lack in terms of formal religious
training with the eagerness that marks their restless attempts
to voice their opinion – in print, on Arabic news channel Al
Jazeera or on Islamonline – speaking of general principles
and modern concerns without making specific reference to the
principles of the established Hanafi, Maliki, Shafi'i or Hanbali
schools of Sunni law (*madhhabs*) and citing few of the classi-
cal works of jurisprudence. The natural consequence of this
development is what Hallaq has described as the 'demise of the
shari'a'.[38] As individual Muslims increasingly interpret Islam
for themselves, a broad spectrum of interpretations emerges that
provide alternative opinions to those of the traditional religious
establishments, making it more and more difficult to say with

reassuring finality what is Islamic and what is not. This would appear to constitute both the biggest dilemma and the greatest challenge for Islam in the modern globalized world.

Related to this combination of a gradual decline of traditional structures, the development of new identities as a consequence of globalization and the increasing fragmentation of religious authority is a phenomenon that Eickelman and Piscatori have termed the 'objectification of Muslim consciousness', a process by which basic questions such as the actual meaning of Islam and how it should affect one's conduct come to the fore in the consciousness of believers.[39] Its concern is with questions of the application of Islamic principle; for example, what does it mean to be Muslim in a world that bears no resemblance at all to the days of the Prophet? The search for the true Islam in the modern world, as the previous section illustrated, is destined to yield an abundance of different answers across the spectrum of existing interpretations that evade easy classification. Given that Islam has no equivalent of the papacy, final judgement lies with the conscience of individual believers. Taken together, these observations lead to the inevitable, if perhaps uncomfortable, conclusion that in practice, if not in theology, there are as many Islams as there are Muslims.

The competition for sacred authority

The increasing number of scholarly – and less scholarly – opinions on what Islam has to say about the present state of world affairs offer those in search of spiritual guidance an unprecedented level of choice. This in turn means that those wishing to share and establish their views as the true meaning of Islam (*'ulama* and Islamists alike) are in direct competition for sacred authority by which to win over the hearts and minds of those whom they wish to convince of the righteousness of their respective missions and agendas. Each attempts to persuade his audience by means of religious symbolism with which all Muslims identify that his interpretation of the sacred scriptures amounts to nothing less than the true will of Allah. Bin Ladin might not have been either a very original thinker or a formally trained religious scholar, but he did have the gift of rhetorical brilliance, which turns his messages into what Lewis described as 'a magnificent piece of eloquent, at times even poetic Arabic prose'.[40] This image of his religiousness is reinforced by, for example, the way he presented himself in the traditional clothing of a devout Muslim, and the air of heroism and personal sacrifice is conferred by stories of the rich businessman who has forsaken the pleasures of a privileged life in the modern world for the sake of his faith. In today's fast-paced environment where superficial impressions all too often replace nuanced, in-depth assessment, he exemplifies all the qualities of an inspirational religious leader: he looks like a true believer, he sounds like a true believer – he must be a true believer.

This is not just superficially effective, however. Bin Ladin's messages reach deeply into the collective consciousness of Muslims around the globe. For example, 'Saudi Arabia' and 'Palestine', central and repeating themes in his many statements, are charged with emotion and symbolism in the Muslim political imagination. Home to the holiest cities in Islam (Mecca and Medina in Saudi Arabia and Jerusalem in Israel/Palestine), they form the setting in which the Prophet lived his life and from which Islam originated. It was in Mecca that the Prophet was born and received his revelations, and it is the destination of the *hajj* (pilgrimage), one of the five pillars of Islam, which Muslims are exhorted to undertake if they are able. Medina, the town where the Prophet and his early followers sought refuge from a plot to assassinate him, became the seat of the first Islamic state, while the year of his migration (*hijra*) marks the first year of the Muslim calendar. Over the years, it has become a special place of devotion, and tradition encourages believers (although it does not require it) to visit the Prophet's mosque. In a similar fashion, Jerusalem occupies a central position in Islam due to its connection to two special journeys of the Prophet: the *isra*, or nocturnal journey, during which it is believed he was taken from Mecca to Jerusalem on a winged horse, and the *mi'raj*, the Prophet's ascension to heaven. As Piscatori explains, 'both Arabian and Palestinian lands are thus special preserves, and, because of this, they take on a wider importance, particularly in the competition for legitimacy that characterizes politics in the Middle East.'[41]

Thus, when bin Ladin calls for the liberation of al-Aqsa Mosque and the Holy Mosque and demands that the foreign armies be driven out of the lands of Islam, he is destined to strike a sentimental chord with his Muslim audience. It would, however, be misleading to accuse him of having exploited these emotionally charged symbols for other purposes. Unlike Saddam Hussein, whose linkage of the Palestinian cause to his own withdrawal from Kuwait in 1991 was, above all, a strategically smart move to attract otherwise unlikely public support across the Arab world,[42] Osama bin Ladin saw the liberation of the holy lands of Islam as a significant milestone towards his ultimate goal of reclaiming the *umma* and restoring the glory of Islam. Palestine is not incidental to the agenda – it *is* the agenda. A survey of his public statements and recruitment videos makes this abundantly clear: what is considered the first of bin Ladin's public pronouncements intended for a wider audience, entitled 'The Betrayal of Palestine' and addressed as a letter to the Chief Mufti of Saudi Arabia, Abdul Aziz ibn Abdullah ibn Baz, decries the endorsement of the 1993 Oslo

Accords as 'a betrayal of the word of God and of the community of the faithful'.[43] The background to the letter is a climate of broader criticism of the *'ulema*-endorsed decision that allowed for the arrival of American troops into the kingdom in 1991, an act that led to the intrusion of Western standards, the corruption of the monarchy and ultimate dependence on the United States, resulting in the sell-out of the Palestinian cause to gratify Washington. The words of bin Ladin convey this message in a far more emotive and persuasive manner:

> No one can be unaware of the tremendous spread of corruption, which has penetrated all aspects of life. ... The political and economic crises that [Saudi Arabia] is suffering, and the crimes that have spread through it like wildfire, are punishment from God....
>
> When the forces of the aggressive Crusader–Jewish alliance decided during the Gulf War – in connivance with the regime – to occupy the country in the name of liberating Kuwait, you justified this with an arbitrary juridical decree excusing this terrible act, which sullied the pride of the *umma* and sullied its honor, as well as polluting its holy places. ...
>
> And it seemed as if you were not satisfied with abandoning Saudi Arabia, home of the two Holy Sanctuaries, to the Crusader–Jewish forces of occupation, until you had brought another disaster upon Jerusalem, the third of the Sanctuaries, by conferring legitimacy on the contracts to surrender to the Jews that were signed by the traitorous and cowardly Arab tyrants....
>
> The legal duty regarding Palestine and our brothers there – these poor men, women and children who have nowhere to go – is to wage *jihad* for the sake of God, and to motivate our *umma* to *jihad* so that Palestine may be completely liberated and returned to Islamic sovereignty.[44]

Far from being afterthoughts or excuses, it is clear that Saudi Arabia and Palestine were central issues from the very beginning. And, while the list of causes gradually widened to include instances of Muslim suffering around the world, and the identification of a central enemy, the cause of all of these ills – first the United States and then the 'Crusader–Jewish alliance' – became more precise, Saudi Arabia and Palestine remained key items on bin Ladin's agenda. Bin Ladin's letter of 23 August 1996, also referred to as the '1996 Declaration of Jihad', which issued an empathetic call to 'expel the Polytheists from the Arabian peninsula', illustrates the development that took place.[45] No longer limited to a Middle Eastern audience, this letter is addressed to 'my Muslim brothers across the world', and broadens the spectrum of his appeals as it invokes incidences of Muslim suffering under the 'blatant imperial arrogance of the United States'[46] from the Middle East, Central Asia and the Horn of Africa to the Caucasus, the Balkans and Southeast Asia. Yet it is telling that in the midst of this litany of desolation, bin Ladin singles out another issue to be of even greater concern – the continued occupation of Saudi Arabia:

> The greatest disaster to befall the Muslims since the death of the Prophet Muhammad is the occupation of Saudi Arabia, which is the cornerstone of the Islamic world, place of revelation, source of the Prophetic mission, and home of the noble Ka'ba where Muslims direct their prayers. Despite this, it was occupied by the armies of the Christians, the Americans and their allies.[47]

The issue at stake for bin Ladin is nothing less than the liberation of the global *umma*, God's favoured community, and the sacred lands of Islam, Saudi Arabia and Palestine, from the grip of the unholy invaders, which is the moral and, above all, religious duty of all believers. Reunited in the name of God, Islam can and will be restored to its former glory:

> I say to our Muslim brothers across the world: your brothers in Saudi Arabia and Palestine are calling for your help and asking you

to share with them in the *jihad* against the enemies of God, your enemies the Israelis and the Americans. They are asking you to defy them in whatever way you possibly can, so as to expel them in defeat and humiliation from the holy places of Islam. God Almighty has said: if they seek help from you against persecution, it is your duty to assist them.[48]

In interviews and letters that appeared later in 1996 and 1997, bin Ladin reinforced and elaborated upon these points in no uncertain terms. In February 1998, the newly formed 'World Islamic Front', under the leadership of bin Ladin, formally condemned US policies as a clear proclamation of war against God, His Messenger and Muslims, and, in an attempt to maximize religious authority,[49] issued the fatwa in support of jihad against America that called for the killing of 'Americans, both military and civilian, wherever possible'.[50] Deeds followed words in August of the same year, in the form of the simultaneous bomb attacks against US embassies in Kenya and Tanzania, providing a foretaste of the terror that would strike at the heart of America in 2001. And while bin Ladin's messages adapted to the changing circumstances on the international arena and the unfolding of the controversial war against terror, the essence of his pan-Islamic rationale remained unchanged. In one of bin Ladin's last audio messages, issued in response to the Gaza tragedy in March 2009, the by now all-too-familiar themes resurface once more.[51] Again bin Ladin talks about the liberation of 'the blessed land', bringing an end to the suffering of the Palestinian people, 'our brothers and sisters in Islam', and defeating the ultimate source of these ills, the 'Crusader–Zionist' alliance by means of jihad. If anything, the way in which bin Ladin addresses his audience repeatedly as 'my *umma*' drives home his transnational, pan-Islamic ambition throughout the address.

Defending Islam: an individual duty

The emotive use of such terminology is, in all likelihood, not simply accidental or merely a sign of personal emotional involvement, but rather an intelligent and ultimately useful rhetorical tool by which bin Ladin individualizes the call to defend the *umma* and Islam to an audience composed of Muslims from a wide variety of nationalities and social backgrounds. By thus interpreting the true meaning of Islam in the present socio-political context – namely, the miserable state of the *umma* as a result of oppressive US policies – bin Ladin leads the audience into a moral endeavour. In other words, he effectively communicates the concept of personal responsibility, namely that it is up to every individual believer to do whatever he (or she) can to rectify this unacceptable situation:

> Oh you who believe! What is the matter with you [plural], that when you are asked to march forth in the Cause of Allah / Jihad, you cling heavily to the earth? Are you [plural] pleased with the life of this world rather than the Hereafter? But little is in the enjoyment of the life of this world as compared to the Hereafter (9:38).
>
> Oh Muslims, do you [plural] want to walk along the straight path and please God? Do you [singular] submit to the will of Allah?[52]

The way in which this question is formulated reveals the significance of the moral endeavour in which the individual in the audience is being invited to take part. The initial part of the question addresses the whole audience, while the second part is directed specifically towards the individual. By moving from speaking to the audience as a whole to addressing the individual, bin Ladin engages every listener in a moral dilemma.

The emphasis on the personal and defensive that is observed here is not only a rhetorical device but is also a way of overcoming the legal requirements for jihad. In the Islamic tradition, the doctrine of jihad is split into two categories: 'defensive' and 'offensive'. Offensive jihad is a collective responsibility to conquer new lands for Islam and convert new peoples to the faith, but one that must be called by the caliph, the recognized leader of the world Islamic community. In the physical absence of the caliph in the present-day environment, bin Ladin did not, contrary to some expectations, take on the role of the new leader of the community. In fact, his ambitions were more modest in that he acted merely to remind his fellow Muslims of the 'personal' jihad, which is not limited merely to striving to be a better Muslim, but also entails the defence of the Islamic faith, the Muslim community and Muslim territory against attacks by non-Muslims. For this action no formal declaration of war is required as it is doctrinally incumbent on each Muslim to contribute to the fight against the attacker to the best of his or her ability. As such, bin Ladin needed no one else's authority to validate his call because doctrine and historical practice void any claim that he was not suitably qualified to lead a jihad in the absence of any religious credentials. For Michael Scheuer, 'Bin Laden's genius lies not in his call for a defensive jihad, but in constructing and articulating a consistent and convincing case that an attack against Islam is under way and is being led and directed by America.'[53] In the light of bin Ladin's rhetorical sophistication, one might conclude that this is only partially true. His construction of the 'umma under attack and in need of rescue' is the first step; his true genius lay in his ability to communicate this in a way that transforms the headline-making, globally significant events of international relations into a personal dilemma that is applicable to every believer. Reclaiming the umma, even by deadly force, thus becomes the obligation of every individual who would call him- or herself a good Muslim – a message which appears to some to be all the more authoritative in a secularized modern world that lacks clear religious guidance.

Reclaiming the *umma*:
the origins of pan-Islamic sentiment

By addressing timely issues of grave concern to the Muslim world, formalizing the return to the traditions of the golden age as a straightforward solution, and authoritatively addressing the entirety of the Muslim community, bin Ladin both powerfully indicted the waywardness of Muslim societies and set out a simple blueprint for action. The likelihood of success in achieving his ultimate goal of restoring the unity of Islam (*tawhid al umma*) by means of jihad – with all of the destruction and bloodshed that are implicit in the indiscriminate nature of the methods he advocated – remains questionable at best, even in the minds of many who sympathize with his aims, yet bin Ladin succeeded in polemicizing modern-day Islam. By calling so forcefully for a return to fundamental Islamic traditions and values, and seeking to interpret them in such a way that they can be applied effectively to the present-day situation, bin Ladin set, with considerable candour, a benchmark by which the status quo can be measured and criticized, and in so doing not only provided religious guidance for the faithful but also brought religious – and, by his standards, righteous – judgement upon a world that currently bears no resemblance to his vision of the golden days of the caliphate. By this light, a more meaningful way to identify the ideological origins of al-Qaeda would be to place it in the context of those issues that have contributed to the emergence of pan-Islam.[54]

Pan-Islam grew up as a response to the double assault of imperialism and decentralization of the Ottoman Empire in

the late nineteenth century. While different proponents such
as Sultan Abdulhamid (1842–1918), polemicists such as Jamal
al-Din al-Afghani (1838–1897), and Western apologists such
as Wilfred Blunt (1840–1922) all contributed to make a vague
idea of Islamic unity a symbol of the modern Islamic condition, it was the Turkish Grand National Assembly that challenged believers and non-believers alike when, in March 1924,
it abolished the caliphate. Kemalists predicted the inevitable
secularization of Muslim societies; devout believers thought
it would weaken Muslims in their interaction with the West;
colonial offices feared that it would stimulate a broad uprising
of the worldwide Muslim community. Although none of these
occurred, the lingering appeal of the notion of Muslim solidarity began to manifest itself and eventually assumed its place in
the formation of modern Muslim states and, more recently, in
attempts to undermine them.[55]

In the years that followed, different perspectives emerged
on the continued significance of the caliphate as a necessary
condition or expression of Muslim unity, ranging from those
wishing to re-establish a purified religious-political institution
(although this in itself was subject to the distortions of the
late Ottoman experience) to those who thought the fusion
of religious and political authority was counterproductive or
even dangerous, and to accommodationists who saw the creation of an international organization among sovereign 'Muslim
states'[56] as being the best way of adapting to post-war conditions. In the face of such diversity, and with no prominent
political leadership to develop the pan-Islamic sentiment into a
reality, 'Pan-Islam seemed at its nadir'.[57] 'Ironically', as Landau
observes, 'among the few who thought that Pan-Islam represented a potent force were foreign officials and military officers
whose duty it was to forestall a Pan-Islamic threat.'[58] However,

although little agreement was reached by the unionists as to how the *umma* was to be constructed, the perception of the spiritual unity of the *umma* remained and firmly established itself as an unquestioned given, readily accepted in line with Qur'anic references to *umma wahida* (one community; e.g. 5:48/53, 16:93/95). In spiritual terms, the idea (and the ideal) of 'unity' (*ittihad-i Islam, al-wahda al-islamiyya*) was cast as essential to Islam, now posited as integral and fundamental and largely divorced from the canonical articulation of concepts such as *khilafa* (the caliphate), *dar al-islam* (the juridical realm of Muslims) and *dhimma* (non-Muslim subjects). Indeed, as Piscatori reminds us, scholarly discussions were remarkably thin on these topics.[59]

In the second half of the twentieth century, the caliphate's political mission gradually disappeared; however, the idea of Islam's political mission did not. In the eyes of many, the *umma* required some form of political expression. Yet whatever broad sense was created of an awareness of a need for Islamic solidarity, it competed with the hesitant but discernible emergence of single-state nationalism (*wataniyya*) in Muslim societies or at least the consolidation of dynastic rules and regimes. In the context of these structural developments, the political goal of a unitary Islamic state resembling the caliphate was replaced by the goal of unity in Islamic state politics.[60] And although Islam has always had a global dimension, it is here that the concept of Islamic, or maybe more appropriately Muslim, solidarity emerged: even if Muslims were not to be united under a single ruler, concern and indeed some form of responsibility for the well-being of all members of the faith, regardless of citizenship, became an article of the modern Islamic condition. Thus, when bin Ladin decried the global suffering of Muslims, he spoke to the core of Muslim consciousness.

In the political sphere, the new sense of Islamic solidarity was expressed in the development of state-based organizations such as the Muslim World Congress, the Muslim World League and the Organization of the Islamic Conference. Yet despite outwardly signalling their support for the noble ideal of Muslim solidarity, critical examination reveals that, in fact, national elites invoked pan-Islam for everything other than pan-Islamic purposes. With one eye on their domestic publics and the other on rival states, they sought to serve as the new patrons of Islam in order to consolidate their individual claims to national power and global leadership. The rivalry between Saudi Arabia, Iran and Pakistan is but one example of this dynamic. Islamist movements like the Muslim Brotherhood, Hamas and the Front Islamique du Salut (FIS), despite vehemently criticizing their respective national leaders for their 'un-Islamic ways', largely did the same, seeking not so much to restore the caliphate as to establish themselves in power within the by now firmly established political form of the nation-state. The political expression of pan-Islam, one might conclude, gradually receded until it became little more than a token commitment to the unity of the faith.

Recognizing these changes in global political organizations and assessing broader socio-political trends, Landau contemplates a renewed surge of Pan-Islamic expression. Writing in late 1989, he concludes, 'As large parts of the world are moving towards more concrete forms of association, Pan-Islamists too may well turn a 120-year-old dream from what seemed to have become a utopia into a political reality.'[61] Taking the analysis into the new millennium, Piscatori explains in 2004:

> As the pan-Islamic dimension appeared to recede, some 'radicals', if you will, have sought to fill the void. They seek, in their view, to reclaim the *umma* from the nation-state and dynastic regimes.

Examples are obvious: Hizb al-Tahrir al-Islami (the Islamic Liberation Party), the Muhajirun (an offshoot of the Hizb al-Tahrir in Britain), Usama Bin Ladin and Ayman al-Zawahiri (leaders of al-Qa'ida). In effect, pan-Islam went underground, re-emerged spectacularly, and, in one virulent form, attacks the status quo in the name of a 'tradition' that has only relatively recently appeared. Bin Ladin's statement of 7 October 2001 dated the current troubles of the Muslim world to eighty years before. Although he did not directly say what the benchmark was, it likely refers to the demise of the caliphate in 1924. This interpretation is consistent with accounts that link European, specifically British, intervention with local secularising regimes – here Atatürk – to explain the collapse of Muslim unity. Today it is the American presence in the Middle East and elsewhere that is particularly harmful because it is both economic and ideological; its attempt to attain market domination is dependent on the curtailing of Islam to a kind of safe, conservative, and largely privatised Islam such as the ruling elites of the Muslim world practice.[62]

Al-Qaeda and the global jihad might not have been exactly what Landau envisioned when he contemplated the determination of pan-Islamists to fulfil their utopian dream. Yet the vision of resurrecting the caliphate that now manifests itself in a perpetual threat of terrorist violence seems to have become a permanent feature of life in the twenty-first century. Although al-Qaeda does not resemble what one would traditionally think of as a political organization, it has become a political reality nonetheless. The key to this realization is to acknowledge the extent to which ideas matter. In the global world in which virtual realities and identities increasingly overlap with and even replace those found in 'real life', it should not come as a surprise that the biggest challenge – real or perceived – to security in the real world comes from the sphere of the imagined, and feared. But where is this leading?

Towards pan-Islamic unity or bitter fragmentation?

Osama bin Ladin, we may conclude, was neither a religious scholar whose rationale originated from any one particular school of thought, nor a particularly innovative thinker. Rather, the logic of his call to global jihad is more adequately explained when placed in the context of broader socio-political developments that have changed the landscape of modern Islam. In fact, a closer look at his statements readily reveals his vision of reclaiming the *umma* from the unholy oppressors with the ultimate goal of re-creating the caliphate to be a contemporary expression of pan-Islamism. Bin Ladin constructed his idea of Islam along the lines of an alternative, individual interpretation that overcomes the ideological rifts within Islam and places the community of faith well above individual states and governments and outside of the influence of all that is un-Islamic. What this lacks in coherence with regard to any definite plans indicating how this community of faith is to be organized in practice, it makes up for in fervour, the logic of which can be summarized as follows: first, we need to overcome the enemies of Islam, namely the Zionist–Crusader invasion, and then everything else will naturally, or maybe by divine intervention, fall into place. With this rationale, bin Ladin falls somewhat short of the more concrete visions of other Pan-Islamists who have expressed their ideas of Islam and the organization of the 'new caliphate' in terms that are more applicable to the reality of the here and now. However, the strength and appeal of bin Ladin's message rests firmly in the powerful belief that utopia is attainable if only all Muslims are willing to try hard enough and play their part in reclaiming the *umma* from the oppressive force of the Zionist–Crusaders. For all its simplicity, it is this kind of idealism that embraces at the very core the growing sense of solidarity among all Muslims and hence so effectively inspires both those who sympathize with bin Ladin's aims and those who wholeheartedly embrace and carry out the global jihad through physical actions. Al-Qaeda and the global jihad have manifested themselves chiefly through what is arguably an exaggerated fear of transnational Islamist networks united in their goal of destroying the West in their pursuit of establishing a new golden age of Islam — an echo of nineteenth-century European anxiety over pan-Islamic anti-colonialism. But is it possible to create a more concrete, real-world presence out of something that is inherently vague and finds its manifestation in the act – in the act of destruction, no less? Or, to put it another way, what is the track record of al-Qaeda in reclaiming the *umma*? An answer to this question warrants a closer look at the reality of al-Qaeda in the post-9/11 world.

FIVE

Al-Qaeda post-9/11: destroyed, weakened or re-emergent?

Every dismissive assumption made about al-Qaeda before September 11 was wrong. So is the assumption that it is in any way receding today: it is still the most dangerous international security threat to both the Western and Islamic worlds. Osama bin Laden has not been driven underground or lost touch with his followers. Al-Qaeda is using the internet extensively to communicate with its supporters and to further its aim of creating new bases from which to organise terrorist attacks. Suggestions that it may have morphed into some kind of 'ideological' or 'inspirational' organisation that merely encourages copycat groups of young Muslims to emulate its greatest 'achievements' are contradicted by its leadership's steady stream of instructions to followers.... [A]l-Qaeda will continue to develop its original aims of trying to defeat the West, carry out regime change in the Muslim world and increase its armies of supporters worldwide, to hasten the advent of its dream of a worldwide caliphate – Muslim state – ruled by al-Qaeda.

Ahmed Rashid, 2006[1]

Since the beginning of the war against terror, news of 'successes', chiefly in the form of the capture or killing of key individuals known to be involved with al-Qaeda, and 'failures', such as detained al-Qaeda members escaping from prison or terror attacks being carried out by groups claiming to be affiliated to al-Qaeda, has regularly made headlines in the Western media. Despite the constant flow of information, the question of how exactly al-Qaeda has fared in the post-9/11 world is difficult to judge. Has it been weakened, almost to the point of being destroyed, so that it is unable to carry out major operations? Or is it re-emergent, stronger and more dangerous now than it was before?

Al-Qaeda: between conflicting assumptions?

As was argued in Chapter 2, the period in which the attacks of 11 September 2001 took place is widely seen as the peak of al-Qaeda's influence and effectiveness. But while the 9/11 attacks are generally perceived as the greatest success, Sageman qualifies them in the light of subsequent events:

> The success of the 9/11 operation backfired on al-Qaeda. There is some evidence that al-Qaeda leadership anticipated a limited U.S. response... This turned out to be a serious miscalculation; the Bush administration decided to freeze al-Qaeda funds and invade Afghanistan to change its regime and deny al-Qaeda any refuge. U.S. Forces, however, did not succeed in eliminating the leadership of al-Qaeda, which escaped through allied Afghan lines during Operation Anaconda.[2]

Indeed, it is possible that bin Ladin and the central leadership or 'hardcore', in Burke's terminology, might not have foreseen that the War on Terror, which began in 2001, would still be ongoing almost ten years later. In the immediate aftermath of the September 11 attacks, the invasion of Afghanistan arguably posed the most troubling development for al-Qaeda. The sympathetic home that they had established, complete with its systems of training camps and total freedom of movement, was lost almost overnight.

Burke argues, 'By the beginning of 2002, it was obvious that the physical assets of al-Qaeda in Afghanistan were destroyed, the personnel scattered. The "al-Qaeda hardcore", the first of our three concentric circles of al-Qaeda, had taken a pounding.'[3] This was evidenced by the more low-key level of subsequent al-Qaeda-attributed attacks, such as the bombing of the Bali nightclub in 2002. Both Burke and Sageman[4] claim that these attacks were initiated locally rather than being orchestrated by the al-Qaeda 'core'. At the same time, however, the US government continued to advance the idea of the immense threat posed by a centralized, global organization.

So what did al-Qaeda look like after the damage it sustained in the course of the War on Terror? This question is the subject of much controversy among different analysts, who either insist on the continued threat from an organized group or contend that the nature of al-Qaeda had been fundamentally transformed. Indeed, since around 2005, 'two seemingly distinct and ostensibly contradictory narratives have emerged regarding the capability, positioning and operational strategy of al-Qaeda'.[5] On the one hand, many government leaders and counter-terrorism experts have asserted that al-Qaeda is steadily getting weaker and is no longer able to plan and carry out large-scale attacks. Supporters of this position point to the shrinking number of al-Qaeda fighters in Afghanistan as a result of the ongoing counter-insurgency campaign, the fact that its funding has all but dried up, and, chiefly, its perceived lack of operational capacity to execute attacks on the scale of 9/11 against the United States and the West. Prominent advocates of this position include Marc Sageman, with his notion of the 'leaderless jihad', and Jason Burke, with his theory of 'freelance combatants', who argue that the main threat no longer comes from the organization called al-Qaeda, but from the bottom up, namely radicalized individuals and groups who meet and plot in their neighbourhoods or via the Internet, who act independently and without any ties to a central organization beyond a shared ideological connection.[6]

On the other hand, the assertion is made that al-Qaeda is on the rise. Arguments in support of this assertion point to al-Qaeda's continued ability to influence and facilitate smaller-scale attacks successfully, of which there are many examples. On 5 November 2009, US Army Major Nidal Hasan opened fire on fellow service personnel at Fort Hood, Texas, killing thirteen people and wounding thirty. Christmas Day 2009 became memorable for Umar Farouk Abdulmuttalab's attempted bomb attack on an airliner en route to Detroit: the bomber succeeded in smuggling explosives on board in his underwear, but was overpowered after they failed to detonate fully and the resulting fire gave him away. 29 October 2010 saw the failure of a plot to blow up two commercial aircraft, after a tip-off led to explosives being found hidden inside the toner cartridges of two laser printers sent as air cargo on flights from Yemen to the United States. Advocates of the view that al-Qaeda is alive and thriving include analysts such as Peter Bergen and Bruce Hoffman, who reject Sageman's notion of a leaderless jihad and insist that al-Qaeda has regrouped in the remote regions of Afghanistan and Pakistan and is not only still active but is in fact resurgent and more dangerous than it has been in several years.[7] Bruce Riedel describes al-Qaeda as 'a more dangerous enemy today than it has ever been before.[8]

Upon closer examination, however, it can soon be seen that these two positions are not as mutually exclusive as they might at first appear. Neither Hoffman nor Riedel deny the changing character of the group. In an interview with the German news magazine *Der Spiegel* in 2006, Hoffman explains:

New structures have emerged. ... There are both new cells inspired by al-Qaida and actual al-Qaida terrorists active today. That is why I think al-Qaida is more dangerous than it was on 9/11. Because you have now a vast sea of self-radicalized Muslims in many places in the Muslim world that aren't necessarily connected with al-Qaida but [are] willing to act. So you still have an al-Qaida organization that is operating on its own but is also seeking to tap into that pool of unhappiness and disaffection.[9]

In a similar fashion, Riedel, writing in *Foreign Affairs*, argues:

[Al-Qaeda] has suffered some setbacks since September 11 2001: losing its state within a state in Afghanistan, having several of its top operatives killed, failing in its attempts to overthrow the governments of Egypt, Jordan, and Saudi Arabia. But thanks largely to Washington's eagerness to go into Iraq rather than concentrate on hunting down al-Qaeda's leaders, the organization now has a solid base of operations in the badlands of Pakistan and an effective franchise in western Iraq. Its reach has spread throughout the Muslim world, where it has developed a large cadre of operatives, and in Europe, where it can claim the support of some disenfranchised Muslim locals and members of the Arab and Asian diasporas. Osama bin Laden has mounted a successful propaganda campaign to make himself and his movement the primary symbols of Islamic resistance worldwide. His ideas now attract more followers than ever.[10]

There is, in fact, agreement about the changing character of al-Qaeda towards a looser array of groups and individuals held together not by formal, organizational ties, but by personal connections and the unity of their ambition to follow the call to jihad. Furthermore, both sets of commentators agree on the seriousness of the threat posed by the fragmented global jihad movement, and that is impossible to locate and inherently unpredictable. The disagreement, and this is hardly surprising in the light of the controversy over the make-up of al-Qaeda pre-9/11, is concentrated very much on the nature of the organizational structure, in particular as to whether a central core or leadership still exists, has re-emerged or is in the process of re-emerging in a particular location to facilitate attacks, or whether the movement is now entirely local, leaderless and fragmented. In the words of Burke, who expressed his disregard for any such core organization:

> The good news is that this [core] al-Qaeda does not exist. The bad news is that the threat now facing the world is far more dangerous than any single terrorist leader with an army, however large, of loyal cadres. Instead, the threat that faces us is new and different, complex and diverse, dynamic and protean and profoundly difficult to characterize.[11]

However, even the divide over the existence of a central core is not as substantial as it might seem. In the bitter exchange following Hoffman's review of Sageman's *Leaderless Jihad*, Sageman, for no apparent reason other than arguably giving in to Hoffman, who relied on intelligence sources to insist on the re-emergence of an al-Qaeda core leadership, eventually changed his mind. In doing so, he effectively undermined the central argument of his book, asserting that he had never intended to say either that al-Qaeda central no longer existed or that it was not dangerous.

Upon closer examination, it becomes clear that the debate surrounding the fate of al-Qaeda post-9/11 is but a continuation of argument regarding the make-up of al-Qaeda pre-9/11, except that it has now become a very public struggle over who speaks most authoritatively on the subject. In this politicized debate, less attention appears to have been paid to the evidence in support of the argument for the continued existence of the central core, which is just as thin, if not thinner, now than it was before. For example, Hoffman's argument that the 'centre holds' is based on National Intelligence Estimate

(NIE) warnings that al-Qaeda had reconstituted, and, as we have seen, this view is reflected in the assessments of other analysts. But how reliable is this information? The National Intelligence Estimate represents the collective best guess of the US intelligence community as to what is likely to happen, or not happen, on the security scene in particular parts of the world. Yet whilst good intelligence is vital, and predictions can be a useful tool, the NIE remains an estimate with no universal truth claim, which has been highly inaccurate in its assessments in the past. Indeed, one of the most controversial estimates in recent years was the one produced in October 2002 concerning Iraq's illicit weapons programmes. As a Senate report later concluded, 'Most of the major key judgments in the report either overstated, or were not supported by, the underlying intelligence reporting.'[12] While the possibility of a re-emergent core leadership of al-Qaeda cannot be ruled out, and it is indeed likely that both the original group and the next generation continue to aspire to greatness, it is important to keep in mind that no indisputable evidence is available. What can be said, however, is that both the former leaders and indeed younger, emerging members of the global jihad have a strong incentive to appear to be as unified as possible, and therefore all statements in this regard which cannot be adequately substantiated should be viewed with a degree of scepticism.

Evidence for – or, rather, examples of – the fragmentation of al-Qaeda and the global jihad are easier to come by. Burke, who maintains that the leaderless jihad was in part a consequence of bin Ladin's advice to his associates to disperse and individually carry out attacks wherever possible, points to the large number of small-scale, low-key attacks that have unfolded since late 2001. They include incidents such as the 2002 suicide attack in a synagogue in Tunisia; the bombings in 2003 of two synagogues, the British Consulate and the local headquarters of HSBC bank in Istanbul, Turkey; the 2005 Amman hotel bombings; the 2007 Algiers bombings; and the aforementioned Fort Hood and Little Rock recruiting office shootings in 2009, to name but a few. Closer examination of the specifics of these attacks reveals a significant variety of different actors, rationales and attributions. Some were committed by individuals in order to assert the continued existence of and threat posed by al-Qaeda, while others were carried out by individuals who either had no apparent connection to the organization or who were connected to local franchises such as the Al-Qaeda Organization in the Islamic Maghreb and acted in response to specific local griev-ances rather than in fulfilment of Osama bin Ladin's original agenda. In the context of the synagogue bombings in Tunisia, the BBC reported:

> A spokesman for Osama bin Laden's al-Qaeda network says the organization was behind a suicide attack at a Tunisian synagogue in April, in which 19 people died. In an audiotape broadcast on the Arabic al-Jazeera television channel, al-Qaeda official Sulaiman Abu Ghaith said the attack was revenge for the deaths of Palestin-ians. Mr Abu Ghaith praised the 11 September attacks on America and warned of more attacks 'in the coming days and months'. The Kuwaiti-born cleric said 98 per cent of al-Qaeda leaders – including Bin Laden – were alive and that Bin Laden would make a statement broadcast on television.[13]

On the surface, this announcement might appear authoritative, representative of an organisation still capable of causing mayhem on a grand and global scale, but on further analysis the impres-sion conveyed by both the statement and the attack itself is one of al-Qaeda in a certain amount of panic, desperate to assert its continued existence and the seriousness of its threat to its followers and enemies alike, in relation to an event that bears little comparison to the magnitude of the New York attacks just seven months before. Has al-Qaeda lived up to Abu Ghaith's claims? Yes and no. Attacks have continued; yet, while some have sent shockwaves through the ranks of the audience, fortunately none has come close to the infamous standards of 9/11, against which they are now measured. Moreover, many of the subsequent attacks, although carried out in the spirit of global jihad, do not support the idea of 'al-Qaeda, the organization/core' as the key facilitator. One such attack that illustrates this is the Madrid train bombings, which consisted of a series of coordinated bombings on the morning of 11 March 2004 that killed a total of 191 people and wounded 1,800. With the world's attention focused on the simultaneous nature of the bombings, the assumption quickly spread that the attacks carried the signature of al-Qaeda, and acceptance of this assumption was augmented by the corollary belief that a larger group had to be behind an attack of such proportions. However, the initial suspicion of a connection to al-Qaeda was never fully established as fact. According to analyst Scott Atran, cited in the *Guardian*'s investigation into the 'worst Islamist attack in European history',

'There isn't the slightest bit of evidence of any operational relationship with al-Qaida,' said Mr Atran. 'We've been looking at it closely for years and we've been briefed by everybody under the sun and … nothing connects them. The overwhelming majority of [terrorist cells] in Europe have nothing to do with al-Qaida other than a vague relationship of ideology. And even that ideology is fairly superficial – it's basically a reaction to what they see as a war on Islam around the world,' he said. But, argued Mr Atran, people needed to believe that something bigger was involved – it was hard to accept that a small, loosely connected group of young men could carry out an attack on this scale without outside assistance. However, 'These young men radicalized themselves.'[14]

The Madrid bombings seem to illustrate the transition towards a fragmented jihad carried out by individuals without a direct connection to an organization or network beyond a shared belief in jihad as a solution to perceived Muslim grievances. They also exemplify the power – both in terms of destruction and loss of life and as instruments of fear – of what might be more adequately described as one-off attacks.

Other terrorist incidents have been attributed to al-Qaeda 'franchises': groups which include individuals with relatively close links to members of the al-Qaeda core, who arguably share the ideology of global jihad espoused by bin Ladin but act mainly within distinctly local geopolitical contexts. One such group is Al-Qaeda in the Maghreb, formerly known as the GSPC (*Groupe Salafiste pour la Prédication et le Combat* – Salafist Group for Preaching and Combat). Although it has allegedly claimed that it supports Osama bin Ladin, the group, which was found to be responsible for the bombings in Algiers in 2007, as well as a number of other local incidents, appears to be more concerned with the goal of overthrowing the Algerian government and the institution of an Islamic state in its place than with the re-establishment of the caliphate and the unity of the global *umma*. And, while the argument can be made that this is not entirely out of touch with the goals of bin Ladin and Zawahiri, it is nonetheless a return to the 'near enemy' that has preoccupied Islamists since the days of Hassan al-Banna, while the explicit focus on the 'far enemy' remains unique to al-Qaeda. At the time of writing, recent political developments in northern Africa have prompted the group to further activity: in January 2011, Al-Qaeda in the Maghreb voiced its support for the demonstrations against the Tunisian government in the hope that the revolution would spread to Algeria. In a 13-minute video, the current leader of the group,

Abu Musab Abdul Wadud, offered military aid and training to the demonstrators, calling on them to overthrow 'the corrupt, criminal and tyrannical' regime and for the establishment of sharia law in the country.[15] Rather than becoming a distraction, the events in Tunisia served Al-Qaeda in the Maghreb's vision by providing the group with a useful opportunity to fan the flames of instability in the region and to attempt to instigate the overthrow of Algerian president Abdelaziz Bouteflika.[16]

In spite of such groups' focus on the local context, some analysts, including Riedel, cited above, saw them as evidence of al-Qaeda's new strength. The group that received most attention until late 2009 is Al-Qaeda in Iraq (AQI). AQI is said to have been founded in 2003 under the leadership of Jordanian militant Abu Musab al-Zarqawi, who declared allegiance to Osama bin Ladin in October 2004. In the light of the seemingly never-ending stream of news of bloody attacks and explosions attributed to the group, it is impossible to ignore the existence of Al-Qaeda in Iraq. On the other hand, it is vital to be cautious about simply attributing every violent incident to al-Qaeda. As Clark Hoyt cautions, 'seeing al-Qaeda in every corner' is more likely to exaggerate the impression of the group than to provide a meaningful assessment of its influence and capabilities.[17] Indeed, a closer look at the AQI's stated objectives and its modus operandi undermines the notion that it might be a group created in the traditional image of al-Qaeda and contributing meaningfully to the fulfilment of its aims.

Right from the start, AQI's goals were distinctly local in character: to force a withdrawal of US-led forces from Iraq; to topple the Iraqi interim government; to assassinate collaborators with the occupation; to marginalize the Shia population and defeat its militias; and subsequently to establish a pure Islamic state.[18] What stands out in an agenda with which Osama bin Ladin might otherwise have been largely sympathetic is the distinct call for confrontation with the Iraqi Shia, which quickly turned what started out as a campaign to liberate Iraq and establish an Islamic state within its borders – which in the big picture could serve as a step towards the establishment of the global caliphate – into a bloody sectarian conflict which endeared AQI neither to the Iraqi public nor to the leaders of al-Qaeda 'central'. Zarqawi's declaration of an all-out war on Shi'ites, coupled with his taking responsibility for the bombing of a Shia mosque in 2005, was promptly answered by a letter believed to have been written by central al-Qaeda leader Ayman al-Zawahiri, which questioned the tactic of indiscriminately attacking Shi'ites in Iraq:

> Many of your Muslim admirers amongst the common folk are wondering about your attacks on the Shia. The sharpness of this questioning increases when the attacks are on one of their mosques... My opinion is that this matter won't be acceptable to the Muslim populace however much you have tried to explain it.[19]

In December 2007, Zawahiri once again emphasized his condemnation of attacks on fellow Muslims in a video in which he defended the idea of making Iraq an Islamic state but distanced himself from the crimes against civilians committed by 'hypocrites and traitors existing among the ranks'.[20] Disagreement about these tactics was not limited to internal disputes among al-Qaeda adherents, however. At the same time, local Sunni tribes and insurgent groups, including the prominent Islamist-nationalist group Islamic Army in Iraq, began to speak of their dissatisfaction with AQI's methods, openly criticizing the fighters for their deliberate targeting of Iraqi civilians. By June 2007, the growing hostility between the foreign-influenced al-Qaeda and Sunni nationalists led to open gun battles between these groups. The severity of the confrontation led several commentators to the conclusion that AQI was 'on the run'.[21]

Upon closer examination, the reality of Al-Qaeda in Iraq is not one that supports the notion of a globally coherent organization gaining strength, but rather one that demonstrates that al-Qaeda as a whole is weakened both by internal disputes and by attacks from other radical Islamic groupings which might otherwise have been its allies.[22] This combination of disunity among al-Qaeda franchises and the outrage expressed by its peers has undermined the coherence of the group and led to significant decline in local support. The impression of emerging strength thus seems to be more the result of a process by which al-Qaeda has become associated with all sorts of violence. In reality, however, the fact that some of al-Qaeda's local offshoots have resorted to the use of violence against fellow-Muslim civilians has undermined the movement's ability either to strengthen its influence or to position itself as a major global and local player.

Thus, by early 2009, al-Qaeda – both the Iraqi franchise and the group as a whole – seemed to have reached its nadir. With the organization internally fragmented, gradually losing public support, and with no high-profile attacks to remind the US and Western audience of its continued threat, those who had asserted that al-Qaeda was in the ascendant, regrouping and gaining strength, seemed to be losing ground. This perception would change, however, with the near-miss attack against a US passenger flight from Amsterdam to Detroit on Christmas Day 2009, which not only renewed the controversy over the continued threat of al-Qaeda but also, after Afghanistan and Iraq's period in the spotlight, propelled the Republic of Yemen into the centre of public attention. According to current theory, al-Qaeda has managed to regroup in the remote tribal areas of the country and is planning attacks on the West from its new base. In December of 2010, the US administration's counterterrorism adviser John Brennan confirmed that the al-Qaeda group based in Yemen poses a greater threat to Americans than any other that claims allegiance to Osama bin Ladin, including the ones based in Pakistan and Iraq. According to Brennan, the Yemen group is 'increasingly active' in its efforts to recruit new terrorists, reaching out even in the United States: 'Al-Qaeda in the Arabian Peninsula is now the most operationally active node of the al-Qaeda network.'[23] Indeed, some commentators have started to suggest that Al-Qaeda in Yemen is the new core of the organization. Is the case of Al-Qaeda in Yemen really so radically different from the rest – or is it yet another attempt at locating an organization 'headquarters'?

'Al-Qaeda in the Arabian Peninsula': evidence of al-Qaeda's (re)emergence?

At a time when al-Qaeda seemed almost to have dropped off the radar, the Christmas Day attack – which, had it been successful, would have caused mass casualties – came as a particularly unpleasant reminder of the potential danger still posed by the movement. It was in many ways the perfect backdrop against which to convince the Western audience that al-Qaeda had not only not gone away but was still operational and as much a threat as ever. The news quickly surfaced that the perpetrator, 23-year-old Nigerian-born, former University College London student Umar Farouk Abdulmutallab, confessed that he had received training for his mission during an extended stay in Yemen. His confession was further supported by the fact that a Yemen-based group calling itself Al-Qaeda in the Arabian Peninsula (AQAP)[24] claimed responsibility for the attack, while Osama bin Ladin embraced the almost-martyr as one of his own.[25] At the same time, it became clear that a number of prior attacks, such as the Fort Hood incident, were also connected to Yemen, the common element being the profound influence apparently exerted on the attackers by the speeches and ideology of radical cleric Anwar al-Awlaki, an American citizen of Yemeni origin who moved back to Yemen in 2004 and has allegedly become a key figure in AQAP. Yemen, so it was concluded, seemed on the verge of becoming the new Afghanistan, turning the fear of a repeat of 9/11 into a much more concrete possibility. So serious was the perceived threat of the situation that actions immediately followed. An international meeting was quickly organized in London on 27 January 2010, with the aim of delivering a strategy to support the Yemeni government in the fight against the looming terrorist threat. On the occasion, US Secretary of State Hillary Clinton called on Yemen's President Ali Abdullah Saleh's government to enact political and economic reforms and to combat AQAP, pledging economic and military assistance for this important task. Nine months after the initial incident, CIA analysts regarded AQAP as the most urgent threat to US security, and senior officials called for an escalation of US operations in the country, including a proposal to add armed CIA drones to a clandestine campaign of US military strikes and the provision of US$1.2 billion in military aid.[26] 'We are looking to draw on all of the capabilities at our disposal'[27] was how the CIA publicly summed up the seriousness of its approach to al-Qaeda's latest manifestation.

In the light of this response and the recent surge in attacks, the outlook for the future seems distinctly worrying. But can al-Qaeda's posturing in Yemen be taken to be a reliable indicator of its capabilities, and is it indeed tangible evidence of the existence of a substantial organization that is once again growing

in strength and potential? Is the fragile nature of the Yemeni
state only of benefit to the group? And does the United States'
response, linking financial aid to an aggressive counterterrorism
campaign, have the potential to undermine the strength and
appeal of al-Qaeda? The task of gaining meaningful insights
into these questions warrants a closer examination of the AQAP
in Yemen. While it would be invidious, in the broader scheme
of things, to concentrate on Yemen to the exclusion of all other
manifestations of al-Qaeda, the situation in Yemen provides
a useful present-day snapshot both of al-Qaeda itself and of
the international community's treatment of the intelligence
it receives and the approach it takes to the threat al-Qaeda
poses.

AQAP: 'compartmentalized and hierarchical'?

A survey of recent media and policy contributions addressing the
issue of al-Qaeda in Yemen reveals an overall consensus regarding the make-up of the group.[28] More commonly referred to as
Al-Qaeda in the Arabian Peninsula, the newly formed group is
considered to be thoroughly 'compartmentalized and hierarchical,
with a distinct division of labour'.[29] The Yemeni Nasir Abd al-
Karim al-Wahayshi (aka Abu Basir) is generally regarded as the
leader. In January 2009, he appeared on a video entitled 'We start
from here and we will meet at al-Aqsa' to announce the merger
of al-Qaeda's branches in Saudi Arabia and Yemen under his
command. Three other men also appeared in the video: a fellow
Yemeni, Qasim bin Mahdi al-Raymi, the alleged military chief
of AQAP, and the Saudis Said al-Shihri, al-Wahayshi's deputy,
and Mohammed al-Awfi, identified as a field commander. In
individual statements they proclaimed that AQAP would target
the near enemy in Sana'a and Riyadh, Western interests in the

region and the West itself.[30] An interview with al-Wahayshi aired on Al Jazeera on 27 January 2010 echoed these sentiments when he explained that '[the West's] crusades against Palestine, Iraq, Afghanistan and Somalia' have been launched from the Arabian Peninsula, and because of this all Western interests in the region and beyond should be targeted. The surge of attempted and successful attacks directed at both Yemenis affiliated with the government and foreign nationals within the country and abroad, and, in particular, the recent publication of what is considered to be AQAP's English-language online journal, *Inspire*, providing detailed guidance on how to kill Americans on US territory, are frequently seen as confirmation of the serious threat posed by the group.[31]

As with all claims about al-Qaeda, however, information is short-lived, contradictory and frequently contested.[32] Even establishing simple facts such as matching names with Guantánamo prison numbers and providing accounts of the physical movements and whereabouts of key figures is an uncertain process, with many sources of evidence subject to debate. Consider the following case: on 19 February 2009, headlines announced that Mohammed al-Awfi, the same high-ranking field commander who had appeared in the AQAP merger video just a month before, had surrendered himself to the Yemeni authorities.[33] Al-Awfi allegedly maintained that 'he did not want to appear in the 24 January video' but was ordered to do so despite his objections. If both he and the reports of his surrender are to be trusted, 'the message [which he had been forced to read on the video] did not represent his viewpoint or ideas'; instead, he 'was told to read it without changes because the wording in the message was carefully chosen'. The veracity of al-Awfi's claims was predictably questioned, as he could quite reasonably be suspected of spinning a gripping yarn in an attempt to redeem himself. It is perhaps unsurprising, therefore, that his version of events was subsequently denied by AQAP, who instead claimed that al-Awfi had been arrested by Yemeni authorities, who in turn had extradited him to Saudi Arabia.[34] Adding further to the speculation, on 23 June 2010, Saudi-owned, London-based *Al-Hayat*, the daily pan-Arab newspaper, carried in its print edition an article by its correspondent in Riyadh, Nasser Al-Hakbani, in which it was claimed that well-informed security sources had revealed to *Al-Hayat* that Qasim al-Raymi, officially named as the 69th most wanted man in Yemen, was the real leader of AQAP. Those sources went on to claim that the supposed leader, Yemeni Nasir al-Wahayshi and his deputy, Saudi Said al-Shihri, both of whom were assumed to be in charge on the basis of their appearance in the aforementioned video, were in fact just figureheads and mere theoreticians who had nothing to do with the day-to-day activities of the organization.[35]

Whether or not the claims and allegations quoted above bear any relation to the truth, it is the fact that such discrepancies and contradictions exist that is of concern in evaluating the nature of, and threat posed by, AQAP. Public statements in the name of AQAP, from videos to online journals, cannot be taken at face value and have to be seen, first and foremost, as an attempt to establish a certain status quo to a wider audience in Yemen and abroad. Thomas Heghammer makes this point convincingly when he concludes that the prominent and widely publicized merger of AQAP might amount to little more than an attempt to gloss over the fact that al-Qaeda's presence in Saudi Arabia had largely been defeated.[36] What can be said with certainty is that AQAP will attempt to appear as unified, competent and powerful as possible. The extent to which this amounts to wishful thinking and mere pretence is another question entirely. The asymmetric appearance of AQAP's confrontation with the Yemeni government and the West belies its true nature: as with al-Qaeda in 2001, the strength of the organization is one based not on physical might but in ideas: not in force of arms or numbers of loyal foot-soldiers but in its intangible, pervasive and insidious ability to manipulate, to instil fear and to generate a response. It is for that reason that even the failed Christmas Day attack can be considered a substantive success.

If gathering meaningful and reliable insights into the leadership of AQAP is difficult, the task of assessing its size or membership in terms of active participants adds another level of ambiguity. In 2009, the Yemeni government claimed that the organization has between 200 and 300 members, and most estimates in the West fall into the same range.[37] It is not clear, however, on what data these assessments are based, and the relative agreement across most assessments might indicate reliance on a working assumption in the absence of empirical evidence. The current estimate has to be viewed with caution as the Yemeni government is utterly dependent on US financial aid that is conditional on combating AQAP, and hence stands to benefit from any exaggeration of the threat.[38] In light of the large number of reported arrests of militants allegedly linked to AQAP, one would have to conclude that the actual number of active members is now significantly lower than it was at the time of the original estimate. But as numbers have remained unchanged and are now at times estimated to be higher than originally believed, it is worth considering the possibility that either the individuals arrested were not the AQAP members they were made out to be or, conversely, that the strategy through which they were detained has generated new recruits.

The difficulty of establishing clarity regarding membership of AQAP is probably best illustrated by the case of US-born and raised Anwar al-Awlaki, widely considered to be AQAP's iconic ideologue.[39] Despite his alleged links with radical Islamists, including the hijackers of 9/11, Awlaki himself has never explicitly associated himself with the organization and has refrained from publishing his statements through AQAP media outlets.[40] His father, former minister of agriculture and president of Sana'a University, has vehemently rejected all accusations that would link his son to the group. This is not to say that the absence of any clear-cut association with AQAP would rule Awlaki out of membership. Rather, his case is a reminder of the more general observation that direct association with AQAP might be of disadvantage to some, while claiming such a connection might be valuable to others.[41] The example of Samir Khan, alleged editor of *Inspire*, and his self-glorifying, article-length confession of being a proud traitor to America is a case in point. In reading his account of his 'closely watched' emigration from the USA to Yemen, in which he repeatedly ridicules the apparent inability of US intelligence to recognize his importance despite the fact that it was evident that he was 'al-Qaeda from the core', one cannot escape the impression of a desperate young man yearning for attention. As ever, the task of evaluating the structure, membership and potential threat of AQAP is impeded by a lack of definite knowledge, which entails considerable reliance upon best guesses and speculation.

Where does this leave any attempt at evaluating Awlaki's position vis-à-vis AQAP and, indeed, the thorny issue of membership more generally? What can be said with certainty about Awlaki is that his public statements echo many of the themes and rationales communicated by Osama bin Ladin, including promotion of a violent global jihad and a stern critique of US foreign policy. Yet, while this might appear to be extremist from a US perspective, anti-American sentiments are deeply engrained in the public consciousness of Yemen, for reasons that have not received much attention in the ongoing debate. The following statement bears this out:

> Our brothers and sisters are suffering in Iraq at the hands of the US invasion. Iraq is on fire. The whole of the Muslim world is on fire. The forces of the crusader control the holy land, eating its riches and controlling its people. And this is happening while Muslims all over the world are attacked.
>
> Oh believers, and the day will come that the Iraqi children will be resurrected and asked for what crime they were killed. What will you say to them?

These words could easily be taken to have fallen from the lips of bin Ladin or Awlaki. After all, as the previous chapter has shown, the plight of the Iraqis under Saddam, at the hands of the Zionist–crusader invasion, through sanctions and during recent wars has been a popular theme in bin Ladin's rhetoric.[42] In fact the quotation is from a speech delivered during Friday prayers in the spring of 2003 in a Sana'a mosque, a place that is not otherwise known to be 'radical'.[43] Seen in the context of public outrage and demonstrations in Yemen against the war in Iraq and various low points in the continuing crisis in Gaza, these public expressions provide some indication of how deeply some of the central messages of al-Qaeda resonate with the wider Yemeni public. Awlaki's rationale is remarkably similar but adds a local dimension to the agenda, criticizing the Yemeni government for allowing foreign interference in the country:

> Yes, I support what Umar Farouk has done after I have been seeing my brothers being killed in Palestine for more than 60 years, and others being killed in Iraq and in Afghanistan. And in my tribe too, US missiles have killed 17 women and 23 children, so do not ask me

if al-Qaeda has killed or blown up a US civil jet after all this. The 300 Americans are nothing comparing to the thousands of Muslims who have been killed.

The Yemeni government sells its citizens to the United States to earn the ill-gotten funds it begs the West for in return for their blood. The Yemeni officials tell the Americans to strike whatever they want and ask them not to announce responsibility for the attacks to avoid people's rage, and then the Yemeni government shamelessly adopt these attacks. For example, the people of Shabwa, Abyan and Arhab have seen the Cruz [*sic*] missiles, and some people saw cluster bombs that did not explode. The state lies when it claims responsibility, and it does so to deny collaboration. US drones continuously fly over Yemen. What state is that which allows its enemy to spy on its people and then considers it as 'accepted cooperation'?[44]

These examples lead to the fundamental challenge in the assessment of and fight against AQAP: how to separate actual members or activists from sympathizers and – just as importantly – how to prevent sympathizers from becoming radicalized and resorting to activism. As unsatisfactory as it may seem, there is no reliable way of identifying who belongs to al-Qaeda in Yemen. Sa'id al-Jamhi, author of *Al-Qaeda fi al-Yaman* (Al-Qaeda in Yemen), attributes this to AQAP's policy of 'maintaining the privacy of its members. Only the identities of the leader, the vice chairman, the military chief, legislative chief, and the media leader are public' (and even these, as has been seen, have to be viewed with a degree of scepticism), while 'the most dangerous and most important ones are unknown'.[45] The idea that members of AQAP are difficult to identify and that its true numbers are hidden by a cloak of secrecy is reinforced by the testimony of an alleged AQAP member interviewed by the *Guardian*. This young man in his mid-twenties lived in a small town in a poor area in the south of the country and had never travelled further than its capital city. When asked whether he considered himself part of al-Qaeda's organization in Yemen, he responded:

> 'We are all connected, all the jihadis are connected,' he opened his arms and pointed at the three of us sitting on the floor. 'One of us is Qaida,' and he pointed at himself, 'the other is protecting him,' and he pointed at me, 'and the other is providing logistics.' And he pointed at the teenager who had brought me there. 'The two,' he pointed at us, 'would only know the Qaida person they are in contact with, and that Qaida person [he pointed at himself] would be the only one in that group to know the leadership.'[46]

Again the impression is given of a large, shadowy network of jihadis in which the members are all connected by a common cause and some form of central leadership, which itself remains hidden and directs attacks at some remove from those who carry them out. But is this really the case? Given that the organization has been so successful in its intention to remain secret in all but name, it is extremely difficult to ascertain whether various reports and testimonies are true in themselves, and impossible to establish to what extent they are representative – indicative of the number of individuals who share this young man's commitment to jihad and, like him, have involved themselves either as 'Qaida' per se, or one of those who could by some measures be said to be on the fringes, yet are essential to AQAP's strategy: a provider of protection, a logistics man, or the next acolyte waiting to be radicalized and become a suicide bomber. Thus the truth about AQAP's capabilities is replaced by claims, counterclaims and uncertain theories, all of which profit from a lack of established facts in their bid for credibility. The benefit for the terrorists is that in the absence of indisputable evidence one way or another, Al-Qaeda in Yemen is what it can make the audience believe it is. And, having seized the initiative in the propaganda war, it is certainly not above inflating its image by elevating individuals into its ranks after the completion of an attack, such as bin Laden's endorsement of the underpants bomber.[47]

AQAP in Yemen: one of many troubles

Instead of focusing on AQAP itself, a meaningful assessment of the threat posed by the group should begin with an overview of the present socio-political situation in the Republic of Yemen as a whole. Yemen, according to recent press coverage, is close to disaster, a fragile, failing, soon-to-be-failed state. Although this view is not without merit,[48] it is useful to be more specific: the statehood of the Republic of Yemen is currently contested by a variety of actors, in terms of both its identity and territorially.[49] Indeed, President Ali Abdullah Saleh's government is currently confronted with a number of interrelated problems that cannot usefully be addressed in isolation from one another.

The first issue is the challenge of effective and sustainable governance, or, in more practical terms, President Saleh's increasingly difficult task of consolidating power. That said, it would be misleading to measure Yemeni politics solely by Western standards and to view it through the lens of modern statehood. The Republic of Yemen is an amalgamation of disparate territories that lacks strong institutions to run the affairs of the state and to provide services to its citizens. Yemeni politics are characterized by rivalry among the elite and extensive networks of personal patronage which effectively determine political loyalty and stability and provide services where the government does not.[50] In large parts of the country, the government is involved in complex negotiations with powerful tribes to co-opt an increasingly dissatisfied and impoverished population and to retain a certain level of political order and control. In practice, this means the provision of money, commercial opportunities and government jobs, in return for which tribes support and take sides with the government. Although this creates a certain level of functionality, it essentially remains an ongoing process of give-and-take bargaining in which the government is at risk of losing influence and control if its resources become insufficient to buy cooperation.[51]

Second, there are two distinct areas of conflict, one at each end of the country, which undermine the effectiveness and legitimacy of the government. One is the Houthi rebellion based in Saada province in the North, bordering Saudi Arabia, which has been ongoing with varying degrees of intensity since 2004.[52] There has been little first-hand reporting of the conflict because of media exclusion from the area, and hence the full extent of military and civilian casualties is unclear.[53] However, reports provided by humanitarian relief agencies speak of 250,000–350,000 internally displaced residents, providing a glimpse into the scale of the conflict.[54] The other area of conflict is the secessionist movement in the southern provinces. Also referred to as the 'South Yemen insurgency', the movement has become known for a series of increasingly violent protests and attacks on government forces since 27 April 2009 (South Yemen's Independence Day) as an expression of rising tension throughout the South.[55] The motivation underlying this movement is one of protest against the government's handling of financial matters, and began when former southern military officials, forced into compulsory retirement, demanded higher pension payments from the government: the protesters accused the Yemeni president of corruption and openly called for independence from his government. It is a sad irony that the government has to rely on its military to suppress the revolt of former military staff over the unfair distribution of financial resources, thereby further draining scarce resources in a manner that is not benefiting the people and that is likely only to add fuel to the flames of public frustration. In the light of the massive budget crisis in Yemen, which is addressed in more detail below, certain potential consequences are neither unforeseeable nor improbable – such as the fragmentation of the country into multiple areas of conflict – if the government was to run out of money to pay the military, on which the fragile cohesion of the country appears to depend.

It is in the context of these conflicts and the ongoing challenge of governance that the problems that place Yemen at the bottom of the list of low-income countries have to be viewed. Present structural challenges include economic recession, staggering poverty, dwindling oil and water resources, rapid population growth and low literacy rates, to name but a few. Nearly half the population lives on less than US$2 per day; national un-employment is at 40 per cent; less than 40 per cent of all Yemeni households have access to safe water and electricity; 50 per cent of all Yemenis are illiterate.[56] The crude death rate and crude birth rate, estimated at 9.0 and 39.7 per 1,000 population, and the fertility rate of 4.1 rank among the highest in the region.[57] State-funded health and education services are abysmal. Cor-ruption and inefficiency, for which the country is notorious (but which have to be seen in the larger context of the nature of its governance) are linked to the government's inability to provide adequate social services at the most basic level. Collectively, these structural challenges translate into a heightened level of public frustration and affect – and are affected by – the conflicts mentioned above. Without wanting to oversimplify the complex dynamics of Yemen's many interrelated problems, it is the lack of sufficient resources that undermines the president's grip on power: his ability to buy political support, provide services to reduce public dissatisfaction and to deal effectively with the conflicts in the country depends upon the scant finances at his disposal. For quite some time, the word on the street has alluded to an increasingly isolated president struggling to maintain vital alliances.[58] The massive protests that erupted in January 2011, in which thousands of Yemenis called for the resignation of President Saleh, only confirm the increasing difficulty of the president's task of holding on to power and keeping the increasingly fragmented country together.[59]

Within this fragile political climate, AQAP appears to add yet another – and, according to some analysts, steadily increasing – challenge to the already troubled regime. At first sight, this is readily confirmed by the recent rise in attacks against government targets as well as a flare-up of anti-government rhetoric from AQAP-related sources. On 30 October 2010, the president publically acknowledged the challenge posed by AQAP in a media statement responding to the latest UPS bomb threat, which originated from Yemen:

> We have a problem with terrorism, specifically the presence of Al-Qaeda, and we continue to pay a high price. We have incurred tremendous losses in the investment and tourism sectors as well as other sectors. The Republic of Yemen lost over 70 martyrs, brave members of our security and armed forces whom Al-Qaeda attacked while serving in security checkpoints.[60]

Whilst the threat of terrorism appears to deal yet another blow to a country already beset by severe challenges, the confrontation of AQAP with the Yemeni government has to be viewed with a degree of caution. During the early 1990s, the Yemeni government, unlike other Arab regimes at the time, welcomed fighters returning from Afghanistan (also known as the 'first generation' of al-Qaeda in Yemen), who integrated into all levels of society and would turn out to be useful allies to counter the influence of 'unbelieving' communists in the South and an 'unbelieving' Shia population in the North.[61] The nature of the relationship arguably changed in response to the government's unrestrained support for the USA in the aftermath of the USS *Cole* incident and the events of 9/11. Yet, despite the recent confrontation, the personal connections and relationships that the government established with jihadis over the years continue to exist and allow room for the negotiation and bargaining on which all policymaking in Yemen relies. And even if relations were to become more strained, the Yemeni government effectively depends on the continuation of the threat posed by AQAP to secure the financial aid from the USA and the West which is vital for its political survival.

Yemen's uneasy role in the war against terror

Yemen, so it is repeatedly stressed in the media, has been – and continues to be – a loyal ally in the war against terrorism: in response to both the attack on the USS *Cole* in Aden in 2000 and the events of 9/11 the Yemeni government went out of its way to demonstrate its support for the USA. Yet to view this support solely as an act of loyalty or indeed agreement with the US position would be to miss the strategic motivations underlying this political move. It must be seen first and foremost as a desire to avoid the mistake that was made in 1990 when Yemen served on the UN Security Council and paid a high price for its failure to back the USA in the build-up to the second Gulf War. A senior American diplomat is on record for relating to his Yemeni counterpart, only minutes after Yemen had cast its infamous vote against military intervention in Iraq, that 'this was the most expensive no-vote you ever cast.'[62] Within days, the USA had effectively stopped its $70 million aid programme to Yemen, and the World Bank and the IMF moved to block loans to the country. By early 1991, over 2 million Yemeni workers had been expelled from Saudi Arabia and the Arab Gulf. By 1992, the price for milk had quadrupled. By 1993, the newly formed republic was descending into civil war.

At a time when the merger of what were formerly North and South Yemen had seen the country embarking on the most egalitarian experiment of democracy in the Arab world, it was American retaliation for a political decision it did not favour, even though that decision was entirely legitimate under the UN Charter, that pulled the political rug from under the feet of Yemen's liberal reformers and directly added to the suffering of the Yemeni people.[63] Although the incident has been quickly forgotten and is certainly no longer on the political radar in the West, it has left the notion of US double standards deeply engrained in the national consciousness of Yemen.

Thus in 2001, the effort of the Yemeni government to show solidarity with the USA backfired dramatically, ironically for both Yemeni and US interests. In what is best described as a frantic attempt to avoid US retaliation and military intervention, the government arrested anybody it suspected of harbouring support for al-Qaeda. In no time, Yemen's jails were filled with young men from all parts of the country who were suspected of supporting terrorism. If they did not support al-Qaeda from the outset, they probably did by the time they were released.[64] The strategy underlying the arrests was twofold: first, Yemen had to be seen to take action on terrorism, and quickly, in order to placate the United States. Second, containment and control were the order of the day: the more people who were detained, with or without evidence against them, the fewer would be left to carry out another attack against US interests and risk making Yemen itself the target of American hostility. There is no shortage of parallels to be found in the overreactions and programmes of arrests carried out by other countries in the course of the fight against terrorism. Overreactions in general, and overly zealous arrests in particular, have done nothing to reduce radicalization – the opposite is the case. The groundwork for radicalization was done most effectively by those who were trying to prevent it.

Yemen's cooperation with Washington was not limited to proclamations of support and public arrests. It also secretly supported a strike conducted by an unmanned CIA drone against Abu Ali al-Harithi, al-Qaeda's head in Yemen at the time, in November 2002. Unfortunately for Yemen, the story was made public when the USA needed a PR boost in the form of a victory in the War against Terror – leaving the Yemeni government betrayed and having to justify its actions to an increasingly frustrated domestic public. It is worth emphasizing that this event, which significantly undermined the public image of the government, played directly into the hands of AQAP, which emphasizes the government's (secret) cooperation with the USA in its rhetoric as a betrayal of the Yemeni people. The way the USA (and indeed the UK – although little of this is discussed in the media) presently conduct their military support in Yemen indicates that little has been learned from mistakes made in previous years. A lack of foresight and critical reflection appears to be the hallmark of counterterrorism policies in Yemen.

With al-Harithi dead and the Americans able to claim a major victory against al-Qaeda, there seemed to be no need for further US involvement in Yemen. Al-Qaeda, it was believed, was largely defeated and the humiliated Yemeni government had merely done its duty and had certainly done nothing that deserved to be recognized or rewarded. This mindset might explain why the USA effectively abandoned Yemen in 2005 when it suspended a US$20 million aid programme, a setback that was compounded by the World Bank's decision to cut back its aid package from $420 million to $280 million.[65] At the time, nobody predicted the crisis that AQAP would later present. In strategic terms, meanwhile, it appeared that US resources were more urgently needed to support the continued military presence in Iraq and Afghanistan.

Although it is not the intention of this book to advocate economic development as a tool for counterterrorism,[66] a history of ignoring the needs and well-being of the Yemeni people and becoming involved only at times when it coincides with other key political interests has done little to endear the USA to the Yemenis, who quite rightly speak of hypocrisy and double standards. As a result, AQAP's criticism of both the government and the USA was always likely to meet a receptive audience.

It is now known that al-Qaeda was never close to defeat in 2002. The escape of twenty-three alleged al-Qaeda militants from a Yemeni prison in 2006 might be viewed as an early sign of the group developing a foothold within the ranks of the Yemeni government. After a campaign of relatively low-level attacks on Yemeni and Western targets within the country, including the US embassy on 17 September 2008, al-Qaeda returned spectacularly to the international stage with the creation of AQAP by the merger of al-Qaeda's Yemeni and Saudi branches, and gained undivided international attention with the Christmas Day attack in 2009. To date, as both recent (attempted) attacks and statements in the name of AQAP indicate, the group's activity appears to be at a new peak: it pursues an ambitious agenda that is both local and global, aspiring to attack the enemy – the USA and its allies, the Yemeni government and other Arab leaders – in Yemen and abroad. The present assumption – or fear – is that the troubled Yemeni state will become the new stronghold of AQAP. Inaction, as several analysts have proclaimed, is not an option.[67] Is this in fact the case or can the situation be viewed differently?

Rethinking the threat of AQAP in Yemen

Whilst care must be taken to avoid downplaying the issue, it is important to place the question of AQAP in the broader context of Islamist politics in Yemen. Although anti-Americanism is a widely shared sentiment, support for violence in general, and that which is likely to cause Yemeni casualties in particular, is not. In a similar way, anti-government sentiments are held across the country – AQAP does not monopolize the issue. In the contested state of Yemen, AQAP has effectively become engaged in a context over political legitimacy, in which it is competing against a number of different actors.

The secessionist movement in southern Yemen is first and foremost a confrontation with the government, which has previously used the jihadis to keep the 'socialist unbelievers' in check. Thus it is not a particular stretch of the imagination to assume that there is little sympathy for AQAP or its particular readings of Islam. In fact, Al Jazeera recently aired a programme in which fighters claiming to be AQAP went out of their way to explain to the secessionists that their war is against the USA and its allies and not against the Yemeni army and fellow Muslims. 'We carry bombs for God's enemies; soldiers, you must know that we do not want to fight you.'[68] They are words that might not carry much weight in the light of AQAP's violent attacks against the military. Rather, a lot more bargaining would have to be done to convince the secessionists (and indeed the wider audience addressed here) to join forces with AQAP in pursuit of a joint goal which has yet to be established and which, in order to be successful, might well have to involve qat rather than guns in the negotiating process.[69] A change or moderation in AQAP's presently narrow interpretation of Islam would most probably be necessary to convince the former socialist unbelievers of the new friendship.

In a similar way, the Shia Houthi rebellion in the North is primarily a confrontation with the government, driven by religious differences regarding the legitimacy of governance in Yemen. The Houthi seek the establishment of an imamate in Yemen but have not, however, advanced a coherent political programme. In fact, the same can be said for AQAP, which has little to offer in terms of a political strategy beyond the espousal of violent jihad. But, despite the shared enemy, there is little love lost between AQAP and the young rebels or 'Believing Youth', whose ideologies are poles apart. Indeed, a report in *The Long War Journal* claims that the Yemeni government has integrated hundreds of al-Qaeda fighters into a militia that has been operating in the northern Saada War since 2004, and that more recently Ayman al-Zawahiri promised Yemen's president more fighters in return for the release of his operatives from prison.[70] While it is difficult to confirm the validity of these statements, it would be reasonable to expect that AQAP and rebels specialized in violence rather than the art of organized, political, give-and-take bargaining are unlikely to search for common ground in a context in which sectarian differences are becoming more profound. Moreover, as bloody conflict has dragged on for years, caused substantial casualties and displaced more than 250,000 residents, the continuation of violent campaigns in pursuit of arguably unrealistic goals is not likely to enjoy a broad base of local support.

These two groups, however, represent only the most visible actors in the Islamist contest over political legitimacy in Yemen.[71] One would naturally take a closer look at the group of Zaydi (moderate, tolerant Shia, closest of all the Shia sects to Sunni Muslims in their beliefs) revivalists – not to be equated with the Houthi rebellion, which is only a fraction of the broader range of opposition groupings that represent a multilayered reaction against the government's anti-Zaydi policies that are gradually eradicating Yemen's Zaydi heritage. There are Zaydis with close ties to Iran, who represent an ideological departure from Yemeni Zaydism and, if Iraq is an example to go by, have clashed violently with al-Qaeda. There is the traditional, religious wing: focused on education; motivated to counter Sunni–Wahhabi influences which have come into Yemen from Saudi Arabia. The different groups within the Zaydi revivalist movement, while also at odds with each other to varying degrees, have little in common with AQAP. Indeed, recent reports from Yemen indicate a growing number of violent clashes between Sunni radicals believed to be associated with AQAP, and comparisons to the beginnings of a sectarian conflict similar to the case of Iraq are beginning to surface.[72]

Adding further diversity to the spectrum of Islamist voices are the Salafis, according to Laurent Bonnefoy an apolitical group formed around the late Muqbil al-Wadi'i, which stands out for its condemnation of violence.[73] More specifically, al-Wadi'i is reported to have been an outspoken critic of jihadists' strategies who accused bin Ladin of having a preference for investing in weapons rather than in mosques. Continuing this position, Muhammad al-Imam, another charismatic member of the group, condemned jihadi violence against the US-led occupation in Iraq.[74] As such, the Yemeni Salafists are in direct opposition to the violence employed by AQAP in the name of Islam.

One group which is well integrated into the social fabric of Yemen is the Muslim Brotherhood, represented in the political arena by the Yemeni Congregation for Reform, or Islah, Yemen's main opposition party. Islah campaigns on a number of issues, ranging from the role of women in society to the pursuit of violence, which are subject to frequent debate.[75] Among the most radical and ambiguous members is Abd al-Majid al-Zindani, who allegedly organized for Yemeni fighters to be sent to Afghanistan during the 1980s and is said to have met bin Ladin on several occasions. Although the USA regards him as a close partner of bin Ladin and supporter of al-Qaeda, his position as a popular mainstream figure is widely respected, while violent militancy does not appeal to many within the party.[76]

The Sufi movement has experienced a significant revival since the late 1990s and is playing an increasingly important role in Yemen's Islamist politics. This is done through two main channels: the communication and teaching of its religious doctrines, and participation in the political arena, where it has challenged the Islah party during previous elections.[77] Along the way, the group has clashed violently with other factions, which has prompted many analysts to describe it as being 'threatened on all sides by government policies and by other Islamist groups'.[78]

Jointly, these different actors represent a multitude of standpoints on the question of governance and political legitimacy in Yemen, thereby providing viable alternatives to the narrow, violent logic of jihad espoused by AQAP. In the power vacuum that emerges as (or if) the influence of the Yemeni government recedes, expressions of differences are bound to become more clearly defined. Indeed, a distinctive feature of the contemporary Yemeni landscape is an accentuation of difference: the self- and cross-identification of Yemenis as Salafis, Zaydis, Sufis, jihadis, and the many variations on these identities. In this context, it is the quality of the internal debate – the process of the emergence of leadership within the Yemeni community, which is difficult to influence from the outside – that will determine the future of AQAP. AQAP's ability to establish itself in the country will therefore depend to a large degree on its ability to manoeuvre effectively in the realm of political bargaining – a task it is poorly equipped to master by the exclusive use of semi-professional explosive devices. Indeed, if the case of Al-Qaeda in Iraq is an example to go by, reliance on violence alone is not a useful indicator for establishing a strong base and is more likely to relegate AQAP to the fringes than to promote it to the centre of public life and political affairs.

The resurgence of al-Qaeda?

Where does this leave the assessment of al-Qaeda in the post-9/11 era? In the immediate aftermath of 9/11 and during the first years of the war against terror, the organization appeared to have suffered a serious blow to its central make-up. While subsequent attacks, some of which smack of a certain amount of desperation, may be viewed as attempts to reaffirm al-Qaeda's continued potency, the group was nonetheless betrayed by its apparent inability to stage another event of any significant magnitude. Yet after a period of calm and relative absence of attacks against Western targets, the debate has – once again – shifted towards the idea that al-Qaeda is resurgent. Triggered by the Christmas Day attack, and further fuelled by the equally creative 'ink cartridge' plot, the focus of the international community has quickly moved to the Yemen, where the latest al-Qaeda franchise, Al-Qaeda in the Arabian Peninsula, is believed to have reorganized into a formally structured organization that is now arguably more dangerous than the original al-Qaeda core and has possibly taken its place. It appears, however, that such assessments are less the result of empirical evidence and more the product of a hasty evaluation of a series of spectacular incidents born of analysts' attempts – assuming or fearing the existence of a larger hand operating behind the scenes – to establish the existence of an organization in a location that had received little attention before, was unknown to most and has become the subject of much orientalized speculation. Upon closer examination, the notion of AQAP as a highly structured and compartmentalized organization is challenged by contradictory and ambiguous accounts about its leadership and membership, as well as its position in Yemen as a whole, where it has effectively become a bit-player in a contest over Islamist politics.

In more analytical terms, the assessment of al-Qaeda by the international community seems to follow a discernible pattern: it is not based strictly on empirical evidence and critical analysis, but instead tends to be reactionary. Assessment follows al-Qaeda's attempted attacks in an ad hoc and post hoc fashion, the necessary result of which is that its conclusions tend to be superficial and simplistic: al-Qaeda exists and is dangerous, because it is obviously able to act and attack. Analysis which suggests that al-Qaeda has been falsely implicated is seldom brought to light, whilst the nuances of the terrorist movement and the complex geopolitical settings in which it has its being are overlooked as excessive reliance on past experience and theories accreted from previous misunderstandings gives birth to new assumptions. Such analysis inadvertently relies on and feeds into the particular ontology of al-Qaeda, one familiar to students of existentialism: the organization not only finds recognition through the execution of attacks, it exists in its violent actions. Hence the attack of Christmas Day 2009 and subsequent events resurrect al-Qaeda as a relevant entity for both its followers and its analysts and observers in the West.

Moreover, the case of Umar Farouk Abdulmutallab and Awlaki's alleged role 'out of Yemen' have – once again – made it possible to construct a geographical location as the narrative centre for the analysis of al-Qaeda. Despite the dubious and contradictory nature of the empirical evidence, popular media and security analysts declared Yemen to be al-Qaeda's new headquarters, from where its actions are guided. While scant regard has been paid to its lack of empirical foundation, this move allows the mainstream view of al-Qaeda to rest on traditional ontological assumptions. While the 'Leaderless Jihad' theory dispersed the source of terror and uncertainty into the midst of Western societies, whereby the terrorist was essentially unidentifiable by virtue of being a member of those societies, the 'discovery' of Yemen as al-Qaeda's new centre once again allows al-Qaeda and its ideology to be seen as rooted in the particular 'oriental' – that is, the eastern-Islamic – nature of such places. Al-Qaeda is therefore once again at risk of no longer being seen as a primarily ideological threat capable of lying 'within our selves' – that is, Western societies – but can safely be 'othered', treated as an issue peculiar to a certain geographical context, and hence understood as resting within societies that are alien, or even hostile, to Western values.

SIX

The future of Al-Qaeda

Though the hardcore – the vanguard – is scattered, and the base is destroyed, the craving for jihad that sent tens of thousands of young men to seek training and jihad in Afghanistan is flourishing. Bin Laden's message makes sense to millions. It is from among these millions that the new wave of terrorists will come. They will be 'freelance' operators who have no obvious connection to any existing group. They will, often, have no previous involvement in terrorism. They may not have access to sophisticated explosives, automatic weapons or rockets, but once they have accepted the radical 'Jihadi Salafist' worldview they will be committed to finding the resources necessary to launch their own violent holy war, whether their weapons be castor beans cooked up to form a basic poison in a flat in north London, a kitchen knife plunged into the chest of a policeman in Manchester, a truck full of Iraqi army explosives or an aircraft full of fuel and passengers. For these men, jihad is a profoundly felt religious duty. It brings them something that nothing else can, and they will not be diverted from it by a few extra bollards outside an embassy or by the destruction of a training camp in a far-off country.

Jason Burke, 2007[1]

A number of individual incidents serve to confirm Burke's prediction that the new manifestation of Islamic terrorism would come from individuals taking it upon themselves to wage jihad: the case of Nidal Malik Hasan, a psychiatrist and major in the US Army who carried out the Fort Hood Shooting in November 2009, which killed thirteen and wounded thirty people; the case of 21-year-old student Roshonara Choudhry, who in May 2010 stabbed the Labour MP Stephen Timms in the stomach during a constituency surgery in revenge for his vote for the war in Iraq; and the case of the 28-year-old Iraqi Swede Taimour Abdulwahab al-Abdaly, Sweden's first suicide bomber, who died among Christmas shoppers in a busy Stockholm street in December 2010 following the partial detonation of the devices he was carrying. These incidents rank as some of the best-known examples of attacks by freelance jihadis, an increasingly common type of terrorist who has been essentially self-radicalized with the help of the Internet, and who operates with no support from overseas networks and has no border to cross to reach the chosen target. In an interview with the *New York Times* following the Fort Hood incident in November 2009, Bruce Hoffman confirmed that such cases were increasing in number and that most of them involved people with no direct ties to terrorist organizations:

> The trend of self-radicalization, which leaders and allies of al-Qaeda have encouraged with a steady stream of inflammatory messages on the Web, is gaining momentum, he said. 'You've had all shapes and sizes, which is a challenge for law enforcement,' Mr. Hoffman said, citing a shooting at a Little Rock military recruitment center, synagogues targeted for attack in the Bronx and foiled bombing schemes in Illinois and Texas, among others.[2]

The notion that these terrorists were individualists acting on their own would not, however, remain unchallenged for long. Investigations into the personal lives and circumstances of the attackers quickly revealed the influence of foreign sources and individuals who would appear to be linked to al-Qaeda. Both Hasan and Choudhry were found to have had contact with Yemen-based cleric Anwar al-Awlaki: the former had communicated with the alleged AQAP member via email, while Choudhry confessed to listening to the cleric's messages online and attributed her decision for the attack to his influence. The suspicion that there was a link between such attacks and Yemen began to emerge, and eventually 'took off', when it became clear during the investigation into the Christmas Day attack that it was possible to trace the bomber Abdulmutallab's radicalization to Awlaki and the newly formed Al-Qaeda in the Arabian Peninsula. In a similar way, Abdaly's attack has been linked to Al-Qaeda in Iraq. As Ranstorp argues,

> Al-Abdaly's disclosure on the farewell tape that he frequently travelled to the Middle East to wage jihad raised the prospect that he had links to more organized terrorist networks in the region. This was strengthened by his affinity to the Islamic State of Iraq on his Facebook page, postings of Shaykh Muhammad al-Maqdisi and multiple credible claims by radical al-Qa'ida affiliated websites that suggested that he belonged to the Islamic State of Iraq.[3]

It is not the intention of this study to deny the potential for larger organizations operating from Iraq and Yemen to be involved in radicalizing Muslims who go on to commit acts of terrorism. What needs to be emphasized, however, is that the belief, first, that such organizations exist and continue to be actively involved in this process of radicalization and recruitment, and, second, that these sources of radicalization can easily be located in certain corners of the Muslim world, is based on connections which are in fact tenuous and can be explained in other ways. A closer look at the cases of the aforementioned attackers illustrates the level of oversimplification inherent in attributing their radicalization to a particular source. In the case of Hasan, the connection to AQAP is based exclusively on an exchange of approximately a dozen emails with Awlaki, while in the case of Choudhry the fact that she listened to the cleric's Internet sermons constitutes an even more slender connection. In both cases, it is more plausible to assume a prior process of radicalization. Individuals do not usually wake up with a sudden desire to become terrorists or sacrifice themselves to the global jihad, but instead have gone through a process of being exposed to radical ideas and coming to identify with them over an extended period of time.[4] Indeed, investigations have revealed a rather extensive history of Hasan's growing engagement with Islamist ideas prior to the shooting and before he ever got into contact with Awlaki. For example, he is on record as having stunned his colleagues during his final year of medical training in 2003 with a formal lecture during which he talked about Islam, especially the need to defend it and the dilemma that this poses for Muslims in the armed forces like himself, rather than speaking about a specific medical issue.[5] There is, in fact, a long record of the process of his radicalization, during which he reportedly became an increasingly devout Muslim, praying several times a week at a mosque, writing papers on topics such as whether the war against terror was a war against Islam and suggesting a form of Muslim resistance. Yet, despite this well-documented process, the interaction with Awlaki somehow takes a central position in the narrative about what caused Hasan to commit a terrorist act. While communication with the cleric might well have been the ultimate trigger for the violent action, it might also have been his imminent military deployment to Afghanistan or some other personal issue unknown to the media and investigators alike that brought Hasan to the point of committing murder. It

is noteworthy that the actual process of Hasan being radicalized – the combination of his deepening devotion to Islam and
his consistent engagement with radical ideas – was paid less
attention by comparison.

A similar process of radicalization which culminated in the
stabbing of the Labour MP has to be assumed in the case of
Choudhry, although relatively little has been reported about
her personal circumstances beyond the fact that she was a
gifted student from a modest background reading English at
King's College London, was fluent in several languages and
volunteered for Islamic charities. On the rationale for her
radicalization, the *Guardian* reported:

> The strongest evidence of the ideological change in Choudhry's
> beliefs and her journey towards an adherence to violent jihad starts
> to appear in late 2009. After her arrest police seized and scoured her
> computers for contacts with jihadists, of which none were found, and
> for details of websites she had visited. She had no known connection
> to any Islamist groups, and there was no evidence she had attended
> meetings or owned any potentially extremist literature. The police
> investigation found that in the last quarter of 2009 Choudhry began
> downloading from the internet sermons and material from Anwar
> al-Awlaki, the Islamist cleric who western officials say is the spiritual
> leader of al-Qaida in the Arabian Peninsula. He preached the need
> for violent action to combat the atrocities of the west against Muslims
> around the world, and urged followers to do what they could, when
> they could, no matter how small.[6]

Maybe the most insightful observation in this brief account
concerns the absence of any known connections to Islamist
groups or other sources of radical teaching. What is emphasized
is Awlaki's role in the process. As the BBC reported, 'the
Muslim student [who acted alone and out of her own volition]
had become radicalized after having watched online sermons by
Anwar al-Awlaki, a radical American Muslim cleric of Yemeni

descent.'[7] Yet it would seem that there are more issues and influences that have the potential to radicalize an individual than can readily be traced by an outside observer. One might, for example, point to the fact that Choudhry studied next door to the academic institution that was attended by the Christmas Day bomber, Nigerian-born Umar Farouk Abdulmutallab, where the Islamic society, of which he was the president, is known for its communication of radical, extremist ideas – a fact that has received no further attention in Choudhry's case. Is it far-fetched to assume that a student could easily have encountered a variety of ideas which sowed the seeds of radicalism while talking to her peers in the library, on the way to class or indeed while watching television news? Of course this is pure speculation and such connections might never have existed. The intention here, however, is neither to prove their absence nor to suggest the most likely process by which these individuals became radicalized. Rather, the aim is to illustrate that the task of mapping with any degree of certainty the process of the development of another person's beliefs and convictions is a complex task that does not allow for the clear and unambiguous identification of triggers beyond that which can be attributed to general trends, which are in themselves influential only to a degree.

Yet, in spite of this complexity, simple 'solutions' abound. New centres have emerged in the popular imagination, from which al-Qaeda radicalizes potential terrorists and recruits them to the global jihad. Yemen is a case in point, but other notional sub-centres, such as a fear of British universities becoming breeding grounds for extremists, have emerged in public and security discourses alike.[8] Upon closer examination, however, the picture is not as clear. Even if the radicalization of the aforementioned attackers was to be attributed first and foremost to Awlaki, localizing the process of radicalization to Yemen remains difficult. Awlaki himself spent most of his life in the USA and only fairly recently returned to Yemen. His contact with Hasan and Choudhry was via email and sermons streaming on the Internet, which are accessible from virtually any location, but ironically not so much from Yemen, where electricity and Internet connections are frequently unreliable. The reach of web-based media such as blogs and instant messaging, and the connections and friendships facilitated by Facebook and Twitter that have started to replace attachments and relationships in the physical world, elude any attempt at localization. Awlaki's presence and the reach of his ideas are not local but global.

Placed in a broader perspective, the world's perception of al-Qaeda continues to shift between the notion of a vague, fragmented network of like-minded individuals connected only by ideology on one hand, and belief in a structured, geographically located organization with a defined core of leadership on the other. As the discussion in the previous chapters has shown, this is not a new phenomenon but one that has characterized discussion of al-Qaeda in the West from the very beginning. As early as MAK, the alleged precursor of al-Qaeda in Afghanistan, the discussion of al-Qaeda was always, to a greater or lesser extent, a search *for* al-Qaeda, driven by the belief, assumption or fear that something bigger had to be out there. Whether this search was driven by the goal to prosecute bin Ladin in his absence, as was the case in the 2001 trial *United States* v. *Usama bin Laden* in the aftermath of the US embassy bombings, or the much larger-scale, all-out war against terrorism in the aftermath of 9/11, in a sense only adds different shades of meaning and potential causalities to the nature of the debate. In each instance, the discussion, which at its core seeks both to rationalize and to prove the existence of al-Qaeda, followed an ad hoc/post hoc model: each time an attack took place, analysts and decision-makers rushed headlong into attempting to identify the enemy. In the process, theories of various geographic centres have evolved to anchor the otherwise elusive nature of al-Qaeda: the first of these was Afghanistan, followed by Iraq, while a new centre is currently emerging in Yemen.

Viewed in this manner, the ongoing debate about al-Qaeda appears to be characterized by a certain degree of resistance and unwillingness to accept the notion that the enemy could be 'among us' rather than 'out there'. Such observations as to how al-Qaeda is conceptualized are more than simply abstract theorizing that bears little resemblance to the real world or the practicalities of ongoing counter-insurgency campaigns. Indeed, this analysis of the tension between global and local spaces can be further expanded into what arguably constitutes one of the most fundamental contradictions that characterize present counterterrorism efforts. For if al-Qaeda indeed presents a global and systemic viral problem, attempts at localizing the organization into a central core are of questionable value. Localized and thus spatially circumscribed intervention is by its very nature ineffective as a way of combating such a threat. Yet, since the beginning of the war against terror and the intervention in Afghanistan, Allied forces have been engaged in a protracted campaign which, as subsequent terrorist attacks have demonstrated, has only temporarily hindered al-Qaeda rather than disrupting it and its affiliates in a decisive fashion.

In fact, the leadership or core has been scattered, only to emerge elsewhere, such as in Iraq, the Maghreb or Yemen – and this is before one considers the far more nebulous dimension of al-Qaeda that has much more to do with ideology and the spread of ideas, which defies any attempt at localization in the first place. Despite this development, in which al-Qaeda is re-emerging and relocating in a manner that is predictable only in so far as it is unpredictable, global and fragmented, the view within defence and security circles that there is a core to be defeated continues to hold. Inherent in this view is the (mis-)understanding that failed or failing states are breeding grounds or safe havens for al-Qaeda, and that in order to fight it a comprehensive concept of security that takes account of the interrelationship between social and political conditions and security has to be deployed.[9] The diagnosis of terrorism as a systemic and viral threat is thus not so much matched as exacerbated by a treatment plan that rearticulates a statist nomatic ontology. Hence, despite the depiction of al-Qaeda in terms of a globalized ideology rather than an organizational structure, the Alliance's discourse continues to rely on the notion of a 'centre' from which attacks are conceived and directed and which therefore stands to be defeated and destroyed. Control of this centre thus is taken to mean control over the dissemination and 'play' of terrorism. Therefore the maxim holds that in order to ensure security in the West and to fight terrorism at the hands of al-Qaeda effectively, action has to be taken in the form of going to the *source* of the attacks – the core of al-Qaeda.

As the analysis of al-Qaeda throughout the chapters of this volume has shown, however, the notion of the centre does not hold. The physical reality of al-Qaeda has evaded and continues to evade attempts at clear and unambiguous specification, disappearing into the shadows when pursued too intensely, only then to reappear by means of another attack, a merger video or online announcement. It takes but a small number of individuals to wave the al-Qaeda flag by announcing or

attempting attacks in the name of jihad to remind the international community of its continued existence and ever-present
threat. The response of those involved in the task of combating
terrorism has, by virtue of their commitment to chasing after
the core of al-Qaeda and keeping it on the run, become predictable: it is inherently reactive, defensive and limited to pursuing
the beast whenever it chooses to rear its ugly head. But this
reactive response is not limited to the kind of cat-and-mouse
game in which the one chasing might eventually run out of
steam. Although the criticism has frequently been voiced that
the US response and the War against Terror as a whole are
playing into the hands of bin Ladin, who allegedly intends to
bleed the US to death, the actual cost in terms of both financial
resources and loss of life, while significant in their own right,
and especially so in the context of an economic crisis, is only
one part of the story.

The other, possibly even more significant, aspect is that
reacting to al-Qaeda by means of all-out war has also been
counterproductive in that it has only further reinforced the
narrative of the USA and its allies as an occupying, oppressive
force that causes suffering to Muslims and is at war with the
Muslim world. Images of violence taking place in Afghanistan and Iraq dominate the media and greatly overshadow the
limited 'good' news, propaganda to some, such as the liberation
of Afghan women and the building of essential infrastructure
like schools and clinics. Indeed, one of the lessons that should
have been learned from the Global War against Terror is that
aggressive confrontation with the enemy – whether in the form
of indiscriminate arrests, indefinite detention or military intervention – has done little to make the USA and the West any
safer from either the anger or the violent attacks of the radical
jihadis. The case of Al-Qaeda in the Arabian Peninsula, the

latest manifestation of the enemy in a somewhat organized manner, and the recent surge in attempted attacks illustrate this point. Again, US intervention in Yemen and manipulation of the Yemeni government constitute one of the most powerful arguments at AQAP's disposal to win favour with an otherwise unsympathetic audience, and one does not need to be a military strategist to appreciate the political potential of the notion of a 'common enemy'. AQAP has effectively exploited the legacy of US intervention in Yemen to support its own legitimacy in the past, and the nature of the US response to date leaves little doubt that it will be able to do so even more effectively in the foreseeable future. With the strength of AQAP dependent on its ability to attract and maintain public support, the continuation of the US kill-or-capture approach that has made Yemen vulnerable to the influence of al-Qaeda in previous years continues to create an advantage for AQAP. In the words of Ted Koppel, commenting on the situation in Yemen in 2010, 'Nine years after 9/11, let's stop playing into the hands of bin Ladin.'[10] A significant part of the war against al-Qaeda is a battle of ideas that cannot be won militarily.

Where does this leave our analysis of al-Qaeda? The idea of the global *umma* – a sense of Muslim solidarity as well as the pan-Islamist notion of reclaiming it – is not likely to go away any time soon. Yet while bin Ladin promoted a kind of generic Islam and idealistic notions of unity by focusing on a common enemy, disunity among Muslims has increased in practice as sectarian and theological differences have hardened. The struggle of Al-Qaeda in Iraq has become the centre stage for bloody disputes between Sunnis versus Shi'ites. Indeed, the brutality and extent of this confrontation has, in some cases, led to the conclusion that sectarianism has become the defining characteristic of modern Islam.[11] Throughout the history of

Islam, Shi'ism has been denounced as heresy by some factions within the community of Sunni Muslims, and continues to be opposed today in such emotive terms that any sense of unity of the *umma* seems to vanish into thin air. The current situation in Iraq and beyond might thus be viewed as simply another flare-up of hostilities that have been smouldering for quite some time. Once again, however, reality is more complex still. As Nelly Lahoud aptly illustrates in her comprehensive analysis of jihadi ideologues, the battle line is not drawn exclusively along the lines of division between Sunnis and Shi'ites. Rather, it is complicated further by doctrinal disputes within the ranks of al-Qaeda, both at the level of leadership and among the jihadis on multiple battlefields in different locations.[12] For Alia Brahimi, this increasing level of fragmentation is the surest indication that al-Qaeda is likely to lose the battle of ideas. With the rise of al-Qaeda 'franchises' in different countries and the introduction of the very bloody reality of sectarian violence, bin Ladin's authority and his goal of both reclaiming and extending the *umma* is challenged by local objectives and increasingly violent means.

> While al-Qaeda's evolution, or devolution, into a diffuse network of affiliates [*sic*] groups has entailed temporary tactical agility, it has simultaneously represented a source of significant weakness for the battle of hearts and minds. The 'operational durability' and 'malleable resiliency' so often posited by Bruce Hoffman have guaranteed the survival of al-Qaeda, certainly, but at the cost of consigning the group to the more radical margins of the *umma*.[13]

Indeed, the extent to which al-Qaeda's jihadis are operating from the margins rather than gaining a strong foothold among the general public is illustrated by other developments in the Middle East. Whilst it may be generally observed that the region is undergoing a swing towards Islam and conservatism, violent, global jihad is but one of many trends currently in development. What has often been overlooked is that the region as a whole is in a period of transition, the likely outcome of which is difficult to predict. Moreover, if Afghanistan and Iraq, as well as the case of Iran in the late 1970s, are examples to go by, then current events in the Middle East will also be extremely hard to influence and direct from the outside. But while it is clear that religion is a crucial component of the unfolding dynamic, it is not one that is necessarily radical and extremist. The popular uprising against repressive regimes that spread throughout the region from Tunisia to Egypt and Yemen from January 2011 illustrates a profoundly different world-view that challenges both popular stereotypes of Islam and an authoritarian religious culture incompatible with liberal ideas and democratic aspirations. In spite of the secularist tone of the uprising, perhaps the most iconic image of this revolution is that of throngs of people in Tahrir Square in Cairo, bowed in prayer, literally hemming in a group of tanks sent there to assert the Egyptian government's authority. This is a radically different image of Islam to what most people in the West are used to seeing: Islam taking on state violence through peaceful protest, a kind of peaceful jihad. This would not be the first time that such a peaceful uprising has occurred in the Muslim world. Previous examples have, however, been much smaller in scale and have not become the focus of attention of the world's media.

As this dynamic of non-violent resistance against the violence of entrenched regimes plays out, it is worth noting that so far Osama bin Ladin and his Egyptian deputy, Ayman al-Zawahiri, have had little to say about the revolution in Egypt and the region as a whole. Whilst they have failed to ignite the flames of worldwide jihad with an ideology of a return to a mythical and pure beginning – their so-called 'golden age of Islam' – and equally failed to usher in the dawn of a new caliphate by means of a strategy of human bombs, IEDs and aeroplanes turned into missiles, a disciplined, forward-thinking, yet amorphous group of young Muslim activists has done so, setting the Middle East on fire with a universal discourse of freedom, democracy and human values, and has pressed home its challenge via a strategy of increasingly calibrated chaos aimed at uprooting some of the region's longest-serving dictators. As one chant in Egypt succinctly put it, playing on the long-standing chants of Islamists that 'Islam is the solution', protesters were heard shouting: 'Tunisia is the solution'. If the street protests in the Middle East and North Africa were to lead to a peaceful transition to a more pluralistic society, it would significantly undermine the broader al-Qaeda narrative which insists that authoritarian pro-American governments should be deposed by violent jihad. Although it is, in a sense, predictable that al-Qaeda is waiting for an opportunity to regain the world's attention through a carefully planned intervention, in the face of the massive revolution of Muslims calling for peaceful, democratic change in the region the jihadis are nowhere to be seen.

It was nonetheless predictable that al-Qaeda was waiting for an opportunity to regain the world's attention through a carefully planned intervention of sorts. On 2 March 2011, the shooting of two US servicemen at Frankfurt airport, the latest incident in the range of small-scale attacks, came as a timely reminder that the jihadis continue to be a force to be reckoned with. Equally predictable, of course, was the subsequent investigation and widespread speculation – drawing from evidence such as his status updates and comments on Facebook – that the 21-year-old perpetrator from Kosovo had links with both Islamist groups in Germany and the al-Qaeda network.[14] Indeed, the fifth issue of the English-language online magazine *Inspire*, allegedly released by the media wing of Al-Qaeda in the Arabian Peninsula later that month, the question of 'Individual Terrorism' was specifically addressed.[15] The articles' main focus, however, was on the uprisings across the Middle East and North Africa. The featured story, under the title 'The Tsunami of Change', allegedly authored by Anwar al-Awlaki, refutes the growing perception that the uprisings are an indication that al-Qaeda is increasingly becoming irrelevant. According to Awlaki, 'The revolution broke the barriers of fear in the hearts and minds that the tyrants couldn't be removed.... Whatever the outcome is, our mujahidin brothers in Tunisia, Egypt, Libya and the rest of the Muslim world will get a chance to breathe again after three decades of suffocation.'[16] Continuing this rationale, al-Zawahiri addresses the 'long and short-term plans' after the protests. Possibly the most direct explanation regarding al-Qaeda's position vis-à-vis the protest is offered by Yahya Ibrahim. In his editorial he makes it abundantly clear that

> Al-Qaeda is not against regime changes through protests but it is against the idea that the change should be only through peaceful means to the exclusion of the use of force. In fact Shaykh Ayman al-Zawahiri spoke in support of the protests that swept Egypt back in 2007 and he alluded to the fact that even if the protests were peaceful, the people need to prepare themselves militarily. The accuracy of this view is proven by the turn of events in Libya. If the protesters in Libya did not have the flexibility to use force when needed, the uprising would have been crushed. It is our opinion that the revolutions that are shaking the thrones of dictators are good for the Muslims, good for the mujahidin and bad for the imperialists of the West and their henchmen in the Muslim world. We are very optimistic and have great expectations of what is to come.[17]

Ibrahim's expression of optimism could never have anticipated the bigger reminder of al-Qaeda's role in current affairs that was about to hit the headlines. On 2 May 2011, President Barack Obama announced the news of Osama bin Ladin's death at the hands of US Special Forces.

The long-term consequences of the permanent removal of al-Qaeda's public face are not yet clear. Initially the news triggered spontaneous celebration in the United States. Justice had at last been done as the leader of al-Qaeda and world's most-wanted terrorist met his rightful end. For some, bin Ladin's death marked the end of an era, the final success in the war against terror and the beginning of the end of the most dangerous terrorist organization in history. But the moment of triumph did not last long. The joyful mood was quickly overshadowed by critical voices questioning the legitimacy of the US kill-or-capture mission, asserting that al-Qaeda continues to pose a considerable threat, and predicting a surge of terror attacks in revenge for bin Ladin's death.

These predictions seem entirely reasonable if al-Qaeda is viewed primarily as an organ of leaderless jihad which, by virtue of having its strength in its ideology rather than in its structure, is naturally resilient to the removal of a single individual, no matter how prominent. But, as had to be expected, many of the newspaper headlines discussing the event focused on the American administration's assertion that Osama bin Ladin was himself a terrorist, was functionally the leader of al-Qaeda, and that he was effectively running the organization from his compound in Abbottabad.

This well-known rationale was – at least at first sight – further supported by a statement issued by 'The al Qaeda Organisation – General Leadership' confirming the death of bin Ladin and pledging to avenge him. But is this the whole truth? Are we the audience now obliged to believe in the existence of the top-down organization? In the midst of the celebrations, the controversy surrounding the death of Osama bin Ladin opens once again the discussion contesting the identity of al-Qaeda. The question remains: What – exactly – is al-Qaeda?

Notes

CHAPTER 1

1. A particularly harsh criticism of the failure to predict the events of 9/11 can be found in Martin Kramer, *Ivory Towers on Sand: The Failure of Middle Eastern Studies in America* (Washington DC: Washington Institute for Near East Policy, 2001).

2. Magnus Ranstorp, 'Mapping Terrorism Studies After 9/11: An Academic Field of Old Problems and New Prospects', in Richard Jackson, Marie Breen Smyth and Jeron Gunning (eds), *Critical Terrorism Studies: Framing a New Research Agenda* (London: Routledge, 2008), p. 23. For a similar assessment of the field, see Magnus Ranstorp, *Mapping Terrorism Research: State of the Art, Gaps and Future Directions* (London: Routledge, 2007).

3. Christina Hellmich, 'Creating the Ideology of Al Qaeda: From Hypocrites to Salafi-Jihadists', *Studies in Conflict and Terrorism*, vol. 32, no. 2, 2008, pp. 111–25.

4. For a critical analysis, see Richard Jackson, *Writing the War on Terrorism: Language, Politics and Counter-Terrorism* (Manchester: Manchester University Press, 2005).

5. Marc Sageman, *Leaderless Jihad, Terror Networks in the Twenty-First Century* (Philadelphia: University of Pennsylvania Press, 2008), p. 13.

6. For reviews and assessments of the field, see Alex Schmid and Albert Jongman, *Political Terrorism: A Guide to Actors, Authors, Concepts, Databases, Theories and Literature* (Amsterdam: North Holland,

1988); Ariel Merari, 'Academic Research and Government Policy on Terrorism', *Terrorism and Political Violence*, vol. 3, no. 1, 1991, pp. 88–102; Andrew Silke, *Research on Terrorism: Trends, Achievements and Failures* (London: Routledge, 2004).

7. Silke, *Research on Terrorism*, p. 188.

8. Martha Crenshaw, 'The Psychology of Terrorism: An Agenda for the 21st Century', *Political Psychology*, vol. 21, no. 2, 2000, p. 405.

9. For a detailed comment on this phenomenon, see Juan Cole, 'A Treatment for Radical Ignorance about Islamic Radicalism', *Chronicle of Higher Education*, 3 March 2006, http://chronicle.com/article/A-Treatment-for-Radical/26858.

10. Ted Gurr, cited in Ranstorp, 'Mapping Terrorism Studies after 9/11', p. 20. For a more comprehensive account, see Ted Gurr, 'Empirical Research on Political Terrorism: The State of the Art and How It Might Be Improved', in R.O. Slater and M. Stohl (eds), *Current Perspectives on International Terrorism* (New York: St. Martin's Press, 1988).

11. Ranstorp, 'Mapping Terrorism Studies after 9/11', p. 26.

12. Ibid., p. 27.

13. Tom Mills, cited in ibid., p. 27. See also David Miller and Tom Mills, 'The Terror Experts and the Mainstream Media: The Expert Nexus and Its Dominance in the News Media', *Critical Studies on Terrorism*, vol. 2, no. 3, December 2009, pp. 414–43.

14. Muhammad Ally, cited in Ranstorp, 'Mapping Terrorism Studies after 9/11', p. 28.

15. Evan Kohlmann, 'Al-Qa'ida's Yemeni Expatriate Faction in Pakistan', *CTC Sentinel*, vol. 4, no. 1, January 2011, pp. 11–15.

16. Ranstorp, 'Mapping Terrorism Studies after 9/11', pp. 28–30.

17. Ibid., p. 29.

18. Martin Bright, 'On the Trail of Osama bin Ladin', *Observer,* 11 May 2003, www.guardian.co.uk/theobserver/2003/may/11/society.politics.

19. *The 9/11 Commission Report: The Final Report of the National Commission on Terrorist Attacks upon the United States* (New York: W.W. Norton, 2004).

20. See, for example, Marc Sageman, *Understanding Terror Networks* (Philadelphia: University of Pennsylvania Press, 2004).

21. Edna Reid, 'Evolution of a Body of Knowledge: An Analysis of Terrorism Research', *Information Processing and Management,* vol. 33, no. 1, 1997, pp. 91–106.

22. Miller and Mills, 'The Terror Experts and the Mainstream Media', p. 414. While some defenders of traditional terrorism studies deny this characterization (see, for example, John Horgan and Michael Boyle, 'A Case against Critical Terrorism Studies', *Critical Studies on Terrorism*, vol. 1, no. 1, 2008, pp. 51–64), it is hard to draw any evidentially based alternative conclusion.

23. During the time of the French Revolution, for example, the Grand Jacobins of the Committee for Public Safety declared themselves 'terrorists' and made 'terror', which was perceived as a contingent necessity, part of daily affairs. Since then, the word 'terrorism', which originally qualified the exercise of state power, has come to signify exactly the contrary – the use of violence in opposition to the state. Alain Badiou, *Infinite Thought: Truth and the Return to Philosophy* (London: Continuum, 2005), pp. 108–10.

24. Andrew Heywood, *Political Theory: An Introduction*, 3rd edn (Basingstoke: Palgrave Macmillan, 2004), p. 79. For a more comprehensive reading of the liberal state, see social contractarians such as John Locke and Jean-Jacques Rousseau.

25. Miller and Mills, 'The Terror Experts and the Mainstream Media', p. 14.

26. James Der Derian, 'The Terrorist Discourse: Signs, States, and Systems of Global Political Violence', in James Der Derian, *Critical Practices in International Theory* (Routledge: London, 2009), p. 69.

27. It was not until 2005 that a collection of bin Ladin's most important statements made between 1994 and 2004 finally became available. While this collection, titled *Messages to the World: The Statements of Osama bin Ladin*, edited and annotated by Bruce Lawrence (London: Verso, 2005), provides one of the most useful insights into the rationale of al-Qaeda to date, it has been surprisingly underutilized. In part, this may be due to the assumption that the phenomenon of bin Ladin's global jihad is already sufficiently understood.

28. Krista Hunt and Kim Rygiel, *(En)Gendering the War on Terror: War Stories and Camouflaged Politics* (Aldershot: Ashgate, 2006), p. xiii.

29. Audrey Cronin, 'How Al-Qaeda Ends', presentation at the IV Jornadas Internacionales Sobre 'Los Finales del Terrorismo', Zaragoza, Spain, 10 November 2010. For a more detailed discussion, see 'How al-Qaida Ends: The Decline and Demise of Terrorist Groups', *International Security,* vol. 31, no. 1, Summer 2006, pp. 7–48.

30. For an excellent discussion of the global jihad and the practice of *takfir*, see Nelly Lahoud, *The Jihadis' Path to Self-Destruction* (London: Hurst, 2010).

31. For a detailed assessment, see Geoff Simmons, *The Scourging of Iraq: Sanctions, Law and Natural Justice* (London: Macmillan, 1996); Irwin Abrams and Wang Gungwu (eds), *The Iraq War and Its Consequences: Thoughts of Nobel Peace Laureates and Eminent Scholars* (Singapore: World Publishing, 2004).

32. Extracts from the interview are available on mainstream Internet sites including YouTube. See, for example: www.youtube.com/watch?v=v36 _zbIQebM.

33. For a detailed analysis of an al-Qaeda recruitment video, see Christina Hellmich, 'Al-Qaeda – Terrorists, Hypocrites and Fundamentalists? The View from Within', *Third World Quarterly*, vol. 26, no. 1, 2005, pp. 39–54.

CHAPTER 2

1. Profile on Al-Qaeda, *Homeland Security*, www.globalsecurity.org/security/profiles/al-qaeda.htm.

2. Xavier Raufer, 'Al-Qaeda: A Different Diagnosis', *Studies in Conflict and Terrorism* 26, 2003, p. 393.

3. Gilles Kepel, *Jihad: The Trail of Political Islam* (Cambridge MA: Harvard University Press, 2002), p. 147.

4. See, for example, Marc Sageman, *Understanding Terror Networks* (Philadelphia: University of Pennsylvania Press, 2004), pp. 2–3; Rohan Gunaratna, *Inside Al Qaeda: Global Network of Terror* (London: Hurst, 2002), pp. 17–18.

5. Biographical detail on Osama bin Ladin, including the date of his birth and the extent of his personal wealth, is subject to controversy and speculation.

6. *The 9/11 Commission Report. The Final Report of the National Commission on Terrorist Attacks upon the United States* (New York: W.W. Norton, 2004), p. 55.

7. Sageman, *Understanding Terror Networks*, p. 35.

8. Gunaratna, *Inside Al Qaeda*, pp. 18–19; emphasis added.

9. Lawrence Wright, *The Looming Tower: Al Qaeda's Road to 9/11* (London: Penguin, 2006), p. 103.

10. *9/11 Commission Report*, p. 55.

11. Ibid., p. 56.

12. Yonah Alexander and Michael S. Swetnam, *Usama bin Laden's al-*

Qaida: Profile of a Terrorist Network (Ardsley NY: Transnational Publishers, 2001), p. 1.

13. *9/11 Commission Report*, p. 56. Comforting as it may be to find some sense of clarity at last, the general consensus regarding the origins of al-Qaeda nonetheless has to be taken with some degree of caution. Upon closer inspection, a tracing of the sources cited above, and on which this account of the origins of al-Qaeda is based thus far, leads to a number of troubling observations. Marc Sageman's section, 'The Afghan Period and the Creation of Al-Qaeda' – a six-page description of the above account providing a total of six distinct references, of which three are articles published in *Al-Sharq al Awsat*, and one in the *Observer*, the contentious testimony of al-Fadl – is remarkable for its similarity to the more detailed account given in the corresponding section in Gunaratna's *Inside Al Qaeda*, which is explicitly referenced. A reference to the same section is also provided by the *9/11 Commission Report*, which, as has been seen, advances the same logic. Admittedly, the corresponding section in Gunaratna's book offers a compelling and plausible account of the period in question. The problem is that many of the sources on which it is based consist of interviews with unnamed intelligence personnel, an alleged member of al-Qaeda, and a manuscript entitled *The Jihad Fixation*, for which no further bibliographical details are provided.

14. Sageman, *Understanding Terror Networks*, p. 36; emphasis added.

15. *United States v. Usama Bin Laden – Indictment*, http://findlaw.com/ news.findlaw.com/cnn/docs/binladen/usbinladen-1a.pdf.

16. Kenneth Katzman, 'AQ: Profile and Threat Assessment: Congressional Research Service', 10 February 2005, www.fas.org/irp/crs/ RS22049.pdf.

17. Raufer, 'Al-Qaeda: A Different Diagnosis', p. 393.

18. Gunaratna, *Inside Al Qaeda*, p. 93.

19. Philippe Migaux, 'Al Qaeda', in Gerard Chaliand and Arnaud Blin, *The History of Terrorism: From Antiquity to Al Qaeda* (San Francisco: University of California Press, 1997), p. 314.

20. Ibid., p. 315.

21. Brad K. Berner, *The World According to Al Qaeda* (New Delhi: Peacock Books, 2005), p. 8.

22. *9/11 Commission Report*, p. 56.

23. Gunaratna, *Inside Al Qaeda*, pp. 95–6.

24. Raufer, 'Al-Qaeda: A Different Diagnosis', p. 394.

25. R.T. Naylor, cited in ibid., p. 394.

26. Jason Burke, *Al-Qaeda: The True Story of Radical Islam* (London: I.B. Tauris, 2007) p. 8.
27. Ibid., p. 6.
28. Ibid., pp. 6–7.
29. Ibid., p. 7.
30. Ibid.
31. Ibid., p. 2.
32. *The Power of Nightmares: The Rise of the Politics of Fear*, Adam Curtis, BBC documentary, Autumn 2004.
33. Sam Schmidt, speaking in ibid.
34. *United States of America* v. *Enaam Arnaout*, full text at http://fl1.find-law.com/news.findlaw.com/hdocs/docs/bif/usarnaout10603prof.pdf.
35. Ibid., p. 21.
36. Ibid
37. Ibid., pp. 33–4.
38. *9/11 Commission Report*, p. 56.
39. Ibid., p. 467.
40. Peter Bergen, *The Osama Bin Laden I Know: An Oral History of Al Qaeda's Leader* (New York: Simon & Schuster), p. 76.
41. Ibid.
42. *United States of America* v. *Enaam Arnaout*.
43. Bergen, *The Osama Bin Laden I Know*, p. 76.
44. Gunaratna, *Inside Al Qaeda*, p. 22.
45. Bergen, *The Osama Bin Laden I Know*, p. 74.
46. Wright, *The Looming Tower*, p. 130.
47. Abdullah Anas, speaking in *The Power of Nightmares: The Rise of the Politics of Fear*.
48. Gunaratna, *Inside Al Qaeda*, p. 23.
49. Abdel B. Atwan, *The Secret History of al Qa'ida* (London: Abacus Book, 2007), p. 68.
50. Wright, *The Looming Tower*, p. 145.
51. Ibid., p. 154.
52. Atwan, *The Secret History of al Qa'ida*, p. 37.
53. G. Kepel, *Jihad: The Trail of Political Islam*, 4th edn (London, I.B. Tauris, 2008), p. 316.
54. Atwan, *The Secret History of al Qa'ida*, p. 38.
55. Bergen, *The Osama Bin Laden I Know*, p. 122.
56. Burke, *Al-Qaeda*, p. 145.
57. Gunaratna, *Inside Al Qaeda*, p. 19.
58. Atwan, *The Secret History of al Qa'ida*, p. 23.
59. Ibid., p. 39.

60. Wright, *The Looming Tower*, p. 169.
61. Gunaratna, *Inside Al Qaeda*, p. 33.
62. Burke, *Al-Qaeda*, p. 145.
63. Wright, *The Looming Tower*, p. 169.
64. Ibid., p. 197.
65. Ibid.
66. Richard Clarke, *Against All Enemies: Inside America's War on Terror* (New York: Free Press: 2004), p. 135.
67. Burke, *Al-Qaeda*, p. 13.
68. Gunaratna, *Inside Al Qaeda*, p. 31.
69. Clarke, *Against All Enemies*, p. 139.
70. Gunaratna, *Inside Al Qaeda*, p. 32.
71. Ibid., p. 35.
72. Wright, *The Looming Tower*, p. 199.
73. *9/11 Commission Report*, p. 59.
74. Sageman, *Understanding Terror Networks*, p. 40.
75. Ibid., p. 40.
76. *9/11 Commission Report*, p. 60.
77. Atwan, *The Secret History of al Qa'ida*, p. 28.
78. Burke, *Al-Qaeda*, p. 17.
79. Ibid., p. 149.
80. *9/11 Commission Report*, p. 60.
81. Wright, *The Looming Tower*, p. 177.
82. Gunaratna, *Inside Al Qaeda*, p. 36.
83. Bergen, *The Osama Bin Laden I Know*, p. 179.
84. Ibid.
85. Migaux, 'Al Qaeda', p. 321.
86. Gunaratna, *Inside Al Qaeda*, pp. 40–41.
87. Burke, *Al-Qaeda*, pp. 167–8.
88. Ibid., pp. 166–7.
89. Ibid., p. xxv.
90. Bergen, *The Osama Bin Laden I Know*, p. 179.
91. For an analysis and a transcript of the interview, see Bruce Lawrence, *Messages to the World: The Statements of Osama bin Ladin* (London: Verso, 2005), pp. 65–94.
92. Ibid., p. 47.
93. Ibid., p. 25. For a detailed analysis of the 1996 fatwa, see Rosalind Gwynne, 'Al-Qa'ida and al-Qur'an: The 'Tafsir' of Usamah bin Ladin', 18 September 2001, http://web.utk.edu/~warda/bin_ladin_and_quran.htm.
94. Lawrence, *Messages to the World*, p. 27.

95. Atwan, *The Secret History of al Qa'ida*, p. 29.

96. Burke, *Al-Qaeda*, p. 155.

97. Osama bin Laden, 1998 Fatwa: 'Jihad against Jews and Crusaders. Statement by the World Islamic Front', www.fas.org/irp/world/para/docs/980223–fatwa.htm.

98. Clarke, *Against All Enemies*, pp. 153–4.

99. The Luxor Massacre took place on 17 November 1997 at Deir el-Bahri, an archaeological site located across the River Nile from Luxor in Egypt. Gunmen from Al-Gama'a al-Islamiyya and Jihad Talaat al-Fath disguised themselves as members of the security forces and attacked in broad daylight, killing and mutilating the bodies of 62 tourists whom they had trapped inside the Temple of Hatshepsut.

100. Clarke, *Against All Enemies*, p. 154.

101. Bergen, *The Osama Bin Laden I Know*, p. 194.

102. Ibid., p. 197.

103. Wright, *The Looming Tower*, p. 261.

104. Ibid., p. 261.

105. Ayman al-Zawahiri, quoted in Atwan, *The Secret History of al Qa'ida*, p. 72.

106. Ibid.

107. Lawrence, *Messages to the World*, pp. 59–60.

108. Notably, bin Ladin uses the word *hukm*, 'ruling', or more specifically 'considered judgement', which carries a less binding authority than a 'juridical decree' (*fatwa*).

109. Lawrence, *Messages to the World*, p. 61.

110. Marc Sageman, *Leaderless Jihad: Terror Networks in the 21st Century* (Philadelphia: University of Pennsylvania Press, 2008), pp. 43–4.

111. *9/11 Commission Report*, p. 67.

112. Ibid.

113. Migaux, 'Al Qaeda', p. 321.

114. Gunaratna, *Inside Al Qaeda*, p. 57.

115. *9/11 Commission Report*, p. 67.

116. Sageman, *Understanding Terror Networks*, p. 48.

117. Wright, *The Looming Tower*, pp. 270–71.

118. Burke, *Al-Qaeda*, p. 7.

119. Clarke, *Against All Enemies*, p. 184.

120. Sageman, *Leaderless Jihad*, p. 48.

121. Ibid., p. 48.

122. Abu Jandal, quoted in Bergen, *The Osama Bin Laden I Know*, p. 253.

123. Ibid., p. 258.

124. *9/11 Commission Report*, chapters 1 and 2.

125. Bergen, *The Osama Bin Laden I Know*, p. 282.

126. Burke, *Al-Qaeda*, p. 235.

127. Clarke, *Against All Enemies*, p. 323.

128. Andreas Behnke, 'Recognizing the Enemy: Terrorism as Symbolic Violence', in Thomas Lindemann and Erik Ringmar (eds), *The Struggle for Recognition in International Relations* (Boulder CO: Paradigm Publishers, 2011).

129. For a more detailed discussion, see Christina Hellmich and Andreas Behnke, *Knowing Al-Qaeda: The Epistemology of Terrorism* (London: Ashgate, 2011).

130. Burke, *Al-Qaeda*, pp. 8–13.

131. Ibid., p. 276.

CHAPTER 3

1. Finding of a Pentagon intelligence team, *Washington Times*, 5 June 2003, www.washingtontimes.com/news/2003/jun/05/2003 0605-011655-2131r.

2. Stephen Schwartz, *The Two Faces of Islam* (New York: Random House, 2002), p. 1.

3. Rohan Gunaratna, *Inside Al Qaeda* (New York: Columbia University Press, 2002), p. 14.

4. Marc Sageman, *Understanding Terror Networks* (Philadelphia: University of Pennsylvania Press, 2004), p. 1.

5. George W. Bush, 'Radio Address of the President to the Nation', 15 September 2001; transcript at www.whitehouse.gov.

6. George W. Bush, 'State of the Union Address', 29 January 2002; transcript at www.whitehouse.gov.

7. Ibid.

8. For a discussion of the neo-Orientalist discourse on terrorism, see Dag Tuastad, 'Neo-Orientalism and the New Barbarism Thesis: Aspects of Symbolic Violence in the Middle East Conflict(s)', *Third World Quarterly*, vol. 24, no. 4, 2003, pp. 591–9. A compelling summary of this logic is also found in the introduction of Anders Strindberg and Mats Wärn, 'Realities of Resistance: Hizballah, the Palestinian Rejectionist and Al-Qa'ida Compared', *Journal of Palestine Studies*, vol. 34, no. 3, Spring 2005, p. 25.

9. For an overview and critique of this hypothesis, see David W. Brannan et. al., 'Talking to Terrorists: Towards an Independent

Analytical Framework of Sub-State Activism', *Studies in Conflict and Terrorism*, vol. 24, no. 1, January 2001, pp. 3–24.

10. Tuastad, 'Neo-Orientalism and the New Barbarism', p. 595. For Tuastad, 'symbolic power' is not only the power to create versions of reality, but also the means of producing distorted images.

11. Similarly, see Richard A. Falkenrath, Robert D. Newman and Bradley A. Thayer, *America's Achilles Heel* (Cambridge MA: MIT Press, 1999), p. 61.

12. For a similar conclusion, see Sageman, *Understanding Terror Networks*, pp. 80–83.

13. Strindberg and Wärn, 'Realities of Resistance', p. 25.

14. Joan Lachkar, 'The Psychological Make-up of a Suicide-Bomber', *Journal of Psychohistory* 20, 2002, pp. 349–67. For attributions to other pathologies, see for example John Rosenberger, 'Discerning the Behavior of the Suicide Bomber', *Journal of Religion and Health*, 42, no. 1, Spring 2003, pp. 13–20; Raphael Israeli, 'Islamikaze and their Significance', *Terrorism and Political Violence*, vol. 9, no. 3, Autumn 1997, pp. 96–121; P. McHugh, 'A Psychiatrist Looks at Terrorism: There's Only One Way to Stop Fanatical Behavior', *Weekly Standard*, 12 December 2001; Jerrold Post, 'Terrorist Psycho-logic: Terrorist Behaviour as a Product of Psychological Forces', in Walter Reich (ed.), *Origins of Terrorism* (Cambridge: Cambridge University Press, 1990); Hervey Cleckley, *The Mask of Sanity* (New York: C.V. Mosby, 1941).

15. Bernard Lewis, *What Went Wrong? Western Impact and Middle Eastern Response* (New York: Oxford University Press, 2002). Scholars like Lewis, Fouad Ajami and Barry Rubin are frequently accused of defining the Middle East according to Western imaginations that underpin the logic of the ongoing war against terrorism. See, for example, Barry M. Rubin, *The Tragedy of the Middle East* (New Haven CT: Yale University Press, 2003); Fouad Ajami, 'Iraq and the Arab's future', *Foreign Affairs*, vol. 82, no. 1, January–February 2003, pp. 2–28.

16. For a comparison of Hamas, Hezbollah and Al-Qaeda, see Strindberg and Wärn, 'Realities of Resistance'. However, the authors, while correctly identifying territorial differences, eventually proceed to place the ideological underpinning of al-Qaeda in Wahhabi theology.

17. Olivier Roy, 'Fundamentalists without a Common Cause', *Le Monde Diplomatique*, 2 October 1998.

18. See, for example, Ruth Wedgwood and Kenneth Roth, 'Combatants or Criminals? How Washington Should Handle Terrorists', *Foreign*

Affairs, May/June 2004. For an extended discussion on the idea of terrorists as rational decision-makers, see Martha Crenshaw, 'The Logic of Terrorism: Terrorist Behaviour as a Product of Strategic Choice', in Walter Reich (ed.), *Origins of Terrorism* (Cambridge: Cambridge University Press, 1990).

19. Gunaratna, *Inside Al Qaeda*, p. 14.

20. For an authoritative discussion of the dynamics of Muslim politics, see Dale Eickelman and James Piscatori, *Muslim Politics* (Princeton NJ: Princeton University Press, 1996).

21. 'Al-Qaeda Not Driven by Ideology', *Washington Times*, 5 June 2003.

22. See, for example, William O. Beeman, 'Fighting the Good Fight: Fundamentalism and Religious Revival', in J. MacClancy, *Anthropology for the Real World* (Chicago: Chicago University Press, 2001); Niklas Luhmann, *Funktion der Religion* (Frankfurt: Piper Verlag, 1977).

23. Schwartz, *The Two Faces of Islam*, p. 1. Other supporters of the Wahhabi hypothesis include: Charles Allen, *God's Terrorists: The Wahhabi Cult and the Hidden Roots of Modern Jihad* (New York: Dacapo Press, 2006); Strindberg and Wärn, 'Realities of Resistance'; Gregory Gause, 'Wahhabism, bin Ladenism and the Saudi-Arabia Dilemma', lecture delivered 25 May 2006, University of California, Los Angeles, www.international.ucla.edu/article.asp?parentid=25057; Stephen Schwartz, 'Wahhabism and Al-Qaeda in Bosnia Herzegovina', *Terrorism Monitor*, vol. 2, no. 20, October 2004.

24. 'Wahhabiyya', *The Encyclopedia of Islam* (Leiden: E.J. Brill, 1960), p. 40.

25. Ibid.

26. Christina Hellmich, 'Al-Qaeda – Terrorists, Hypocrites and Fundamentalists? The View from Within', *Third World Quarterly*, vol. 26, no. 1, 2005, pp. 39–54.

27. See also Maha Azzam, 'Al-Qaeda: The Misunderstood Wahhabi Connection and the Ideology of Violence', *Royal Institute of International Affairs*, Briefing Paper no. 1, February 2003.

28. For an alternative view, see Natana DeLong-Bas's extensive study of Wahhabism's founding father, which rejects the conventional idea that the movement is a radical departure from the mainstream of Islam. Natana Delong-Bas, *Wahhabi Islam: From Revival and Reform to Global Jihad* (London: I.B. Tauris, 2004).

29. Ibid., p. 248.

30. Bernard Haykel, 'Radical Salafism: Osama's Ideology', *Dawn*, 2001, www.muslim-canada.org/binladindawn.html.

31. Menahem Milson, 'Reform v. Islamism in the Arab World Today', *Special Report* 34, 15 September 2004, Middle East Media Research Institute (MEMRI), www.memri.org/bin/articles/cgi?Page/archives Area/srIDSR3404.

32. Guy Sorman, *Les enfants de Rifaa: musulmans et modernes* (Paris: Fayard, 2003), p. 62.

33. Yahya Michot, *Mardin: Hégire, fuite du péché et 'demeure de l'Islam'* (Beyrouth: Albouraq, 2004).

34. James Piscatori, 'Preface', in ibid., p. xiv.

35. See also Michot, *Mardin*, p. 130.

36. See, for example, Daniel Benjamin and Steven Simon, *The Age of Sacred Terror* (New York: Random House, 2002); Henri Laoust, *Essai sur les doctrines sociales et politiques de Taòkâi-d-Dâin Aòhmad b. Taimâiya, canoniste òhanbalite, né á Harrâan en 661/1262, mort á Damas en 728/1328* (Cairo: Imprimerie de l'Institut francais d'archâeologie orientale, 1939); Johannes Jansen, *De radicaal-islamistische ideologie: van Ibn Taymiyya tot Osama ben Laden*, speech, Faculty of Letters, University of Utrecht, 3 February 2004; David Zeidan, 'The Islamic Fundamentalist View of Life as a Perennial Battle', *Middle East Review of International Affairs*, vol. 5, no. 4, 2001, pp. 251–69.

37. Laoust, 'Essai sur les doctrines sociales et politiques' and 'L'influence d'Ibn Taymiyya', in A. Welch and P. Cachia (eds), *Islam: Past Influence and Present Challenge* (Edinburgh: Edinburgh University Press, 1979), pp. 15–33; T. Michel, 'Ibn Taymiyya, Islamic Reformer', *Studia Missionalia, 34: Reformateurs religieux, Christianisme et les autres religions* (Rome: Gregorian University Press, 1985), pp. 213–32; Basheer M. Nafi, 'Abu al-Thanna' al-Alusi: An Alim, Ottoman Mufti and Exegete of the Qur'an', *International Journal of Middle East Studies* 34, 2002, pp. 465–94, and 'Tasawuf and Reform in Pre-Modern Islamic Culture: In Search of Ibrahim al-Kurani', *Die Welt des Islam*, vol. 42, no. 3, Leiden, 2002, pp. 307–55.

38. Quintan Wiktorowicz, 'Anatomy of the Salafi Movement', *Studies in Conflict and Terrorism* 29, 2006, pp. 207–39; Anders Strindberg, 'The Enemy of my Enemy', *The American Conservative*, 2 September 2006; Katharina von Knop, 'The Female Jihad: Al-Qaeda's Women', *Studies in Conflict and Terrorism* 30, 2007, pp. 397–414; Sageman, *Understanding Terror Networks*; Haykel, 'Radical Salafism: Osama's Ideology'; Quintan Wiktorowicz and John Kaltner, 'Killing in the Name of Islam: Al-Qaeda's Justification for September 11', *Middle East Policy Council Journal*, vol. 10, no. 2, 2003; Jeffery Cozzens and

Ian Conway, 'The 2005 Los Angeles Plot: The New Face of Jihad in the US', *Terrorism Monitor*, vol. 4, no. 2, 26 January 2006.

39. Sageman, *Understanding Terror Networks*, p. 1.

40. Ibid., p. 1.

41. Ibid., p. 8.

42. Ibid., p. 9.

43. Wiktorowicz, 'Anatomy of the Salafi Movement', p. 207.

44. Ibid.

45. Ibid.

46. For an extensive discussion of the variety within Salafism, see Roel Meijer, *Global Salafism: Islam's New Religious Movement* (London: Hurst, 2009). See, for example, Adis Duderija, 'Islamic Groups and their Worldviews and Identities: Neo-Traditional Salafis and Progressive Muslims', 2006, www.understanding-islam.com/related/text.asp?type=rarticle&raid=442.

47. 'Salafiyah', *The Encyclopedia of Islam* (Leiden: Brill, 1960), p. 463.

48. Ibid.

49. Ibid.

50. See, for example, Jeffery B. Cozzens, 'Identifying Entry Points of Action in Counter Radicalization – Countering Salafi-Jihadi ideology through Development Initiatives', *DIIS Working Paper* No. 2006/6, 2006, Danish Institute of International Studies, Copenhagen, Denmark; Quintan Wiktorowicz, 'The New Global Threat:Transnational Salafis and Jihad', *Middle East Policy Council*, vol. 8, no. 4, 1 December 2001; Haykel, 'Radical Salafism: Osama's Ideology'.

51. 'Salafiyah', *The Encyclopedia of Islam*, p. 463.

52. Ibid., p. 465.

53. Sageman, *Understanding Terror Networks*, p. 9.

54. 'Salafism and Qutbism', http://en.wikipedia.org/wiki/Wahhabi; accessed 12 February 2007.

55. Sayyid Qutb, *Fi Zilal al-Qur'an* (In the Shade of the Qur'an), trans. M.A. Salahi and A.A. Shamis (London: MWH London Publishers, 1979). An interesting discussion of Qutb's interpretation is Ronald Nettler's 'Guidelines for the Islamic Community: Sayyid Qutb's Political Interpretation', *Journal of Political Ideologies*, vol. 1, no. 2, 1996, pp. 183–96.

56. For a detailed discussion of the history of pan-Islam, see Jacob M. Landau, *The Politics of Pan-Islam* (Oxford: Oxford University Press, 1994).

57. James Piscatori, 'The Turmoil Within', *Foreign Affairs,* May/June 2002, www.foreignaffairs.org/2002/the-turmoil-within.html.

58. Ibid.
59. Hassan al-Turabi, quoted in Dale Eickelman and James Piscatori, *Muslim Politics* (Princeton NJ: Princeton University Press, 1996), p. 43.
60. James Piscatori, 'Islam, Islamists and the Electoral Principle in the Middle East', *ISIM Papers* (Leiden: ISIM, 2000), p. 46.

CHAPTER 4

1. For the full text of the declaration, see Bruce Lawrence, *Messages to the World* (London: Verso 2005), pp. 23-30.
2. Pew Global Attitudes Project, 'Islamic Extremism: Common Concern for Muslim and Western Publics', 14 July 2005, http://pewglobal.org/reports/display.php?ReportID=248.
3. Ibid.
4. Pew Global Attitudes Project, 'Global Unease with Major World Powers and Leaders', 27 June 2007, http://pewresearch.org/pubs/524/global-unease-with-major-world-powers-and-leaders.
5. Zogby International, 'Impressions of America 2004: How Arabs in 6 Countries View America', June 2004, www.zogby.com/features/features.cfm?ID=218.
6. For a detailed analysis, see John L. Esposito and Dalia Mogahed, *Who Speaks For Islam? What a Billion Muslims Really Think* (New York: Gallup Press, 2007).
7. Gallup Survey, 'U.S. Approval Gains Nearly Erased in Middle East/North Africa', 30 September 2010, www.gallup.com/poll/143294/Approval-Gains-Nearly-Erased-Middle-East-North-Africa.aspx.
8. See, for example, William O. Beeman, 'Fighting the Good Fight: Fundamentalism and Religious Revival', in Jeremy MacClancy (ed.), *Anthropology for the Real World* (Chicago: University of Chicago Press, 2001).
9. Quoted in Bruce Lawrence, *Messages to the World: The Statements of Osama bin Ladin* (London: Verso, 2005), p. xvii.
10. Peter L. Bergen, *The Osama Bin Laden I Know: An Oral History of Al Qaeda's Leader* (New York: Simon & Schuster, 2006), p. 216.
11. For Behnke, the attacks of 9/11 were all about the final achievement of recognition. For a more detailed analysis, see Andreas Behnke, 'Recognizing the Enemy: Terrorism as Symbolic Violence', in Thomas Lindemann and Erik Ringmar (eds), *The Struggle for Recognition in International Relations* (Boulder CO: Paradigm Publishers, 2011).

12. Bruce Lawrence, *Messages to the World: The Statements of Osama bin Ladin* (London: Verso, 2005).

13. Polly Curtis and Martin Hodgson, 'Student Researching al-Qaida Tactics Held for Six Days', *Guardian*, 4 May 2008, www.guardian. co.uk/education/2008/may/24/highereducation.uk.

14. www.amazon.com/Al-Qaeda-Training-Manual/dp/1414507100/ref= sr_1_1?s=books&ie=UTF8&qid=1294942028&sr=1-1; accessed 12 January 2011.

15. Again, it needs to be emphasized that these are not exclusive categories and that the latter does not apply to the perception of all Muslims.

16. Excerpt from bin Ladin's statement issued 14 February 2003 (on the day of Eid al-Adha). The 53-minute audio tape was circulated on various websites and excerpts were reprinted in the Saudi-owned newspaper *Al-Hayat*. For a complete translation, see Lawrence, *Messages to the World*, pp. 187–206.

17. According to Islamic tradition, the Prophet was brought by night from Mecca to the Dome of the Rock (or *miraj*), Jerusalem, from where he ascended to heaven.

18. The *qibla* is the direction that should be faced when a Muslim prays. Muslims all praying towards the same place is traditionally considered to symbolize the unity of all Muslims worldwide under the Law of God.

19. Extract from bin Ladin's interview with CNN reporter Peter Arnett in March 1997. The quote is taken from Lawrence, *Messages to the World*, pp. 46–7. For a full account of this encounter, see Peter L. Bergen, *Holy War Inc.: Inside the Secret World of Osama bin Laden* (New York: Simon & Schuster, 2001).

20. Review of 1998 Reports Concerning Threats by Osama bin Ladin to Conduct Terrorist Operations Against the United States and/or Her Allies, p. 3 of 43, www.danmahony.com.

21. World Islamic Front, 'Declaration of Jihad', published in Lawrence, *Messages to the World*, p. 61.

22. Nelly Lahoud, *The Jihadis' Path to Self-Destruction* (London and New York: Hurst/Columbia University Press, 2010) provides a nuanced discussion of the rise and fall of the Kharijites and compares the internal dynamics to the contemporary phenomenon of global jihadism. For broad historical background, see for example Wael B. Hallaq, *The Origins and Evolution of Islamic Law* (Cambridge: Cambridge University Press, 2005).

23. See also Lawrence, *Messages to the World*, p. xix.

24. 'Declaration of Jihad', ibid., p. 25.

25. For a detailed analysis of the 'global *umma*', see Peter Mandaville, *Transnational Muslim Politics: Reimagining the Umma* (London: Routledge, 2003).

26. Interview with Yosri Fouda, 24 November 2008.

27. Michael Mann, *Incoherent Empire* (London: Verso, 2003), p. 169, cited in Lawrence, *Messages to the World*, p. xx.

28. ABC, 'Interview: Osama Bin Laden, May 1998', Frontline: Hunting Bin Laden, www.pbs.org/wgbh/pages/frontline/shows/binladen/who/interview.html#video.

29. For a brief discussion of the separation of religion and politics in the history of Islam, see Dale Eickelman and James Piscatori, *Muslim Politics* (Princeton NJ: Princeton University Press, 1996), pp. 51–3. For a more extensive version, see M.Q. Zaman, *Religion and Politics under the Early Abbasids* (Leiden: Brill, 1997), pp. 1–32.

30. See, for example, William O. Beeman, 'Fighting the Good Fight: Fundamentalism and Religious Revival', in J. MacClancy, *Anthropology for the Real World* (Chicago: Chicago University Press, 2001).

31. James Piscatori, *Islam in a World of Nation States* (Cambridge: Cambridge University Press, 1986).

32. Qur'an 3:7.

33. Qur'an 17:86.

34. Critical voices include such scholars as Mu'tazila in the eighth century, Sayyid Ahmad Khan in the nineteenth century, and Ghulam Ahmad Parwez in the twentieth century. For a more detailed discussion, see for example Richard C. Martin, Mark R. Woodward and Dwi S. Atmaja, *Defenders of Reason in Islam: Mutazilism from Medieval School to Modern Symbol* (Oxford: Oneworld, 1997); George F. Graham, *The Life and Work of Sir Syed Ahmed Khan* (Karachi: Oxford University Press, 1974).

35. Piscatori, *Islam in World of Nation States*, p. 4.

36. Eickelman and Piscatori, *Muslim Politics*, pp. 37–45.

37. Turabi, quoted in ibid., p. 43.

38. Hallaq, *The Origins and Evolution of Islamic Law*.

39. On the objectification of Muslim consciousness, see Eickelman and Piscatori, *Muslim Politics*, pp. 37–42.

40. B. Lewis, 'License to Kill', *Foreign Affairs*, November–December 1998.

41. James Piscatori, *Islamic Fundamentalism and the Gulf Crisis* (Chicago: American Academy of Arts and Sciences, 1991), p. 5.

42. For a nuanced discussion of Saddam and the political symbolism of Islam, see ibid., pp. 1–27.

43. Lawrence, *Messages to the World*, p. 3.

44. Extracts from bin Ladin's letter to bin Baz, 'The Betrayal of Palestine', in ibid., pp. 6–9.

45. Ibid., p. 23.

46. Ibid.

47. Ibid., p. 25.

48. Ibid., p. 30.

49. Again, the idea of 'religious authority' has to be treated with caution. The common understanding is that bin Ladin lacks the necessary religious qualifications to issue authoritative legal opinions. Strictly speaking, this is correct, but it is equally important that we see this statement in the light of broader development of the gradual demise of the sharia and an increasing number of people who take it upon themselves to interpret sacred sources. And while it is true that bin Ladin's fatwa does not comply with traditional authority, the final interpretation, in practical rather than theological terms, is in the eye of the beholder.

50. Lawrence, *Messages to the World*, p. 61.

51. Full text of the statement is available on the Jihadica Blog, http://worldanalysis.net/modules/news/article.php?storyid=368; accessed 7 April 2009.

52. Cited in Christina Hellmich, 'Al-Qaeda – Terrorists, Hypocrites and Fundamentalists? The View from Within', *Third World Quarterly*, vol. 26, no. 1, pp. 48–9.

53. Michael Scheuer, *Imperial Hubris* (Dulles: Brassey's, 2004), p. 138.

54. For the most comprehensive account of pan-Islam, see Jacob M. Landau, *The Politics of Pan-Islam: Ideology and Organization* (Oxford: Clarendon Press, 1990). For an excellent summary of the historical developments and a nuanced assessment of the state of pan-Islam in the new millennium, see James Piscatori, 'Imagining Pan-Islam', in Shahram Akbarzadeh and Fethi Mansouri (eds), *Islam and Political Violence* (London: I.B. Tauris 2007).

55. For a detailed account, see Piscatori, 'Imagining Pan-Islam', pp. 27–8.

56. Ibid., p. 28. Conservative opinion was represented by Muhammad Rasid Rida (1865–1935), who in his compilation *al- Khilafa wa'l-imama al-uzma* [The Caliphate or the Greatest Imamate] (Cairo: Matba'at al-Manar, 1923) made the case for a restoration. Radical opinion was represented by 'Ali 'Abd al-Raziq (1888–1966), who, in

his *al-Islam wa usul al-hukum* [Islam and the Foundations of Government] (Sousse/Tunis: Dar al-Ma'arif li'l-Tiba'a wa'l-Nashr, 1999), expressed doubts about the need for a caliphate. Realist opinion was expressed by Abd al-Raziq Sanhoury's *Le Califat: son évolution vers une société des nations orientales* (Paris: Paul Geuthner, 1926).

57. Landau, Jacob M. Landau, *The Politics of Pan-Islam* (Oxford: Oxford University Press, 1994), p. 217.
58. Ibid., p. 216.
59. Piscatori, 'Imagining Pan-Islam', p. 29.
60. Ibid., pp. 248-9.
61. Landau, *The Politics of Pan-Islam*, p. 311.
62. Piscatori, 'Imagining Pan-Islam', p. 32-3.

CHAPTER 5

1. Ahmed Rashid, 'Don't Think al-Qaeda is on the Back Foot, It Will Be on the March in 2007', *Telegraph,* 31 December 2006, www.telegraph.co.uk/news/worldnews/1538251/Dont-think-al-Qaeda-is-on-the-back-foot-it-will-be-on-the-march-in-2007.html.
2. Marc Sageman, *Understanding Terror Networks* (Philadelphia: University of Pennsylvania Press, 2004), p. 52.
3. Jason Burke, *Al-Qaeda: The True Story of Radical Islam* (London: I.B. Tauris, 2007), p. 261.
4. Sageman, *Understanding Terror Networks*, p. 52.
5. Alex Gallo, 'Understanding al-Qaeda's Business Model', *CTC Sentinel*, vol. 4, no. 1, January 2011, p. 15.
6. For the defining works of this argument, see Marc Sageman, *Leaderless Jihad: Terror Networks in the 21st Century* (Philadelphia: University of Pennsylvania Press, 2008); and Burke, *Al-Qaeda*.
7. Bruce Hoffman, 'The Myth of Grass-Roots Terrorism', *Foreign Affairs*, May/June 2008. See also Elaine Sciolino and Eric Schmitt, 'A Not Very Private Feud over Terrorism', *New York Times*, 8 June 2008, www.nytimes.com/2008/06/08/weekinreview/08sciolino. html.
8. Bruce Riedel, 'Al-Qaeda Strikes Back', *Foreign Affairs*, May/June 2007, www.foreignaffairs.com/articles/62608/bruce-riedel/al-qaeda-strikes-back.
9. Yassin Musharbash, 'Al-Qaida Is More Dangerous Than it Was on 9/11', interview with terrorism expert Bruce Hoffman, *Der Spiegel*, 10 October 2006, www.spiegel.de/international/0,1518,441695,00.html.
10. Riedel, 'Al-Qaeda Strikes Back'.
11. Burke, *Al-Qaeda*, p. 1.

12. Cited in 'Times Topic: National Intelligence Estimate', *New York Times*, http://topics.nytimes.com/top/reference/timestopics/organizations/i/us_intelligence_community/national_intelligence_estimates/index.html?inline=nyt-classifier.

13. 'Al-Qaeda Claims Tunisia Attack', *BBC News*, 23 June 2002, http://news.bbc.co.uk/1/hi/world/middle_east/2061071.stm.

14. Paul Hamilos, 'The worst Islamist attack in European history', *Guardian*, 31 October 2007, www.guardian.co.uk/world/2007/oct/31/spain.

15. Ennahar Online, 'Al-Qaeda Supports the Events in Tunisia and Algeria', 14 January 2010, www.ennaharonline.com/en/news/5541.html.

16. For a nuanced discussion of AQIM and the War of Succession, see Oliver Guitta, 'Al Qaeda's War of Succession in the Maghreb', *Atlantic Community Organization,* 19 January 2011, www.atlantic-community.org/index/articles/view/Al_Qaeda%27s_War_of_Succession_in_the_Maghreb.

17. 'Seeing Al-Qaeda Around Every Corner', *New York Times,* 8 July 2007, www.nytimes.com/2007/07/08/opinion/08pubed.html?_r=2&oref=login.

18. Al-Qaeda leaders have proclaimed Iraq a major front in their global terrorist campaign. *Office of the Director of National Intelligence*, 9 July 2005; full text available in English translation at www.dni.gov/press_releases/letter_in_english.pdf.

19. Ibid.

20. Some of the best examples of communication difficulties contributing strategic missteps are the various letters from al-Qaeda Central leaders to commanders in Iraq, and notes from Al-Qaeda in Iraq leaders to their various commanders once internal communication mechanisms began to break down in early 2007. See Ayman al-Zawahiri, 'Letter from al-Zawahiri to al-Zarqawi, dated 9 July 2005', released by the Office of the Director of National Intelligence, 11 October 2005, www.globalsecurity.org/security/library/report/2005/zawahiri-zarqawi-letter_9jul2005.htm; Atiyah abd al-Rahman, 'Note to Zarqawi', 12 November 2005, www.ctc.usma.edu/harmony/pdf/CTC-AtiyahLetter.pdf; Abu Yahya al-Libi (Yunus al-Sahrawi), 'A Message to Mujahid Leader Abu Mus'ab Al-Zarqawi from Abu-Yahya Yunis Al-Sahrawi, 'Jihadi Websites, 20 November 2005; Bill Roggio, 'Letters from al-Qaeda Leaders Show Iraqi Effort is in Disarray', *Long War Journal*, 11 September 2008, www.defenddemocracy.org/index.php?option=com_content&task=view&id=11782255&Itemid=353.

21. Joe Klein, 'Is al-Qaeda on the Run in Iraq?', *Time* Magazine, 23 May 2007, www.time.com/time/nation/article/0,8599,1624697,00.html.

22. For an excellent discussion of this theme and the state of al-Qaeda more generally, see Assaf Moghadam and Brian Fishman (eds), *Self-Inflicted Wounds: Debates and Divisions within Al-Qa'ida and its Periphery* (New York: Harmony Project: Combating Terrorism Center at West Point, 2010), www.ctc.usma.edu/Self-Inflicted per cent20Wounds.pdf.

23. Larry Shaughnessy, 'U.S. Official: Al Qaeda in Yemen Bigger Threat than in Pakistan', *CNN*, 17 December 2010, http://articles.cnn.com/ 2010–12–17/us/al.qaeda.yemen_1_aqap-al-qaeda-yemen?s=PM:US.

24. Throughout this chapter, the acronym AQAP is used to refer to 'Al-Qaeda in the Arabian Peninsula', indicating the merger of al-Qaeda's Yemeni and Saudi branches in 2009.

25. Brian Ross and Richard Esposito, 'Abdulmutallab: More Like Me in Yemen. Accused Northwest Bomber Says More Bombers On the Way', *ABC News*, 28 December 2009, http://abcnews.go.com/ Blotter/abdulmutallab-yemen-northwest-flight-253–terror-suspect/ story?id=9430536; Jason Keyser, 'Bin Laden Endorses Bomb Attempt on US Plane' *ABC News*, 24 January 2010, http://abcnews. go.com/International/wireStory?id=9647388.

26. Eric Schmitt and Scott Shane, 'U.S. Divided on Aid to Counter Qaeda Threat in Yemen', *New York Times*, 15 September 2010, www. nytimes.com/2010/09/16/world/middleeast/16yemen.html_r.

27. Quoted in Greg Miller and Peter Finn, 'CIA Sees Increased Threat from al-Qa'ida in Yemen', *Washington Post*, 24 August 2010.

28. See, for example, Murad al-Shishani, 'An Assessment of the Anatomy of al-Qaeda in Yemen: Ideological and Social Factors', *Terrorism Monitor*, vol. 8, no. 9, March 2010; Jane Novak, 'Arabian Peninsula Al-Qaeda Groups Merge', *The Long War Journal*, 26 January 2009, www.longwarjournal.org/archives/2009/01/arabian_peninsula_al.php; Leela Jacinto, 'Key Figures in Al-Qaeda's Yemeni Branch', *France 24*, 5 January 2010; Stephen Kurcy, 'Five Key Members of Al-Qaeda in Yemen', *Christian Science Monitor*, www.csmonitor. com/World/Middle-East/2010/1102/Five-key-members-of-Al-Qaeda-in-Yemen-AQAP/Nasir-al-Wuhayshi-head-of-AQAP.

29. Barak Barfi, 'Yemen on the Brink? The Resurgence of Al-Qaeda in Yemen', *New America Foundation,* January 2010, p. 2, www.newamerica.net/publications/policy/yemen_on_the_brink.

30. Aired on Al Jazeera, 29 January 2009.

31. On the recent surge of attacks, see for example Saeed al-Batati, 'Al-Qaeda Renews Attacks in Yemen', *Arab News*, 12 October 2010, http://arabnews.com/middleeast/article159019.ece. The full version

of *Inspire* is available at http://info.publicintelligence.net/Inspire-Fall2010.pdf.

32. Even vague assumptions are frequently reported as facts. For example, Anwar al-Awlaki's death was widely announced in May 2010, only to be retracted shortly after (www.hurriyetdailynews.com/n.php?n=al-qaeda-in-yemen-announces-new-leader-ex-gitmo-prisoner). For a detailed discussion of the challenge of knowing al-Qaeda, see Christina Hellmich and Andreas Behnke, *Knowing Al-Qaeda: The Epistemology of Terrorism* (London: Ashgate, 2011).

33. 'Yemen Captures Al Qaeda Commander, a Former Guantanamo Detainee', *Associated Press* and *Fox News*, 17 February 2009, www.foxnews.com/story/0,2933,494784,00.html; 'Saudi Al-Qaeda Leader Outlines New Strategy and Tactics of Al-Qaeda in the Arabian Peninsula', *Terrorism Monitor*, vol. 7, no. 9, April 2009.

34. Munir Mawari, 'Uncertainty Surrounds the Arrest of al-Qaeda Financier in Yemen', *Terrorism Monitor*, vol. 7, no. 19, July 2009.

35. Nasser al-Hakbani, 'Al-Rimi is the Real Leader of Al-Qa'idah in Yemen', *Al-Hayat*, 23 June 2010.

36. Thomas Heghammer, 'Jihad in Saudi Arabia and Yemen', presentation at IISS, London, 30 September 2010. For a detailed discussion of Jihadism in Saudi Arabia, see Thomas Heghammer, *Jihad in Saudi Arabia* (Cambridge: Cambridge University Press, 2010).

37. A quick search produces estimates ranging from 200 to 1,500 members or cells. See, for example, David Sanger and Mark Mazetti, 'New Estimate of Strength of Al Qaeda Is Offered', *New York Times*, 30 June 2010, www.nytimes.com/2010/07/01/world/asia/01qaeda.html; Jane Merrick and Kim Sengupta, 'Yemen: The Land with More Guns than People', *Independent*, 20 September 2009, www.independent.co.uk/news/world/middle-east/yemen-the-land-with-more-guns-than-people-179.

38. The Yemeni government has repeatedly been accused of forcing confessions from detained individuals. On forced confessions and torture in Yemen, see for example the International Federation for Human Rights' report, *Yemen: In the Name of National Security – Human Rights Violations in Yemen*, www.fidh.org/IMG/pdf/Yemen.pdf; and Amnesty International's report, *Yemen: The Rule of Law Sidelined in the Name of Security*. September 2003, www.amnesty.org/en/library/asset/MDE31/006/2003/en/084dc66b-d6a7-11dd-ab95-a13b602c0642/mde310062003en.html.

39. For more details on Anwar al-Awlaki, see Katherine Zimmerman, 'Militant Islam's Global Preacher: The Radicalizing Effect of Sheikh

Anwar al Awlaki', *Critical Threats Project*, 12 March 2010, www. criticalthreats.org/yemen/militant-islams-global-preacher-radicalizing-effect-sheikh-anwar-al-awlaki.

40. His interpretation of the 'Fatwa of Mardin', a controversial piece that has received much attention from Islamists and religious scholars alike, included in the recent version of *Inspire*, appears to have been selected/copied from another source and included by the editors. For an excellent discussion of different interpretations of the Mardin Fatwa, see Yahya Michot, *Mardin: Hégire, fuite du péché et 'demeure de l'Islam* (Beirut: Albouraq, 2004).

41. The fact that he was tried *in absentia* should not necessarily be interpreted as 'proof' of his AQAP connection, but has to be viewed as part of the government's effort to demonstrate its cooperation with the USA, who placed him on the terrorist kill-or-capture list.

42. For translations of bin Ladin's messages, see Bruce Lawrence, *Messages to the World: The Statements of Osama bin Laden* (London: Verso, 2005).

43. Christina Hellmich, 'The *Khutba* as Medium for the Communication of Islamic Fundamentalism: The Case of Yemen', M.St. thesis, Oxford University, 2003.

44. Anwar al-Awlaki in an interview with Al Jazeera, 7 February 2010. Full text available at http://english.aljazeera.net/focus/2010/02/2010271074776870.html.

45. Sa'id Ubayd al-Jamhi, *al-Qa'ida fi al-Yaman* (Sana'a: Maktaba al-Hadara, 2008). A summary of his findings in English, provided by Zaid al-Alaya'a, 'Al-Qaeda in Yemen', 20 July 2010, *Yemen Today*, is available at www.yemen-today.com/go/special_reports/5327.html.

46. Ghaith Abdul-Ahad, 'Al-Qaida in Yemen: Poverty, Corruption and an Army of Jihadis Willing to Fight', *Guardian*, 22 August 2010, www.guardian.co.uk/world/2010/aug/22/ al-qaida-yemen-ghaith-abdul-ahad.

47. Rick Nelson, senior fellow at the Center for Security and International Studies, Washington DC, quoted in Rachel Martin, 'From Osama to Obama – Bin Laden Delivers New Threats', *ABC News*, 24 January 2010, http://abcnews.go.com/WN/osama-bin-laden-addresses-president-obama-audio-tape/story?id=9650267.

48. No agreement exists as to whether Yemen is about to implode or merely experiencing another period of political turmoil.

49. For a theoretical discussion of contested statehood, see Deon Geldenhuys, *Contested States in World Politics* (Basingstoke: Palgrave Macmillan, 2009).

50. On the nature of Yemeni politics, see for example Sarah Phillips, *Yemen's Democracy Experiment in Regional Perspective* (Basingstoke: Palgrave Macmillan, 2008).

51. It is also worth keeping in mind that the frequently mentioned 'lawless regions' of Yemen are not the wild, empty spaces they are often made out to be, but areas that are governed by tribal law (*urf*). For Yemeni tribalism, see Paul Dresch, *Tribes, Government and History in Yemen* (Oxford: Clarendon Press, 1989); R.B. Serjeant, *Studies in Arabian History and Civilisation* (London: Variorum, 1981). For a Yemeni account of the tribes and their role in society, see Fuad al-Salahi, *Thulathiyya al-Dawla w'al-Qabila w'al-Mujtama' al-Madani* (Taiz: Markaz al-Malumat, 2001).

52. For the Houthi rebellion, see Samy Dorlian, *Les Filières Islamistes Zaydites au Yémen*, Master's thesis, Université Paul Cézanne, Aix en Provence, 2005; and International Crisis Group, *Yemen: Defusing the Saada Time Bomb*, 27 May 2009. For Zaydism, see Rudolf Strothman, *Kultus der Zaiditen* (Strasbourg: K.J. Trübner, 1912), and *Das Staatsrecht der Zaiditen* (Strasbourg: K.J. Trübner, 1912); Cornelis van Arendonk, *Les Débuts de L'Imamate Zaidite au Yemen* (Leiden: E.J. Brill, 1960); Wilferd Madelung, *Der Imam al-Qasim ibn Ibrahim und die Glaubenslehre der Zaiditen* (Berlin: De Gruyter, 1965); Bernard Haykel, *Revival and Reform in Islam: The Legacy of Muhammad al-Shawkani* (New York: Cambridge University Press, 2003).

53. Maysaa Shuja al-Deen, 'Media Absent from Yemen's Forgotten Conflict', *Arab Media Society* 8, Spring 2009, www.arabmediasociety. com/?article=714.

54. UNHCR struggles to help the internally displaced in northern Yemen; www.unhcr.org/4ab3a7d49.html.

55. Stephen Day, *The Political Challenge of Yemen'sSouthern Movement*, Carnegie Paper, 29 March 2010, http://carnegieendowment.org/publications/index.cfm?fa=view&id=40414.

56. For a quick overview of structural challenges, see 'Yemen: 10 reasons to worry', www.nato.int/docu/review/2010/Yemen/Yemen_10_reasons_to_worry/EN/index.htm.

57. The numbers in Yemeni health-care indicators differ substantially from source to source. The data presented here, representing a middle ground, is taken from the WHO International Health Indicator webpage, 2003, www.208.48.190.WHO/WHD/Countryprofile -Yem. htm. For comparison, see UNICEF Yemen, 2006, www.unicef.org/infobycountry/yemen_statistics.html.

58. If the notion holds that any politician, not to mention one who is desperate, will do whatever it takes to stay in power, then Amnesty International's observations of the surge in human rights violations, including unlawful killings of those accused of links to Southern Movement activists, Houthi rebels and al-Qaeda, arbitrary arrests, torture and unfair trials will not come as a surprise. See www.amnesty.org/en/news-and-updates/report/yemen-abandons-human-rights-name-countering-terrorism-2010-08-24.

59. 'Anti-government Rallies Hit Yemen', Al Jazeera, 27 January 2011, http://english.aljazeera.net/news/middleeast/2011/01/201112710 0660857.html.

60. Embassy of the Republic of Yemen, Washington DC, Media Office, 'Situation in Yemen', Press Update, 2 November 2010.

61. An example is Tariq al-Fadli, leader of the *mujahidin* (fighters) in Afghanistan, who later was appointed by the president to the Majlis al-Shura, the upper house of the parliament.

62. Geoff Simons, *The United Nations* (London: Macmillan, 1995), p. 168.

63. Ibid.

64. On radicalization in prisons, see for example Peter Neumann, 'Prisons and Terrorism Radicalisation and De-radicalisation in 15 Countries', in M. Cuthbertson, *Prisons and the Education of Terrorists*, policy report published by the International Centre for the Study of Radicalisation and Political Violence (ICSR), London, 2010, http://icsr.info/publications/.papers/1277699166PrisonsandTerrorism Radicalisation and Deradicalisationin15Countries.pdf; or James Beckford, Daniele Joly and Farhad Khosrokhavar, *Muslims in Prison: Challenge and Change in Britain and France* (Basingstoke: Palgrave Macmillan, 2005).

65. In 2008, Yemen was placed thirteenth on the Fund for Peace's 'Failed State Index', which measures political and economic factors that threaten central authority, including a state's ability to provide basic services, government corruption, economic development and human rights. Fund for Peace, 'Failed State Index', www.fundforpeace.org/web/index.php?option=com_content&task=view&id=99&Itemid=140.

66. On the disconnect between state-building and counterterrorism, see Karin von Hippel, 'The Roots of Terrorism: Probing the Myths', *Political Quarterly*, vol. 73, no. 1, 2002, pp. 25–39.

67. Christopher Boucek, *Yemen: Avoiding a Downward Spiral*, Carnegie Paper, September 2009, www.carnegieendowment.org/publications/index.cfm?fa=view&id=23827.

68. Extended extracts from the report are available at www.youtube. com/watch?v=G7RElWMRdRk.

69. The video also provides insights into the public reaction to the bombing, authorized by a joint US/Yemeni in which Yemeni children were among the victims.

70. Jane Novak, 'Yemeni al-Qaeda leader: State Conducts Terror Attacks', *The Long War Journal*, 3 December 2008, www.longwarjournal.org/archives/2008/12/yemeni_al_qaeda_lead_2.php.

71. For a detailed overview of different Islamist actors in Yemen, see Laurent Bonnefoy, 'Varieties of Islamism in Yemen: The Logic of Integration under Pressure', *Middle East Review of International Affairs*, vol. 13, no. 1, 2009.

72. Jeffrey Fleishman, Yemen: Car Bomb Targeting Shiite Tribesmen Kills 17, *Los Angeles Times*, 24 November 2010, http://latimesblogs.latimes.com/babylonbeyond/2010/11/a-car-bomb-exploded-along-a-procession-of-shiite-muslims-in-northern-yemen-killing-at-least-15-people-and-raising-concerns.html.

73. For details on this group, see Laurent Bonnefoy, 'Les relations religieuses transnationales contemporaines entre le Yémen et l'Arabie Saoudite: un salafisme importé?' Ph.D. dissertation, IEP, Paris, 2007.

74. On al-Wadi'i's criticism of Osama bin Ladin, see also Lia Brynjar, 'Destructive Doctrinairians: Abu Musab al- Suri's Critique of the Salafis in the Jihadi Current', in Roel Meijer (ed.), *Global Salafism: Islam's New Religious Movement*, London: Hurst, 2009, pp. 249–68.

75. For a detailed discussion of Islah, see Jillian Schwedler, 'The Yemeni Islah Party: Political Opportunities and Coalition Building in a Transitional Polity', in Quintan Wiktorowicz (ed.), *Islamist Activism: A Social Movement Theory Approach* (Bloomington: Indiana University Press, 2003), pp. 205–29; and Jillian Schwedler, *Faith in Moderation: Islamist Parties in Jordan and Yemen* (Cambridge: Cambridge University Press, 2007).

76. For details on Zindani, see Gregory Johnsen, 'Profile of Sheikh Abd al-Majid al-Zindani', *Terrorism Monitor*, vol. 4, no. 7, 2006, pp. 3–5.

77. Alexander Knysh, 'The Tariqa on a Landcruiser: The Resurgence of Sufism in Yemen', *Middle East Journal*, vol. 55, no. 3, 2001, pp. 399–414.

78. Bonnefoy, 'Les relations religieuses transnationales contemporaines entre le Yémen et l'Arabie Saoudite'. See also 'Contextualizing the Salafi–Sufi Conflict (from the Northern Caucasus to Hadramawt)', *Middle Eastern Studies*, vol. 43, no. 3, 2007, pp. 503–30.

CHAPTER 6

1. Jason Burke, *Al-Qaeda: The True Story of Radical Islam* (London: I.B. Tauris, 2007), p. 276.

2. Scott Shane and James Dao, 'Investigators Study Tangle of Clues on Fort Hood Suspect', *New York Times,* 14 November 2009, www.nytimes.com/2009/11/15/us/15hasan.html?_r=3.

3. Magnus Ranstorp, 'Terrorist Awakening in Sweden?', *CTC Sentinel,* vol. 4, no. 1, January 2011.

4. For a more detailed discussion on the process of radicalization, see Christina Hellmich, 'The Physiology of Al-Qaeda', in Magnus Ranstorp, *Understanding Violent Radicalisation* (London: Routledge, 2009).

5. The presentation, originally released by the *Washington Post*, is available on the NEFA website, www.nefafoundation.org/miscellaneous/Hasan2.pdf.

6. Vikram Dodd, 'Profile: Roshonara Choudhry', *Guardian,* 10 November 2010, www.guardian.co.uk/uk/2010/nov/02/profile-roshonara-choudhry-stephen-timms.

7. 'Woman Jailed for Life for Attack on MP Stephen Timms', BBC News, 3 November 2010, www.bbc.co.uk/news/uk-england-london-11682732.

8. See, for example, James Brandon, 'British Universities Continue to Breed Extremists', *CTC Sentinel*, vol. 4, no. 1, January 2010.

9. For a critique of the failed-state theory, see Karin von Hippel, 'The Roots of Terrorism: Probing the Myths', *Political Quarterly*, vol. 73, no. 1, 2002.

10. Ted Koppel, 'Nine Years after 9/11, Let's Stop Playing into bin Laden's hands', *Washington Post,* 12 September 2010, www.washingtonpost.com/wpdyn/content/article/2010/09/09/AR2010090904735.html?hpid=opinionsbox1.

11. For a comprehensive analysis, see Vali Nasr, *The Shia Revival: How Conflicts within Islam Will Shape the Future* (New York: W.W. Norton, 2006).

12. Nelly Lahoud, *The Jihadis' Path to Self-Destruction* (London: Hurst, 2010).

13. Alia Brahimi, 'Crushed in the Shadows: Why Al Qaeda Will Lose the War of Ideas', *Studies in Conflict and Terrorism,* vol. 33, no. 2, 2010, p. 106.

14. Anna Mulrine, 'Does Shooting at Frankfurt Airport Follow Pattern of Simpler Attacks?', *Christian Science Monitor,* 2 March 2011, available at www.csmonitor.com/USA/Military/2011/0302/Does-shooting-

at-Frankfurt-Airport-follow-pattern-of-simpler-attacks.

15. Full text of the 2011 spring issue of *Inspire* is available at www.adl. org/main_Terrorism/inspire_issue_5_aqap.htm.
16. Anwar al-Awlaki, 'The Tsunami of Change', ibid., pp. 50–53.
17. Yahya Ibrahim, 'Protest Focus', ibid. p. 5.

Bibliography

Abd al-Raziq, A. (1925) *Al-Islam wa usul al-hukum* [Islam and the Foundations of Governance], Sousse/Tunis: Dar al-Ma'arif li'l-Tiba'a wa'l-Nashr.

Abdul-Ahad, G. (2010) 'Al-Qaida in Yemen: Poverty, Corruption and an Army of Jihadis Willing to Fight', *Guardian*, 22 August.

Abrams I., and W. Gungwu (eds) (2004) *The Iraq War and Its Consequences: Thoughts of Nobel Peace Laureates and Eminent Scholars*, Singapore: World Publishing.

Ajami, F. (2003) 'Iraq and the Arab's Future', *Foreign Affairs*, vol. 82, no. 1, January–February.

Al-Alaya'a, Z. (2010) 'Al-Qaeda in Yemen', *Yemen Today*, 20 July.

Al-Hakbani, N. (2010) 'Al-Rimi is the Real Leader of Al-Qa'idah in Yemen', *Al-Hayat*, 23 June.

Al-Raziq al-Sanhoury, A. (1926) *Le Califat: son évolution vers une société des nations orientales*, Paris: Paul Geuthner.

Al-Salahi, F. (2001) *Thulathiyya al-Dawla w'al-Qabila w'al-Mujtama' al-Madani*, Taiz: Markaz al-Malumat.

Al-Shishani, M. (2010) 'An Assessment of the Anatomy of al-Qaeda in Yemen: Ideological and Social Factors', *Terrorism Monitor*, vol. 8, no. 9, March.

Alexander, Y., and M.S. Swetnam (2001) *Usama bin Laden's al-Qaida: Profile of a Terrorist Network*, Ardsley, NY: Transnational Publishers.

Allen, C. (2006) *God's Terrorists: The Wahhabi Cult and the Hidden Roots of Modern Jihad*, New York: Dacapo Press.

Amnesty International (2003) *Yemen: The Rule of Law Sidelined in the Name of Security*, September.

Atwan, A.B. (2007) *The Secret History of al Qa'ida*, London: Abacus Books.

Azzam, M. (2003) 'Al-Qaeda: The Misunderstood Wahhabi Connection and the Ideology of Violence', *Royal Institute of International Affairs,* Briefing Paper no. 1, February.

Alain Badiou (2005) *Infinite Thought: Truth and the Return to Philosophy*, London: Continuum.

Barfi, B. (2010) 'Yemen on the Brink? The Resurgence of Al-Qaeda in Yemen', *New America Foundation*, January.

Beckford, J., D. Joly and F. Khosrokhavar (2005) *Muslims in Prison: Challenge and Change in Britain and France*, Basingstoke: Palgrave Macmillan.

Beeman, W.O. (2001) 'Fighting the Good Fight: Fundamentalism and Religious Revival', in J. MacClancy, *Anthropology for the Real World*, Chicago: Chicago University Press.

Behnke, A. (2011) 'Recognizing the Enemy: Terrorism as Symbolic Violence', in T. Lindemann and E. Ringmar (eds), *The Struggle for Recognition in International Relations*, Boulder CO: Paradigm.

Bergen, P.L. (2001) *Holy War Inc.: Inside the Secret World of Osama bin Laden*, New York: Simon & Schuster.

Bergen, P.L. (2006) *The Osama Bin Laden I Know: An Oral History of Al Qaeda's Leader*, New York: Simon & Schuster.

Berner, B.K. (2005) *The World According to Al Qaeda*, New Delhi: Peacock Books.

Bin Laden, O. (1998) Fatwa: 'Jihad against Jews and Crusaders. Statement by the World Islamic Front'.

Bonnefoy, L. (2007) 'Les relations religieuses transnationales contemporaines entre le Yémen et l'Arabie Saoudite: un salafisme importé?' Ph.D. dissertation, IEP de Paris.

Bonnefoy, L. (2009) 'Varieties of Islamism in Yemen: The Logic of Integration under Pressure', *Middle East Review of International Affairs*, vol. 13, no. 1.

Boucek, C. (2009) *Yemen: Avoiding a Downward Spiral*, Washington DC: Carnegie Endowment, September.

Brahimi, A. (2010) 'Crushed in the Shadows: Why Al Qaeda Will Lose the War of Ideas', *Studies in Conflict and Terrorism*, vol. 33, no. 2.

Brandon, J. (2010) 'British Universities Continue to Breed Extremists', *CTC Sentinel*, vol. 4, no. 1, January.

Brannan, D.W., et. al. (2001) 'Talking to Terrorists: Towards an Independent Analytical Framework of Sub-State Activism', *Studies in Conflict and Terrorism* vol. 24, no. 1.

Bright, M. (2003) 'On the Trail of Osama bin Ladin', *Observer*, 11 May.

Brynjar, Lia (2009) 'Destructive Doctrinairians: Abu Musab al- Suri's Critique of the Salafis in the Jihadi Current', in Roel Meijer (ed.), *Global Salafism: Islam's New Religious Movement*, London: Hurst, pp. 249–68.

Burke, J. (2007) *Al-Qaeda: The True Story of Radical Islam*, London: I.B. Tauris.

Bush, G.W. (2001) 'Radio Address of the President to the Nation', 15 September.

Bush, G.W. (2002) 'State of the Union Address', 29 January.

Clarke, R. (2004) *Against All Enemies: Inside America's War on Terror*, New York: Free Press.

Cleckley, H. (1941) *The Mask of Sanity*, New York: C.V. Mosby.

Cole, J. (2006) 'A Treatment for Radical Ignorance about Islamic Radicalism', *Chronicle of Higher Education,* 3 March.

Cozzens, J.B. (2006) *Identifying Entry Points of Action in Counter Radicalization – Countering Salafi-Jihadi Ideology through Development Initiatives*, DIIS Working Paper No. 2006/6, Copenhagen: Danish Institute of International Studies.

Cozzens, J., and I. Conway (2006) 'The 2005 Los Angeles Plot: The New Face of Jihad in the US', *Terrorism Monitor*, vol. 4, no. 2.

Crenshaw, M. (1990) 'The Logic of Terrorism: Terrorist Behaviour as a Product of Strategic Choice', in W. Reich (ed.), *Origins of Terrorism*, Cambridge: Cambridge University Press, 1990.

Crenshaw, M. (2000) 'Current Research on Terrorism: The Academic Perspective', *Political Psychology*, 21 February.

Cronin, A.K. (2006) 'How al-Qaida Ends: The Decline and Demise of Terrorist Groups', *International Security*, vol. 31, no. 1, Summer.

Cronin, A.K. (2010) 'How Al-Qaeda Ends', presentation at IV Jornadas Internacionales Sobre 'Los Finales del Terrorismo', Zaragoza, 10 November.

Curtis, A. (2004) *The Power of Nightmares: The Rise of the Politics of Fear*, BBC documentary.

Curtis, P., and M. Hodgson (2008) 'Student Researching al-Qaida Tactics Held for Six Days', *Guardian,* 4 May.

Cuthbertson, I.M. (2004) 'Prisons and the Education of Terrorists, *World Policy Journal*, vol. 21, no. 3, Fall.

Day, S. (2010) 'The Political Challenge of Yemen's Southern Movement', Carnegie Paper, Washington DC, 29 March.

Delong-Bas, N. (2004) *Wahhabi Islam: From Revival and Reform to Global Jihad*, London: I.B. Tauris.

Der Derian, J. (2009) 'The Terrorist Discourse: Signs, States, and Systems of Global Political Violence', in J. Der Derian, *Critical Practices in International Theory*, London: Routledge.

Dodd, V. (2010) 'Profile: Roshonara Choudhry', *Guardian*, 10 November.

Dorlian, S. (2005) *Les Filières Islamistes Zaydites au Yémen*, Master's thesis, Université Paul Cézanne, Aix-en-Provence.

Dorlian, S. (2009) *Yemen: Defusing the Saada Time Bomb*, International Crisis Group, Middle East Report No. 86, 27 May, www.observatori.org/paises/pais_64/documentos/86_yemen_defusing_the_saada_time_bomb.pdf.

Dresch, P. (1989) *Tribes, Government and History in Yemen*, Oxford: Clarendon Press.

Duderija, A. (2006) *Islamic Groups and their World-views and Identities: Neo-Traditional Salafis and Progressive Muslims*, Leiden: Brill.

Eickelman, D.F., and J.P. Piscatori (1996) *Muslim Politics*, Princeton NJ: Princeton University Press.

Encyclopedia of Islam, The (1960) Leiden: E.J. Brill.

Esposito, J.L., and D. Mogahed (2007) *Who Speaks For Islam? What a Billion Muslims Really Think*, New York: Gallup Press.

Falkenrath, R.A., R.D. Newman and B.A. Thayer (1999) *America's Achilles Heel*, Cambridge, MA: MIT Press.

Fleishman, J. (2010) Yemen: Car Bomb Targeting Shiite Tribesmen Kills 17, *Los Angeles Times*, 24 November.

Gallo, A. (2011) 'Understanding al-Qaeda's Business Model', *CTC Sentinel*, vol. 4, no. 1, January.

Gallup Survey (2010) 'U.S. Approval Gains Nearly Erased in Middle East/North Africa', September.

Gause, G. (2006) 'Wahhabism, bin Ladenism and the Saudi-Arabia Dilemma', lecture, University of California, Los Angeles, 25 May.

Geldenhuys, D. (2009) Contested *States in World Politics*, London: Palgrave Macmillan.

Graham, G.F. (1974) *The Life and Work of Sir Syed Ahmed Khan*, Karachi: Oxford University Press.

Guitta, O. (2011) 'Al Qaeda's War of Succession in the Maghreb', *Atlantic Community Organization*, 19 January.

Gunaratna, R. (2002) *Inside Al Qaeda: Global Network of Terror*, London: Hurst.

Gurr, T.R. (1988) 'Empirical Research on Political Terrorism: The State of the Art and How It Might Be Improved', in R.O. Slater and M. Stohl (eds), *Current Perspectives on International Terrorism*, New York: St. Martin's Press.

Gwynne, R. (2001) *Al-Qa'ida and al-Qur'an: The 'Tafsir' of Usamah bin Ladin*, Tennessee: University of Tennessee Press.

Hallaq, W.B. (2005) *The Origins and Evolution of Islamic Law*, Cambridge: Cambridge University Press.

Hamilos, P. (2007) 'The Worst Islamist Attack in European history', *Guardian*, 31 October.

Haykel, B. (2001) 'Radical Salafism: Osama's Ideology', *Dawn*, www.muslim-canada.org/binladindawn.html.

Haykel, B. (2003) *Revival and Reform in Islam: The Legacy of Muhammad al-Shawkani*, New York: Cambridge University Press.

Heghammer, T. (2010) *Jihad in Saudi Arabia*, Cambridge: Cambridge University Press.

Heghammer, T. (2010) 'Jihad in Saudi Arabia and Yemen', presentation at IISS, London, 30 September.

Hellmich, C. (2003) 'The *Khutba* as Medium for the Communication of Islamic Fundamentalism: The Case of Yemen', M.St. thesis, Oxford University.

Hellmich, C. (2005) 'Al-Qaeda – Terrorists, Hypocrites and Fundamentalists? The View from Within', *Third World Quarterly*, vol. 26, no. 1.

Hellmich, C. (2008) 'Creating the Ideology of Al Qaeda: From Hypocrites to Salafi-Jihadists', *Studies in Conflict and Terrorism*, vol. 32, no. 2.

Hellmich, C. (2009) 'The Physiology of Al-Qaeda', in Magnus Ranstorp (ed.), *Understanding Violent Radicalisation*, London: Routledge.

Hellmich, C., and A. Behnke (2011) *Knowing Al-Qaeda: The Epistemology of Terrorism*, London: Ashgate.

Heywood, A. (2004) *Political Theory – An Introduction*, 3rd edn, Basingstoke: Palgrave Macmillan.

Hoffman, B. (2008) 'The Myth of Grassroots Terrorism', *Foreign Affairs*, May–June.

Horgan, J., and M. Boyle (2008) 'A Case Against Critical Terrorism Studies', *Critical Studies on Terrorism*, vol. 1, no. 1.

Hoyt, C. (2007) 'Seeing Al-Qaeda around Every Corner', *New York Times*, 8 July.

Hunt, K., and K. Rygiel (eds) (2006) *(En)Gendering the War on Terror: War Stories and Camouflaged Politics*, Aldershot: Ashgate.

International Federation for Human Rights (2010) *Yemen: In the Name of National Security – Human Rights Violations in Yemen*, www.fidh.org/IMG/article_pdf/article_a7447.pdf.

Israeli, R. (1997) 'Islamikaze and Their Significance', *Terrorism and Political Violence*, vol. 9, no. 3, Autumn.

Jacinto, L. (2010) 'Key Figures in Al-Qaeda's Yemeni Branch', *France 24*, 5 January.

Jackson, R. (2005) *Writing the War on Terrorism: Language, Politics and Counter-Terrorism*, Manchester: Manchester University Press.

Jansen, J. (2004) *De radicaal-islamistische ideologie: van Ibn Taymiyya tot*

Osama ben Laden, speech, Faculty of Letters, University of Utrecht, 3 February.

Johnsen, G. (2006) 'Profile of Sheikh Abd al-Majid al-Zindani', *Terrorism Monitor*, vol. 4, no. 7.

Katzman, K. (2005) 'AQ: Profile and Threat Assessment: Congressional Research Service', 10 February, www.fas.org/irp/crs/RS22049.pdf.

Kepel, G. (2002) *Jihad: The Trail of Political Islam*, Cambridge MA: Harvard University Press.

Kepel, G. (2008) *Jihad: The Trail of Political Islam*, 4th edn, London, I.B. Tauris.

Keyser, J. (2010) 'Bin Laden Endorses Bomb Attempt on US Plane', *ABC News*, 24 January.

Klein, J. (2007) 'Is al-Qaeda on the Run in Iraq?' *Time* magazine, 23 May.

Knysh, A. (2001) 'The Tariqa on a Landcruiser: The Resurgence of Sufism in Yemen', *Middle East Journal*, vol. 55, no. 3.

Knysh, A. (2007) 'Contextualizing the Salafi–Sufi Conflict (from the Northern Caucasus to Hadramawt)', *Middle Eastern Studies*, vol. 43, no. 3.

Kohlmann, E. (2011) 'Al-Qa'ida's Yemeni Expatriate Faction in Pakistan', *CTC Sentinel*, vol. 4, no. 1, January.

Koppel, T. (2010) 'Nine Years after 9/11, Let's Stop Playing into bin Laden's Hands', *Washington Post*, 12 September.

Kramer, M. (2001) *Ivory Towers on Sand: The Failure of Middle Eastern Studies in America*, Washington DC: Washington Institute for Near East Policy.

Kurcy, S. (2010) 'Five Key Members of Al-Qaeda in Yemen', *Christian Science Monitor*, 2 November.

Lachkar, J. (2002) 'The Psychological Make-up of a Suicide-Bomber', *Journal of Psychohistory* 20.

Lahoud, N. (2010) *The Jihadis' Path to Self-Destruction*, London and New York: Hurst/Columbia University Press.

Landau, J.M. (1990) *The Politics of Pan-Islam: Ideology and Organization*, Oxford: Clarendon Press, 1990.

Laoust, H. (1939) *Essai sur les doctrines sociales et politiques de Taòkâi-d-Dâin Aòhmad b. Taimâiya, canoniste òhanbalite, né á Harrâan en 661/1262, mort á Damas en 728/1328*, Cairo: Imprimerie de l'Institut francais d'archâeologie orientale.

Laoust, H. (1979) *Essai sur les doctrines sociales et politiques* and *L'influence d'Ibn Taymiyya*, in A. Welch and P. Cachia (eds.) *Islam: Past Influence and Present Challenge*, Edinburgh: Edinburgh University Press.

Lawrence, B. (2005) *Messages to the World: The Statements of Osama bin Ladin*, London: Verso.

Lewis, B. (1998) 'License to Kill', *Foreign Affairs*, November–December.

Lewis, B. (2002) *What Went Wrong? Western Impact and Middle Eastern Response*, New York: Oxford University Press.

Luhmann, N. (1977) *Funktion der Religion*, Frankfurt: Piper Verlag.

Madelung, W. (1965) *Der Imam al-Qasim ibn Ibrahim und die Glaubenslehre der Zaiditen*, Berlin: De Gruyter.

Mahony, D. (1998) Review of 1998 Reports Concerning Threats by Osama bin Ladin to Conduct Terrorist Operations against the United States and/or her Allies, www.danmahony.com.

Mandaville, P. (2003) *Transnational Muslim Politics: Reimagining the Umma*, London: Routledge.

Mann, M. (2003) *Incoherent Empire*, London: Verso.

Martin, R.C., M.R. Woodward and D.S. Atmaja (1997) *Defenders of Reason in Islam: Mutazilism from Medieval School to Modern Symbol*, Oxford: Oneworld.

Mawari, M. (2009) 'Uncertainty Surrounds the Arrest of al-Qaeda Financier in Yemen', *Terrorism Monitor*, vol. 7, no. 19, July.

McHugh, P. (2001) 'A Psychiatrist Looks at Terrorism: There's Only One Way to Stop Fanatical Behavior', *Weekly Standard*, 12 December.

Meijer, R. (ed.) (2009) *Global Salafism: Islam's New Religious Movement*, London: Hurst.

Merari, A. (1991) 'Academic Research and Government Policy on Terrorism', *Terrorism and Political Violence*, vol. 3, no. 1.

Merrick J., and K. Sengupta (2009) 'Yemen: The Land with More Guns Than People', *Independent,* 20 September.

Michel, T. (1985) 'Ibn Taymiyya, Islamic Reformer', in *Studia Missionalia, 34: Reformateurs religieux, Le Christianisme et les autres religions*, Rome: Gregorian University Press.

Michot, Y. (2004) *Mardin: Hégire, fuite du péché et 'demeure de l'Islam*, Beirut: Albouraq.

Migaux, P. (2007) 'Al Qaeda', in G. Chaliand and A. Blin, *The History of Terrorism: From Antiquity to Al Qaeda*, San Francisco: University of California Press.

Miller, D., and T. Mills (2009) 'The Terror Experts and the Mainstream Media: The Expert Nexus and its Dominance in the News Media', *Critical Studies on Terrorism*, vol. 2, no. 3, December.

Miller, G., and P. Finn (2010) 'CIA Sees Increased Threat from al-Qa'ida in Yemen', *Washington Post*, 24 August.

Milson, M. (2004) 'Reform v. Islamism in the Arab World Today', *Special Report* 34, Middle East Media Research Institute (MEMRI), 15 September.

Moghadam, A., and B. Fishman (eds) (2010) *Self-Inflicted Wounds: Debates and Divisions within Al-Qa'ida and its Periphery*, New York: Harmony Project: Combating Terrorism Center at West Point.

Musharbash, Y. (2006) 'Al-Qaida is More Dangerous Than it Was on 9/11', interview with terrorism expert Bruce Hoffman, *Der Spiegel*, 10 October.

Nafi, B.M. (2002) 'Abu al-Thanna' al-Alusi: An Alim, Ottoman Mufti and Exegete of the Qur'an, *International Journal of Middle East Studies* 34.

Nafi, B.M. (2002) 'Tasawuf and Reform in Pre-Modern Islamic Culture: In Search of Ibrahim al-Kurani', *Die Welt des Islam*, vol. 42, no. 3.

Nasr, V. (2006) *The Shia Revival: How Conflicts within Islam Will Shape the Future*, New York: W.W. Norton.

Nettler, R. (1996) 'Guidelines for the Islamic Community: Sayyid Qutb's Political Interpretation', *Journal of Political Ideologies*, vol. 1, no. 2.

Neumann, P. (2010) *Prisons and Terrorism Radicalisation and De-radicalisation in 15 Countries*, policy report published by the International Centre for the Study of Radicalisation and Political Violence (ICSR), London.

9/11 Commission (2004) *The 9/11 Commission Report: The Final Report of the National Commission on Terrorist Attacks upon the United States*, New York: W.W. Norton.

Novak, J. (2008) 'Yemeni al-Qaeda leader: State Conducts Terror Attacks', *The Long War Journal*, 3 December.

Novak, J. (2009) 'Arabian Peninsula Al-Qaeda Groups Merge', *The Long War Journal*, 26 January.

Pew Global Attitudes Project (2005) *Islamic Extremism: Common Concern for Muslim and Western Publics*, July.

Pew Global Attitudes Project (2007) *Global Unease with Major World Powers and Leaders*, June.

Phillips, S. (2008) *Yemen's Democracy Experiment in Regional Perspective*, London: Palgrave Macmillan.

Piscatori, J.P. (1986) *Islam in a World of Nation States*, Cambridge: Cambridge University Press.

Piscatori, J.P. (1991) 'Islamic Fundamentalism and the Gulf Crisis', Chicago: American Academy of Arts and Sciences.

Piscatori, J.P. (2000) *Islam, Islamists and the Electoral Principle in the Middle East*, ISIM Papers, Leiden: ISIM.

Piscatori, J.P. (2002) 'The Turmoil Within', *Foreign Affairs*, May/June.

Piscatori, J.P. (2007) 'Imagining Pan-Islam', in S. Akbarzadeh and F. Mansouri, *Islam and Political Violence*, London: I.B. Tauris.

Post, J. (1990) 'Terrorist Psycho-logic: Terrorist Behaviour as a Product of Psychological Forces', in W. Reich (ed.), *Origins of Terrorism*, Cambridge: Cambridge University Press.

Qutb, S. (1979) *Fi Zilal al-Qur'an* (In the Shade of the Qur'an), trans. M.A. Salahi and A.A. Shamis, London: MWH Publishers.

Ranstorp, M. (2007) *Mapping Terrorism Research: State of the Art, Gaps and Future Directions*, London: Routledge.

Ranstorp, M. (2008) 'Mapping Terrorism Studies after 9/11: An Academic Field of Old Problems and New Prospects', in R. Jackson, M. Breen Smyth and J. Gunning (eds), *Critical Terrorism Studies: Framing a New Research Agenda*, London: Routledge.

Ranstorp, M. (2011) 'Terrorist Awakening in Sweden?', *CTC Sentinel*, vol. 4, no. 1, January.

Rashid, A. (2006) 'Don't Think al-Qaeda Is on the Back Foot, It Will Be on the March in 2007', *Telegraph*, 31 December.

Rasid Rida, M. (1923) *Al- Khilafa wa'l-imama al-uzma*, Cairo: Matba'at al-Manar.

Raufer, X. (2003) 'Al-Qaeda: A Different Diagnosis', *Studies in Conflict and Terrorism* 26.

Reid, E. (1997) 'Evolution of a Body of Knowledge: An Analysis of Terrorism Research', *Information Processing and Management*, vol. 33, no. 1.

Riedel, B. (2007) 'Al-Qaeda Strikes Back', *Foreign Affairs*, May/June.

Roggio, B. (2008) 'Letters from al-Qaeda Leaders Show Iraqi Effort is in Disarray', *Long War Journal*, 11 September.

Rosenberger, J. (2003) 'Discerning the Behavior of the Suicide Bomber', *Journal of Religion and Health*, vol. 42, no. 1, Spring.

Ross, B., and R. Esposito (2009) 'Abdulmutallab: More Like Me in Yemen. Accused Northwest Bomber Says More Bombers On the Way', ABC News, 28 December.

Roy, O. (1998) 'Fundamentalists without a Common Cause', *Le Monde Diplomatique*, 2 October.

Rubin, B.M. (2003) *The Tragedy of the Middle East*, New Haven CT: Yale University Press.

Sageman, M. (2004) *Understanding Terror Networks*, Philadelphia: University of Pennsylvania Press.

Sageman, M. (2008) *Leaderless Jihad: Terror Networks in the Twenty-First Century*, Philadelphia: University of Pennsylvania Press.

Sanger, D., and M. Mazetti (2010) 'New Estimate of Strength of Al Qaeda Is Offered', *New York Times*, 30 June.

Saudi–US Relations Information Service (2009) 'Saudi Al-Qaeda Leader Outlines New Strategy and Tactics of Al-Qaeda in the Arabian Peninsula', *Terrorism Monitor*, vol. 7, no. 9, April.

Scheuer, M. (2004) *Imperial Hubris*, Dulles: Brassey's.

Schmid, A., and A. Jongman (1988) *Political Terrorism: A Guide to Actors, Authors, Concepts, Databases, Theories and Literature*, Amsterdam: North Holland.

Schmitt, E., and S. Shane (2010) 'U.S. Divided on Aid to Counter Qaeda Threat in Yemen', *New York Times*, 15 September.

Schwartz, S. (2002) *The Two Faces of Islam*, New York: Random House.

Schwartz, S. (2004) 'Wahhabism and Al-Qaeda in Bosnia Herzegovina', *Terrorism Monitor*, vol. 2, no. 20, October.

Schwedler, J. (2003) 'The Yemeni Islah Party: Political Opportunities and Coalition Building in a Transitional Polity', in Q. Wiktorowicz (ed.), *Islamist Activism: A Social Movement Theory Approach*, Bloomington: Indiana University Press.

Schwedler, J. (2007) *Faith in Moderation: Islamist Parties in Jordan and Yemen*, Cambridge: Cambridge University Press.

Sciolino, E., and E. Schmitt (2008) 'A Not Very Private Feud over Terrorism', *New York Times*, 8 June.

Serjeant, R.B. (1981) *Studies in Arabian History and Civilisation*, London: Variorum.

Shane, S., and J. Dao (2009) 'Investigators Study Tangle of Clues on Fort Hood Suspect', *New York Times*, 14 November.

Shaughnessy, L. (2010) 'U.S. official: Al Qaeda in Yemen Bigger Threat Than in Pakistan', CNN, December 17.

Shuja al-Deen, M. (2009) 'Media Absent from Yemen's Forgotten Conflict', *Arab Media Society* 8, Spring.

Silke, A. (2004) *Research on Terrorism: Trends, Achievements and Failures*, London: Routledge.

Simon, B., and S. Simon (2002) *The Age of Sacred Terror*, New York: Random House.

Simons, G.L. (1995) *The United Nations*, London: Macmillan.

Simons, G.L. (1996) *The Scourging of Iraq: Sanctions, Law and Natural Justice*, London: Macmillan.

Sorman, G. (2003) *Les enfants de Rifaa: musulmans et modernes*, Paris: Fayard.

Strindberg, A. (2006) 'The Enemy of My Enemy', *The American Conservative*, 11 September.

Strindberg, A., and M. Wärn (2005) 'Realities of Resistance: Hizballah, the Palestinian Rejectionist and Al-Qa'ida Compared', *Journal of Palestine Studies*, vol. 34, no. 3, Spring.

Strothman, R. (1912) *Kultus der Zaiditen*, Strasbourg: K.J. Trübner.

Strothman, R. (1912) *Das Staatsrecht der Zaiditen*, Strasbourg: Trübner.

Tuastad, D. (2003) 'Neo-Orientalism and the New Barbarism Thesis: Aspects of Symbolic Violence in the Middle East Conflict(s)', *Third World Quarterly*, vol. 24, no. 4.

Ubayd al-Jamhi, S. (2008) *al-Qa'ida fi al-Yaman*, Sana'a: Maktaba al-Hadara.

United States v. *Usama Bin Laden* Indictment, http://.findlaw.com/news. findlaw.com/cnn/docs/binladen/usbinladen-1a.pdf

United States v. *Usama bin Laden*, Trial Transcript, Jamal al Fadl Witness Testimony, 06/02/2001: http://news.findlaw.com/legalnews/us/terrorism/cases/background.html

United States vs. *Usama bin Laden* Trial Transcript Day 8, http://cryptome.org/usa-v-ubl-08.htm

United States v. *Enaam Arnaout*, http://fl1.findlaw.com/news.findlaw.com/hdocs/docs/bif/usarnaout10603prof.pdf

Van Arendonk, C. (1960) *Les Débuts de L'Ima'mate Zaidite au Yemen*, Leiden: E.J. Brill.

Von Hippel, K. (2002) 'The Roots of Terrorism: Probing the Myths', *Political Quarterly*, vol. 73, no. 1.

Von Knop, K. (2007) 'The Female Jihad: Al-Qaeda's Women', *Studies in Conflict and Terrorism* 30.

Wedgwood, R., and K. Roth (2004) 'Combatants or Criminals? How Washington Should Handle Terrorists', *Foreign Affairs*, May/June.

Wiktorowicz, Q. (2001) 'The New Global Threat: Transnational Salafis and Jihad', *Middle East Policy Council*, vol. 8, no. 4, 1 December.

Wiktorowicz, Q. (2006) 'Anatomy of the Salafi Movement', *Studies in Conflict and Terrorism* 29.

Wiktorowicz, Q., and J. Kaltner (2003) 'Killing in the Name of Islam: Al-Qaeda's Justification for September 11', *Middle East Policy Council Journal*, vol. 10, no. 2.

Wright, L. (2006) *The Looming Tower: Al Qaeda's Road to 9/11*, London: Penguin.

Zaman, M.Q. (1997) *Religion and Politics under the Early Abbasids*, Leiden: Brill.

Zeidan, D. (2001) 'The Islamic Fundamentalist View of Life as a Perennial Battle', *Middle East Review of International Affairs*, vol. 5, no. 4.

Zimmerman, K. (2010) 'Militant Islam's Global Preacher: The Radicalizing Effect of Sheikh Anwar al Awlaki', *Critical Threats Project*, 12 March.

Zogby International (2004) *Impressions of America 2004: How Arabs in 6 Countries View America*, June.

Index